WOMEN RESHAPING HUMAN RIGHTS

WOMEN RESHAPING HUMAN RIGHTS

How Extraordinary Activists Are Changing the World

MARGUERITE GUZMAN BOUVARD

A Scholarly Resources Inc. Imprint
Wilmington, Delaware

First published 1996
Printed and bound in the United States of America

Scholarly Resources Inc.
104 Greenhill Avenue
Wilmington, DE 19805-1897

Sources for Illustrations

Chapters 1, 2, 4, 7, 9, 10, and 15: Paula Chandoha
Chapter 3: Jodi Freeman, *Earth Times*
Chapter 5: Provided by Daisy L. Bates
Chapter 6: Sigrid Estrada (reprinted courtesy of Simon & Schuster)
Chapters 8 and 14: Shelley Kjonstad
Chapter 11: Marguerite Guzmán Bouvard
Chapter 12: UN Photo 188850/E. Schneider
Chapter 13: © Andrea Mistri
Chapter 16: *Earth Times*
Chapter 17: Photojournalists of newspapers of the Mothers of the Plaza de Mayo

The author gratefully acknowledges the above-mentioned sources for permission to reproduce the photographs in this book.

Library of Congress Cataloging-in-Publication Data

Bouvard, Marguerite Guzmán, 1937–
Women reshaping human rights : how extraordinary activists are changing the world / Marguerite Guzmán Bouvard.
p. cm.
Includes bibliographical references.
ISBN 0-8420-2562-6 (cloth : alk. paper). — ISBN 0-8420-2563-4 (pbk. : alk. paper)
1. Human rights. 2. Civil rights. 3. Women human rights workers—Biography. 4. Women civil rights workers—Biography. I. Title.
JC571.B6735 1996
323'.092'2—dc20 96-5126
[B] CIP

∞The paper used in this publication meets the minimum requirements of the American National Standard for permanence of paper for printed library materials, Z39.48, 1984.

For Pierre, Laurence, Michele,

Neil, and Mary,

always the center

Acknowledgments

With gratitude to all those who helped me in so many different ways: Dr. George Tomeh, Majed Tomeh, Marilyn Ewer, Zhu Hong, Mona Harrington, Nancy Levy-Konesky, Patsy Robertson, Eva Brantley, Leopoldo Brizuela, and Ada Alessandro. Also, my thanks to the members of my family: my husband, who provided technical support; my son Pierre, who provided me with travel and accommodations; my daughter Laurence, whose skills as a linguist and editor are reflected throughout the book; and my niece, Professor Michele Cloonan, for her organizing talents and for helping with documentation.

Contents

Introduction: Women Transforming the Battle for Human Rights

WOMEN HAVE LONG BEEN ACTIVE in the fight for human rights at all levels and on many fronts: in resistance during wartime, in struggles against colonialism and authoritarian governments, and, within democratic societies, in seeking their just claims and those of people excluded from the political community as defined by the largely male elite. That women's achievements, their concepts of human worth, and their methods of attaining justice have been largely overlooked by the male political and human rights establishment makes it all the more urgent to air their voices.

Women's accomplishments have received little notice because the very language and concept of rights derives from a liberal political tradition focused on the public activities of male citizens. The major documents defining these claims—the Virginia Declaration of Rights, precursor to the American Declaration of Independence of 1776, the Bill of Rights in the American Constitution, and the French Declaration of the Rights of Man and the Citizen—were all modeled on the natural rights theory of John Locke, the seventeenth-century English philosopher, who characterized individual prerogatives as political and civil freedom to be guaranteed by the state. Underpinning this definition are a number of assumptions with which women activists have taken issue. The most crucial objection women have raised is to the assumption that the fundamental political being is an autonomous individual, a view that ignores the importance of relationships and social settings that enhance or constrict human dignity.

Locke's theory of individual rights makes a distinction between the public and the private sphere, thus abstracting human beings from their familial, social, economic, and cultural ties. A long line of political thinkers, beginning with Plato and Aristotle, have associated the public sphere with the distinctly human and the private with the natural, representing the family as focused on particularistic and, hence, inferior concerns that are often in conflict with the superior and more universal preoccupations of the public sphere. Locke's philosophy presupposes that individuals are self-sufficient units who may acquire freedom and justice before the state while ignoring their relationship with family, ethnic group, or religion. However, as women are keenly aware, these are areas in which individuals may either flourish or experience oppression.

Furthermore, the Lockean characterization of rights as civil and political locates all power within the state, which must either be constrained from interfering in individual lives or create legislation to ensure individual freedom. However, this concept of the state unmediated by nongovernmental institutions ignores the fact that relations within religious, social, and economic groups are also defined by power. The family unit can function in an authoritarian manner, denying the individual freedom supposedly guaranteed by the state; institutions such as banks, cartels, and multinationals can control or supersede national laws by crossing boundaries. They also frequently collude with the state at the expense of ethnic communities and the poor as evidenced in the chapters in this volume that recount women's struggle for environmental justice.

While based on civil and political liberties derived from eighteenth-century political theory, the Universal Declaration of Human Rights adopted by the UN General Assembly in 1948 also includes a list of economic, social, and cultural rights incorporated in the International Covenant of Economic, Social, and Cultural Rights; the European Social Charter; and various national constitutions. These prerogatives reflect a major trend during the nineteenth century that led to the development of a socialist doctrine requiring the state to ensure basic standards of health, welfare, education, and workers' rights. However, these declarations do not include instruments or political documents that allow the individual the recourse of petition; they merely impose general obligations on states to work toward the attainment of these claims.

Although many political thinkers have seen a conflict between civil rights and the fulfillment of basic social and economic needs, women activists believe that, without the latter, it is impossible to enjoy political freedom. The women profiled in this book have stressed that individual abuses of rights are inseparable from the social and economic structures that perpetuate or create injustices. Eva Brantley, for instance, recounts the differing goals of the women and the men in the Polish Solidarity movement, with the former insisting upon social and economic guarantees and the latter focused primarily on political rights.

Women's alternative approaches to human rights have been largely ignored by historical and political analysts and the media. As a professor in a women's college, I grappled with the problem of finding material that reflected female work in this field. One solution was to bring women activists to the classroom, and it proved highly successful as my students were presented with a version of reality that they shared and responded to enthusiastically. As a result, I decided to bring these voices to a wider audience and to help carve out a space for broadened perspectives on rights by means of this book. Despite their official invisibility, I found scores of female activists in the Boston area. One of them, Vera Laska, had been a colleague of mine for many years. I was also able to interview women from other parts of the United States and the world as they traveled to talk about their work. In fact, narrowing the choice proved difficult given the number of remarkable people engaged in such work.

Notable among them, although her work has not been included in studies of male colleagues, is Vera Laska, who as a teenager joined the fight against the Nazi occupation of Czechoslovakia during World War II. Similarly, Eva Brantley, who served as legal counsel to Lech Walesa as the Solidarity movement toppled the Polish Communist regime, rarely appears in accounts of that period. Yet, her role in helping to achieve Polish democracy was only a single episode in a long career spanning different countries. During the same period when Solidarity was organized, Annette Lu Hsiu-Lien, a young woman in Taiwan, confronted the military government of that country and also founded a women's movement in a traditional, male-dominated society that brooked no dissent. She suffered a long prison term because of these efforts, but, upon her release, she plunged back into the struggle for a democratic government. Moreover, although the dissident movement in China may be dominated by men such as Wei Jingsheng, Bao Zunxin, and Liu Xiaobo, Dai Qing is nevertheless a powerful voice for justice in China, a woman who insists upon fighting the Communist Party's grip upon the media and the government.

The struggle against Western imperialism, which began after World War II, also prompted a reexamination of relations among ethnic groups within individual countries. Just as nationalist movements have their pantheon of heroes, the liberation of suppressed races and ethnic groups are usually associated with a male leadership. But Daisy Bates of the civil rights movement in the United States; Hanan Ashrawi, a Palestinian activist; Awiakta, a Cherokee activist who has sought to preserve the cultural heritage of her people; and Navanethem Pillay, a South African human rights lawyer, have all contributed in powerful ways to the achievement of justice for their people.

Furthermore, women have broadened the concept of human dignity to include new aspects, including the right not to be poisoned by toxic wastes. Given that women responsible for family well-being are directly concerned about the effects of hazardous deposits in their neighborhoods, they have been at the forefront of efforts to keep these materials out of their immediate surroundings. Dollie Burwell characterized her struggle to keep PCBs (polychlorinated biphenyls) away from her neighborhood as a continuation of the civil rights movement.[1] Juana Beatrice Gutiérrez and the Mothers of East Los Angeles also have defined human dignity as the right to ensure that their communities not serve as dumping grounds for harmful substances. Women such as Grace Thorpe of the Sauk and Fox Tribe have pointed out that poor and ethnic communities have been the target of governmental programs for the storage of hazardous materials, and they are working to reverse that trend. Because few people in her country cared to raise their voices on behalf of the environment, Dai Qing initiated a campaign to protect natural resources from the authoritarian and irresponsible policies of Communist Party leaders.

Given the fact that existing perceptions of human rights have been modeled on male experiences, women's claims have been either marginalized or ignored by the institutions charged with monitoring the status of rights. In her work as director of the UN Fourth World Conference on Women, Gertrude Mongella of Tanzania cited the problem of equality as the central issue facing women and the source of the many rights violations that they suffer. This perception has been the model for groups such as Equality Now, founded by Jessica Neuwirth of the United States and Navanethem Pillay of South Africa, to address the problems of protecting women. The South African also has created the Advice Desk for Abused Women to confront the particular issues facing women in her country. Zhu Hong has chosen the route of literature to reveal the problems women face within the family, society, culture, economy, and politics of the Chinese Communist regime.

Because women have been active in caring work, they are concerned with the flourishing of generations and view children's rights as crucial to social well-being and to the future of the species. Describing her work with UNICEF (United Nations Children's Fund), Liv Ullmann recounts how her role as a mother has enabled her to make the connection between her own child and children around the world. The International Gathering of Mothers and Women in Struggle, founded in March 1994 by the Argentine Mothers of the Plaza de Mayo (an organization of mothers created to protest the disappearance of their children during the time of the military junta of 1976–1983), has formulated an ongoing strategy to influence governments around the world toward policies of life and peace rather than war.

While addressing diverse problems, each of the women presented in this book brings a radical and alternative approach to human rights based upon female views of the polity and of morality as well as a continuity between the public and private spheres. These women regard human rights as enmeshed in all the factors that impinge upon our daily lives not only at the state level but also in the economic, social, and religious arenas. Women activists are seeking to transform the assumptions, discourse, and goals of the international human rights movement and, by implication, the power structures of states and international organizations. While recognizing the importance of liberal theory in rescuing the individual from governmental and nationalistic tyranny, they believe that there is yet another stage to traverse in order for democracy to achieve its full realization. Individual dignity must be part of relationships characterized by mutual respect, which foster both personal growth and the ongoing development of these ties. As a result, relationships cannot be off-limits to the state, and the state must be proactive in assuring individual rights within such areas as the family and religious groups, including among its most important goals the flourishing of future generations.

There is a reluctance in the mainstream human rights organizations within the United Nations, such as the Commission on Human Rights, and in nongovernmental organizations (NGOs), such as Amnesty International, to address the social and economic problems of a structural nature that negate the possibility of exercising civil and political rights, a point women activists have been emphasizing for a number of years. As does Jessica Neuwirth, women feel that much of current human rights practice concerns itself with the symptoms rather than the causes of human rights violations. Responding to clear cases of gross violations where victims are suffering in a socially visible way and where abusers can be identified and required to desist is much easier than responding to abuses stemming from economic and social arrangements that can only be addressed by fundamental changes.

Gertrude Mongella speaks of the necessity for revolutionary transformations to ensure the broad definition of human rights outlined by women. In the chapter devoted to her work for the Conference on Women, she stresses the need for across-the-board changes in all the structures that govern our lives and for a more balanced view of rights that accounts for the female as well as the male outlook. Her perspective is reflected in the work of the other women profiled in this book, whose human rights agendas are all inclusive and continually evolving in response to new issues.

Women activists have developed an alternative political style to achieve their goals. Often their efforts have been focused on establishing links between nations in conflict, such as Hanan Ashrawi's ties with Israeli women's peace groups, or the International Gathering of Mothers and Women in Struggle, which includes women from the warring factions of the former Yugoslavia as well as Israeli and Palestinian mothers. Equality Now honors diverse cultures with its Muslim, South African, and American directors and its networking with groups around the world. Zhu Hong sees her work as informing Chinese and American women about each other's achievements so that both cultures may benefit in their struggle for women's human rights. Like the feminist philosopher Virginia Held, these women stress the usefulness of dialogue to further the political process, allowing all perspectives to be heard and accounted for while remaining sensitive to the divisions of race, class, and ethnicity.[2]

Key to these women's strategy is the manner in which information obtained from the field is used. Equality Now maintains a two-way channel of information and expertise with local women's groups around the world. Both Eva Brantley and Jessica Neuwirth insist that such information not be appropriated by distant organizations for their own purposes, as done by the mainstream human rights institutions, but rather that the use of such data remain a local decision. Eva points out that local communities often never find out what happens to the information that they provide to either international institutions or NGOs.

While the expertise for engaging in human rights activities has been the privilege of an educated elite in both the mainstream organizations and the NGOs, women's human rights organizations have seen the sharing and gathering of information as a means of empowering the victims of abuse. Juana Gutiérrez and the Mothers of East Los Angeles worked diligently to educate their community about the implications of the proposed oil pipeline that would traverse their neighborhood as well as the ramifications of the construction of an incinerator and the storage of toxic wastes, so that the ordinary person could communicate with the media and play a significant role in reform. Having witnessed how scientific information can be manipulated for political purposes, Dollie Burwell decided to interview experts hired by her own community to assess the condition of the PCBs stored in her neighborhood rather than to rely upon state-sponsored scientists. As president of the Native American Coalition on the Environment, Grace Thorpe believes her role is to gather the latest information on the storage and transport of nuclear waste and to circulate it as widely as possible. Women working for human rights have sought to democratize knowledge and to prevent its use to uphold privilege and domination.

People such as Eva Brantley, Dai Qing, and Zhu Hong, and activist groups such as Equality Now or the Mothers of East Los Angeles, have created organizations that contrast with the more hierarchical and centralized human rights associations. Whether dedicated to obtaining environmental justice or to women's human rights, these groups have established decentralized associations, creating structures that are flexible and capable of mobilizing people as issues arise. Thus, they incorporate the values women depend upon in the household, where they continually face the complex problems of childrearing and socialization as well as deal with issues imposed from the outside. Eva Brantley works at the grassroots level, helping to establish local organizations that can then operate independently, while Awiakta speaks of people as connected within a web in which no one role is more important than another. Rather than adopting the conventional model of elitism, exclusivity, and bureaucracy, women activists have opted for more fluid organizations that allow rapid decision making and universal participation. Contrary to the general view within traditional human rights organizations, they regard these features as sources of strength and commitment.

An inextricable part of this organizational style is its basis on mutual respect and trust and the belief that leadership is a matter of connection rather than domination, as in the examples of the Mothers of East Los Angeles, the International Gathering of Mothers and Women in Struggle, and Equality Now. Similarly, within these groups the method of problem solving is one of consensus building and using nonconfrontational negotiating techniques. Because many women's concept of self is intrinsically connected to relationships to others, they perceive their own interest as lying in the welfare of these ties; therefore, they emphasize cooperation rather than individual self-advancement, believing that the process of attaining human rights is as important as the goal.

The women who tell their stories in this book speak from the immediacy of their own experiences and achievements. They provide models of new forms of power with a strong ethical strain that connects thought and feeling. Awiakta refers to a unified thinking, which signifies an understanding of cause and effect and a recognition that we are connected in our common humanity. She explains that the Native American way of "speaking from the heart" means that there is no separation between heart, mind, and spirit, as there can be no compartmentalizing among the various aspects of our lives.

Therefore, while morality has been characterized by some male philosophers as rational theories for ideal societies, women human rights activists have broadened the concept to include feeling as well as thought, practicing the ethics of caring. In the search for objectivity and the fear of distorting passions, most male theoreticians have sought to discount the emotions as unreliable. While there are morally harmful emotions such as prejudice, hatred, and egotism, these women believe that feeling should be added to reasoning and that emotions have their own intelligence, helping us to understand complex moral issues and how to act in the face of them. Vera Laska's decision to join those resisting the National Socialists was fueled by outrage at the Nazis' brutality, an anger that sparked highly creative and ingenious actions. Vera has always insisted that becoming a member of the Resistance was not a rational, considered act, which does not mean that one should abandon reason or general principles, but rather that these elements should be compatible with particular judgments based on empathy and concern instead of solely on rational calculation or abstract reasoning regarding hypothetical situations.[3]

Women's experience has been notably absent from moral theory: that understanding is not limited to the law, state, and public policy, but includes bringing up children, caring for the vulnerable, and cultivating social relations. It is the women who suffer firsthand the effects of environmental problems, war, and economic and social policies on their families and relationships, and who insist that these issues be taken into account in assuring human dignity. As Gertrude Mongella points out, females have been excluded from policymaking regarding war and conflict resolution, and, as Grace Thorpe emphasizes, women need to be included in the decision to create industries that do not produce harmful waste. Navanethem Pillay insists that for human beings to be free they need more than the absence of interference guaranteed by the liberal tradition. They must have access to decent jobs, minimum incomes, affordable housing, and medical care. However, as with classic liberalism, the collectivism of Marxism does not acknowledge that women's and men's perceptions are diverse. Women feel that what is needed is not the relinquishing of privacy at the expense of community but the fostering of both individual self-realization and social responsibility.

One of the key experiences ignored by moral philosophers is that of mothering. Native Americans, such as Awiakta, and the feminist philosopher Sara Ruddick have revealed that love and thought are deeply connected in the process of mothering. Mothers' lives are filled with conflict, yet they develop ways of dealing with it that are consistent with the goals of protecting and socializing their children. Through their efforts, they have found the means to achieve peace without violence, a peace not of conflicting members who go their separate ways but rather one through which the human connections between persons are restored.[4] Women such as the members of the International Gathering of Mothers and Women in Struggle see their efforts as a positive source of peacemaking. They have learned to seek change through organization, pressure, and persuasion rather than through violence.

Although mothers around the world often identify with their communities and are not able to make the leap of sympathy with other cultures and races, the women profiled in this book make a strong case for political motherhood. Hanan Ashrawi insists that politics and motherhood are inseparable and that a real mother not only has a vision for her children but also wants to work for their future, ensuring them a life of peace, freedom, and dignity. Since their creation in 1979 the Mothers of the Plaza de Mayo have revised the concept of motherhood to include political mentoring and working to establish governments that assure justice. Liv Ullmann suggests that we look at the faces of suffering children across the world as if they were our own. The political mothers represented here bring to their activism a concern not only for their children's prospects but also for those of distant children. While rooted in the particular situations of their communities or ethnic groups, they have formed alliances at the national and international level, demonstrating how working to protect ethnic and neighborhood concerns enables them to bridge the distance between the individual and the universal. It is also the compassion particular to women's experience that has prepared them to move with such ease from the local to the global. Dollie Burwell has brought her environmental knowledge and concerns to the women of South Africa. Although Eva Brantley has no children of her own, by working with children in India and in Afghanistan she reveals what it is like to be a citizen of the world, as does Liv Ullmann in her activities with UNICEF. Whether seeking environmental justice, national liberation, or women's human rights, these activists have demonstrated to what extent their neighborhood or national struggles are globally linked.

Some feminists have argued that emphasizing motherhood means imprisoning women in the biology-as-destiny argument. However, the women who have chosen political motherhood have pointed out the importance of choice in reproduction, which is denied to women in most societies, and of the recognition of giving birth as a significant cultural, economic, and social contribution to states and to the world. As Gertrude Mongella notes, giving birth can be either a joyous or a bitter experience depending upon the availability of social and cultural support. Awiakta and Mrs. Mongella provide us with views of the balance and flourishing of both male and female in partnership and in the rearing of children. They regard interdependence as a component of autonomy. Women seeking to break free of oppressive relationships, whether in the family or caused by traditional law, are not seeking isolation but new and satisfactory relations.

The women whose experiences are detailed in this book have entered the battle for justice at all stages in the life cycle, discounting images of girls and the elderly as ineffective. Vera Laska joined the Resistance when she was only fifteen years old, Dollie Burwell became involved in voter registration at the age of twelve, and Jessica Neuwirth first became active in Amnesty International when she was fourteen. Eva Brantley's human rights work was inspired by her imprisonment at the age of nineteen. Dai Qing and Annette Lu Hsiu-Lien abandoned successful careers to work for political change. Grace Thorpe was already retired when she decided to fight the placement of nuclear waste on Indian lands. Along with Juana Gutiérrez and Awiakta, she is a grandmother.

While the dominant male culture may find this fact jarring, we have as a paradigm Native American history and the government of Native peoples, where older women enjoy an important role, where public and private are complementary rather than contradictory, and where matters of home and family are given equal weight with matters of state. Cherokee women, for example, have a long record of entitlement to participate in the highest questions of tribal affairs. They are landowners and supervisors, and older female members make significant contributions by bringing their wisdom to bear on important issues and calling other leaders to account. Therefore, although Western philosophers have identified public life as a space reserved for males, women are drawing upon ancient and living history when they enter the political arena. Rather than intruding upon a so-called male preserve, in their concern for achieving freedom and dignity in diverse situations, they are claiming roles that they have played throughout millennia.

Part I of this book focuses upon women leaders in the opposition against authoritarian and totalitarian governments on the left and right of the political spectrum. Women were key leaders and members of the Resistance against National Socialism in Europe, yet their contributions have been ignored. This neglect prompted Vera Laska, who had been a teenage member of the underground and spent years in various Nazi concentration camps, to write *Women in the Resistance and the Holocaust,* which chronicles her own efforts and those of the many unsung heroines of that period.

In confronting the Kuomintang government's martial law in Taiwan, Annette Lu Hsiu-Lien risked her life speaking out on behalf of human rights and publishing several books criticizing the regime. She was also ahead of her time in regarding women's human rights as an important part of the search for freedom, acting as founder and leader of the Taiwanese feminist movement. Eva Brantley and Dai Qing fought leftist totalitarian governments in Poland and in China. Eva also has worked with democracy movements in Communist East Germany and the former Yugoslav republics and has lobbied on behalf of the Coalition for Democracy in China at the UN Commission on Human Rights. Dai abandoned a life of privilege within the Communist Party elite to launch an independent study of party documents that would reveal the dark underside of the revolution. She also, through her writing and her organization of concerned scientists opposed to the projected damming of the Yangtze River, is working to protect the environment on behalf of her own people and the rest of the world from the authoritarian and irresponsible policies of the Communist Party leaders. As a journalist, historiographer, and writer of short stories, she took on the government single-handedly.

Part II deals with struggles against racial and ethnic oppression. Women have long been active in the movements against Western imperialism and in organizations seeking racial justice within nations. Although anticolonial uprisings began soon after World War II, a 1960 UN resolution defining national self-determination as a human right quickened the pace, tripling UN membership and sparking battles for racial justice within nations. Despite the fact that women ranked prominently among those who fought cultural domination within their own countries, it is the male leaders who are remembered: the civil rights movement in the United States has been portrayed as male led even though it includes within its ranks women such as Rosa Parks, Septima Clark, and Daisy Bates, to name just a few. Daisy Bates rose to national prominence as a result of a historic Supreme Court ruling in 1954 that separate education for blacks and whites was not equal, and that public schools should therefore become integrated. As a consequence, she moved to the forefront of integration efforts, acting as mentor to the nine children who were the first to enter all-white schools in Little Rock, Arkansas, and braving death threats and intimidation.

Hanan Mikhail Ashrawi, leader of the Palestinian delegation to the peace talks in Washington between 1991 and 1993, was one of the first of her people to recognize that in order to achieve peace and independence, the Israelis and Palestinians must learn to coexist, thus demonstrating women's special capabilities for cooperation rather than confrontation. While working for the independence of her people, she is also active on behalf of pluralism and economic and social justice within Palestinian society.

Cherokee activist Awiakta has struggled to keep the history of her people alive within a society that not only has sought to eliminate Native Americans but also has tried to render the survivors invisible and to destroy their traditions. Through her work, Awiakta upholds the vision of a truly just world in which no single culture predominates, a balance and a flourishing of both male and female attributes is provided, and future generations and nature are included in the concept of rights.

Navanethem Pillay was the first black woman to start a law practice in the province of Natal in South Africa, in 1967. She used that position to work for human rights, spending over twenty years involved in political trials on behalf of some of the most notable opponents of apartheid. She viewed these court battles as opportunities to challenge unjust laws and provide public exposure for political grievances in a society that prohibited dissent. Throughout her career, Navanethem Pillay not only has fought racial discrimination against the black community but also has espoused the rights of all cultures.

Part III articulates a hitherto neglected human claim, the right not to be poisoned by toxic wastes. Dollie Burwell regarded her battle against the dumping of PCBs in her neighborhood as one of assuring her people's dignity. Beginning with the organization of a local protest, she soon gained national attention and the support of the leaders of the National Association for the Advancement of Colored People as well as members of Congress. While Dollie's organization was unsuccessful in preventing the state of North Carolina from burying PCBs three miles from her home and near a primary school, her efforts resulted in a series of investigations into decisions regarding the storage of hazardous waste. A General Accounting Office study sponsored by an African-American congressman who marched with Dollie revealed that all the hazardous and toxic waste facilities in the South were located in predominantly black and poor communities. Those findings sparked an enquiry by the Commission for Racial Justice of the United Church of Christ, thereby uncovering environmental injustice on a national scale.[5]

Modeled on the Argentine Mothers of the Plaza de Mayo, the Mothers of East Los Angeles have defined human dignity as the right to live in a safe environment that is also free of toxic wastes. Juana Gutiérrez, president of the Santa Isabel chapter, and hundreds of neighborhood mothers drew upon their organizational experience within their neighborhoods to successfully combat the placement of an incinerator, an oil pipeline, and a prison in their community. They became a powerful political force, forming coalitions with environmental groups across the state and nation and confounding the white establishment's perceptions of Mexican Americans.

Grace Thorpe, a member of the Sauk and Fox Tribe and a seventy-three-year-old grandmother, regards the dumping of nuclear wastes on Indian land as the final assault in a long series of oppressive policies aimed at eliminating the Native American population. Through her tireless efforts, she persuaded fifteen of seventeen tribes to refuse the burial of nuclear wastes on their land, and she also has worked closely with Nuclear Free America and other environmental groups disseminating information on the problems involved in the disposal of nuclear materials.

Part IV highlights activists seeking to ensure women's human rights. These women have particularly difficult obstacles to overcome: the key institutions concerned with the guarantee of human rights at the international and regional levels are dominated by a male membership and hence have rendered interpretations of such instruments as the Universal Declaration of Human Rights that focus on direct infringement of individual rights by the state, ignoring or marginalizing violations suffered by women. Many of the abuses that females endure are connected to disadvantages they face in economic, social, and cultural arenas, where denial of their worth is often regarded either as of little consequence or as too sensitive to handle. International institutions, for instance, fear that attention to infringements such as female circumcision or women's position within Islam may elicit accusations of cultural imperialism.

The center of international human rights practice is located within the UN system, in Geneva-based political and expert bodies such as the UN Commission on Human Rights, and also within regional systems such as the Inter-American Court of Human Rights in San José, Costa Rica, and the European Court of Human Rights in Strasbourg. In these bodies, political and civil claims enjoy a privileged position, strengthened by significant resources, prestige, and a male-oriented discourse. Furthermore, there is an institutional separation between organizations concerned with human rights and those concerned with women's issues. The Commission on the Status of Women and the Committee on Elimination of Discrimination against Women were located in Vienna until their removal to New York City in 1993, and thus the Geneva-based bodies are often unaware of what is occurring within these institutions. Many UN bodies obtain much of their information about human rights violations from the NGOs that form part of the Geneva or U.S. human rights community. The networks of women's organizations working in areas of gender-specific abuses have limited access to these forums and are not sought out by those responsible for gathering information. Therefore, the relevance of gender to both the definition and responses to violations of rights has been neglected within the mainstream.[6] While Amnesty International has made the greatest progress in this regard, publishing a report on human rights abuses against women, its approach is still the traditional one of suggesting reactive, rather than proactive, measures.[7]

Women have pointed out that if issues of gender rather than general maltreatment would be raised by bodies inquiring into torture in a country, the abuses that females are subjected to would come to light. These acts of mistreatment include violations at the hands of private individuals acting in a private capacity and, more insidiously, the denial of access to social and economic benefits and opportunities. The latter is due not only to discrimination but also to the fact that economic and social institutions are typically modeled on male experience and life patterns.[8] Among other abuses determined by gender are dowry deaths, forced prostitution and trafficking in women, mail-order-bride networks, the denial of equal rights to participate in political life, the harassment of politically active women, the denial of reproductive rights, and unequal access to health care and adequate food. The fact that these abuses may go unaddressed may be traced to the state's responsibility for allowing a social and legal system in which such violations may remain unrecognized.

The UN Commission on Human Rights typically issues general comments identifying the most important dimensions of civil and political claims. These opinions have provided no recognition that gender is a significant aspect of individual rights or that it can affect the choice of methods adopted by states to protect individuals within their jurisdiction. For example, there are no references to the effect of claims to privacy on women's struggle for control over their reproductive lives, or that people's entitlement to nondiscriminatory treatment by legal systems includes women's relations to criminal justice systems as victims and defendants of crime. UN rapporteurs often compile reports without making the slightest reference to the fact that women suffer gender-specific abuses, such as rape, in addition to the same violations experienced by men.[9]

Women human rights scholars and activists note that sexism is a widespread structural problem; equality is not the freedom to be treated without regard to sex, but freedom from systematic subordination because of gender.[10] What has been offered to women in industrialized societies is the opportunity to become like men. Women, however, do not universally wish to shed their particular identities. Furthermore, they consider their own experiences within the family and society, where they are often subjected to various forms of abuse as well as economic and social oppression, central to human rights; therefore, they are working to create public awareness of these problems and to provide remedies.

As director of the UN Fourth World Conference on Women, Gertrude Mongella has claimed that until the male power structure at all governmental levels is transformed to include females' unique perspectives as well as their active involvement, there can be no notable progress in women's conditions. While the conference also focused on development and peace—two areas that have a profound impact on female lives—it stressed that there can be no significant improvement in these spheres without women's participation and vision.

Equality Now was founded by Jessica Neuwirth and Navanethem Pillay to address women's human rights. That organization uses Amnesty International's techniques of publicizing cases of human rights violations and seeking to influence governmental policies so that they acknowledge specific abuses against females as cause for seeking political asylum. It also promotes mass campaigns on behalf of women's rights. Equality Now is run on an entirely voluntary basis, receiving information on infringements of female claims from around the world through its Women's Action Network, which serves as a two-way channel of communication and helps coordinate global actions.

Through the creation of the Advice Desk for Abused Women and her work in the law, Navanethem Pillay has grappled with the multiple issues confronting South African women. She also has sought to assure the dignity of women through her efforts to educate diverse sectors of the population and by creating a network of community organizations that provide sources of relief for women as well as promoting their full participation in all aspects of society.

By compiling anthologies of stories by Chinese women and translating these works into English, Zhu Hong has provided a voice for females who have existed virtually at the whim of men and who have been silenced throughout history. She believes that literature is a powerful means of social criticism as well as a way of revealing alternate courses of being and perceiving. As do many of the activists profiled in this book, she sees her battle for female rights as reflecting women's views of morality.

Part V considers the human rights of children as the key to the survival of humanity. Women involved in seeking justice, peace, and human dignity believe that it is of primary concern to create social and economic arrangements and environmental conditions in which children will be properly nurtured. Along with the feminist philosopher Virginia Held, they believe that the well-being of children should be at the center of moral, political, social, and economic planning rather than remain at the periphery of both thought and policy.[11] These activists do not imply that women should be relegated to birthing and child care, but instead that national and international governmental entities, along with NGOs, should place the current and future generations of children at the center of their concerns.

Liv Ullmann has always insisted upon the centrality of community and close relationships in her work with UNICEF and the struggle for rights. She sees these ties as an antidote to the powerlessness many people feel in the face of the difficulty and complexity of assuring human dignity around the world and, as such, also reaffirms the significance of individual gestures. Upholding the compassion and personal involvement in the problems of distant societies needed to guarantee the rights of all human beings, she thus reminds us of the spiritual dimension of human rights work.

In March 1994 the International Gathering of Mothers and Women in Struggle was formed. Included in that movement were fourteen organizations of political mothers: women fighting against authoritarian governments; women confronting disastrous environmental policies such as the radiation leaks from Chernobyl in Kiev; mothers working on behalf of peace in Israel, Palestine, and the former Yugoslav republics; mothers working against drugs in Spain; mothers of the *disappeared* in Brazil, Honduras, Guatemala, and the Western Sahara; and mothers against the Mafia in Italy. They met in Paris in order to pool their expertise and experience, develop a permanent movement to achieve their national goals, and help create societies in which all human beings might prosper. Although the newly formed organization planned to hold yearly meetings, the next conference was postponed until the spring of 1996 because of limited finances. In the interval between meetings, the national groups assist each other in carrying out their programs, whether supplying Sarajevo with food and medicine or helping the Mama 86 in Kiev gather signatures aimed at closing down the Chernobyl nuclear reactor. As in the Native American tradition, the mothers of nations have reassumed their roles as guarantors of justice and monitors of ethics in the public realm.

Whether as political mothers, individuals, or organizational activists, women often have been disregarded by the male establishment. However, through their actions and the space they have claimed for their ideas, they have proved that they are far from powerless. On the contrary, they have demonstrated that while governments at all levels have tried to exclude their experience and their presence within the institutions of power, they have nevertheless made great strides not only in creating a more humane and livable world but also in presenting us with new models of ethical action.

Notes

1. PCBs are in the family of halogenated aromatic hydrocarbons and also contain DDT and dioxin, some of the most toxic substances known to exist. See Mary-Jane Schneider, *Persistent Poisons: Chemical Pollutants in the Environment* (New York: New York Academy of Sciences, 1979), 13.

2. Virginia Held, *Feminist Morality: Transforming Culture, Society, and Politics* (Chicago: University of Chicago Press, 1993), 39.

3. Ibid., 35.

4. Ibid., 154.

5. Commission for Racial Justice, United Church of Christ, *Toxic Wastes and Race in the United States: A National Report on the Racial and Socio-Economic Characteristics of Communities with Hazardous Waste Sites* (New York: Commission for Racial Justice, 1987).

6. Andrew Byrnes, "Women, Feminism, and International Human Rights Law—Methodological Myopia, Fundamental Flaws, or Meaningful Marginalisation? Some Current Issues," *The Australian Year Book of International Law* 12 (1992): 208–9.

7. Amnesty International USA, prepared statement, Hearings on Human Rights Abuses against Women before Subcommittee on Human Rights and International Organizations, Committee on Foreign Affairs, U.S. House of Representatives, 101st Cong., March 21, 1990.

8. Byrnes, "Women, Feminism, and International Human Rights Law," 214.

9. Ibid., 219.

10. Hilary Charlesworth, Christine Chinkin, and Shelly Wright, "Feminist Approaches to International Law," *American Journal of International Law* 85 (1991): 632.

11. Held, *Feminist Morality*, 56.

Part I

Confronting Authoritarian Governments

1 / Vera Laska

VERA LASKA'S HOME IN SUBURBAN Weston, Massachusetts, looks like any other in that area, surrounded by trees and a patch of lawn. However, inside her study are books and papers reaching the ceiling and photographs of her mentors and role models from academia and politics. She and I were colleagues for many years before I learned about her past as a teenage member of the Resistance against the Nazis in wartime Czechoslovakia. The only inkling she gives of her history is the fact that she always says what she thinks and speaks to the heart of the matter, regardless of the consequences. She is a totally free spirit who acts from inner conviction, whose quiet and casual demeanor and wry sense of humor belie an accomplished scholar and a woman of extraordinary courage.

Vera Oravec was born in Kosice, Czechoslovakia, and lived with her mother after her parents divorced. She remembers loving school as a child, being avidly curious about everything, and reading voraciously. She did not excel in high school, however, because she loved volleyball and skiing and was a champion swimmer. It was at Charles University that her talents as a student would bloom.

There was not much money in Vera's household, and therefore, when only thirteen, she took advantage of her great facility for languages and began giving private lessons in German. When the Hungarians occupied Kosice in 1939, a number of high Hungarian officers wanted their children to learn the language, and thus Vera had quite a number of them as her students. Her job served as a useful cover and as a good source of information for the Resistance.

Vera's career in the underground started casually and came about because of her known prowess in skiing. Someone approached her about some escaped French prisoners of war who wanted to go to Hungary and needed a person to help them across the border over the mountains. She agreed without any hesitation, feeling that she would have done anything to spite the Nazis. By the time she had taken three such trips across the mountains, she realized that she was in the Resistance. Although only fifteen at the time, she was not the youngest member of her small group of Resisters. Her fluency in Czech, Slovak, Hungarian, and German facilitated her work as did her intimate knowledge of the countryside.

In the 1940s there were two groups of people who were fleeing from the Nazis in her country and whom Vera helped ferry to their destinations. After the defeat of France, there were many French prisoners of war in German camps and also in camps in German-occupied Poland. A number of them managed to escape via the Polish-Slovak border into Slovakia, through the Slovak-Hungarian border into Hungary, then into Yugoslavia, to Beirut, and around the Mediterranean and into southern France, where they eventually joined the Free French. Also attempting to escape were Jews persecuted by the collaborationist government in Slovakia. Vera was part of an "underground railroad" that shepherded both French prisoners of war and Jews across the border. It was a chain operation and only a small number of the Resistance workers knew where it began or ended. For security reasons all that Vera knew was the stop before and the stop after.

Night after night, often in the freezing cold, Vera escorted groups of people across the border from 1940 to 1943. Although only a teenager, she learned a great deal about human foibles. Despite her warnings to the people she helped across the border, some insisted on bringing along useless material possessions. She and her little band of guides learned to carry hand shovels to dig holes for discarded objects, aspirin to keep children sleepy, and ropes with loops for a handhold.[1] She experienced many close calls during these dangerous crossings. During one of her trips leading a transport of men to Yugoslavia through Kiskunhalas, her right foot froze. Nevertheless, she and another young girl managed to guide the band of twenty-eight to a safe house in Belgrade.[2]

In the spring of 1943, Vera was betrayed. She considers the fact that she was able to continue for so long a record, because generally Resistance workers were caught after barely six months. Someone had seen too much and observed her group. They were all captured. She never found out who it was.

Vera spent two years in the concentration camps of Auschwitz, Gross-Rosen, and Dora-Nordhausen. Her first human contact at Auschwitz was with a female guard who hit her across the mouth with a belt buckle and broke her teeth. Vera has described that experience as a place where all values changed, where "to steal was an art or a virtue, and where in all that grayness, death was a lark."[3] She narrowly escaped the gas chambers herself. A Slovak friend from her high school recognized her even though Vera's head had been shaved and she had lost much weight. Her friend Magda had a privileged position within the camp, working in a barracks sorting shoes, jewelry, eyeglasses, and everything else that had been confiscated from the inmates. As soon as she saw Vera, she pushed her toward the latrines with kicks and curses and told her to stay there and clean. She kept up the barrage of abuse for two days, insisting that Vera continue scrubbing. When Magda finally told her she had finished her task, Vera emerged to discover that her entire block had vanished up the chimneys while she had been spared.

Dora-Nordhausen had a huge munitions factory of several stories hidden underground beneath the barracks for prisoners. It was an international slave labor center with prisoners from France, Belgium, Czechoslovakia, Poland, and Hungary. Vera and some of her fellow inmates were assigned the task of measuring the diameters of small duralumin rings. They deliberately mismeasured millions of them, and Prime Minister Winston Churchill later acknowledged that this sabotage prevented many V-2 missiles from exploding over London.

After her liberation from the concentration camp, Vera immediately contacted former Czech political prisoners from Camp Dora.

They obtained an automobile and painted a large red cross on it, with the words "Czechoslovak Red Cross." In the trunk of that car were Camp Dora's prisoner lists and SS correspondence. These files constituted the basis for the Czechoslovak War Crimes Investigation Commission for which Vera served as executive secretary.

When Vera finally returned to Prague after the war, the mood was jubilant. However, her father had been shot and her mother had died in Auschwitz. She started to look for her friends, most of whom were either in the underground or in England, although some were even in the Czechoslovak Legion in the USSR. Little by little the news filtered in from London: out of two dozen of her close friends, only four were still alive. This news was a heavy blow to endure when everyone around her was celebrating the end of the hostilities.

Vera found an apartment in Prague and began work with the War Crimes Commission. Because she was with the commission, she was told she could go to the central location where German prisoners were gathered and take one out for the day to clean her apartment. This opportunity gave her a chance to express revenge. Accordingly, she brought out a German woman to help her with housework. However, after one day Vera felt sorry for the woman and wound up giving her something to eat, although she did not have much food herself, and sending her right back.

While working full-time with the commission, Vera went to Charles University in Prague to study philosophy and history. Then, on the recommendation of two of her professors, she was sent to the United States in 1946 on a fellowship given by the Institute of International Education. She studied at the University of Chicago, earning her doctorate in American history in 1959. There she served as a foreign students counselor and also met her future husband, Andy Laska. They became the parents of two sons: Tom, who later was killed in an automobile accident on the way to attend graduate school; and Paul, whom they adopted after Tom's death.

The Laskas lived in Cuba, Brazil, and Chicago before settling in New England, where in 1966 Vera joined the faculty at Regis College; there she has taught American and diplomatic history and has earned the love of a generation of students. From the time she settled in Massachusetts, Vera was active in helping refugees from Communist Czechoslovakia. When the regime was toppled and replaced by a democratic system, she returned for a semester in 1993 to her beloved Charles University as a Fulbright professor of American history. She was accompanied by her husband, who serves as a director of the Citizens Democracy Corps.

Among Vera's many publications is *Women in the Resistance and in the Holocaust.* She was in the midst of preparing another book when she realized that most of the studies of the Resistance and the Holocaust had been written by men, and that they seldom pointed out the important role of women in resisting National Socialism. These works did not mention the fact that it was women who contributed the gunpowder for sabotage in Auschwitz, that the head of one of the large Resistance networks in France was a woman, and that women had special gifts that made them very effective in such work. Vera claims that women reacted differently than men, could maintain poker faces better than could men, were able to pretend more effectively, and were ingenious in using the materials at hand for sabotage. She also has noted that women behaved in a different manner from men within the concentration camps and, therefore, had a better survival rate. When the guards would spit on them or physically abuse them, the women would remain expressionless. On the other hand, the men, more apt to talk back or to try to retaliate, were being shot more frequently. Vera's book has earned these brave women a place in history and has provided important role models.

Vera has written that her wartime experiences have given her a deep appreciation of life and an ability to enjoy the simplest things, and that she no longer worries about the small problems of everyday life that bother most people. "I rejoice over the laughter of a child and the beauty of a book. Paradoxically, I am capable of enjoying happiness more than those who did not savor the wages of fear. I gained the gift of knowing how to live life to the fullest, body and soul. I carry in me constantly the awareness that I want to see and hear and know as much and as many people as possible, for knowledge is power and knowledge is happiness. Above all, I cherish my freedom to listen and to speak without fear."[4] Rather than being wracked by bitterness, Vera regards her survival of the concentration camps as a triumph over her captors. She has used her experience to urge people to treasure life and work for freedom.

VERA SPEAKS

I became involved because my deepest beliefs, my moral and patriotic values, directed me to resist evil. I could not sit on the sidelines and play possum, pretending that I did not see the outrages committed all around me.

"Paradoxically, people become aware of human rights when they are denied them, or when they see their fellow human beings denied them. But one can live one's entire life ignoring the plight of others, not noticing that some people are less fortunate than ourselves, just because they believe in a different god or because their forebears had different ethnic roots.

It is hard to conceive that in this shrinking world with the communication revolution of the last few decades, so many people can remain so insular. Yet when I think back on my own early years, I was just as insular. I lived for school, which I loved because it satisfied much of my curiosity, and for sports because they brought me such pleasure.

If there was injustice around me, I was not aware of it. I grew up in a town in Czechoslovakia where several ethnic groups lived in peace side by side. In my school, in my sports clubs, Czechs and Slovaks, Germans and Hungarians mixed without any friction. Nor did religion erect barriers between us. I did not even find out that one of my closest friends was Jewish until the Nazis pinned a yellow star on her coat. I hated that stamp of discrimination on her as much as she did.

My school years were happy ones. For most of my friends and me, the process of learning was a challenge. But it was my philosophy professor who gave direction to my life. He was a pupil of Tomas G. Masaryk, the philosopher and humanitarian who was also the liberator-president of the country after its creation in 1918. Whether he was expounding ethics or metaphysics, Professor Jan B. Kozak's every sentence was permeated with deep concern about human decency and the importance of democracy. He stressed these two major values in relations between individuals and nations. He did not preach against Nazism or Communism. He warned against any kind of totalitarianism. With his index finger pointing at the class, he emphasized the moral law in [the German philosopher Immanuel] Kant's categorical imperative: Do not do unto others what you do not want others to do unto you.

We lived in a democratic Czechoslovakia. The Czechs were nicknamed the Yankees of Europe. Our constitution was drafted in 1918 on a park bench near the White House in Washington, DC, and was similar to the American constitution. One difference was that Masaryk insisted that women should have an equal vote with men; thus, female suffrage arrived for Czechoslovak women before it was won for American women.

I never experienced any discrimination because of my sex. As a matter of fact, I eventually received the highest fellowship available in the country, the Masaryk Award, established from the personal funds of the president. This is not to say that there was no discrimination against women. When confronted with my wish to go to college, my own father replied that women have no business studying and that I should learn how to sew. I still chuckle now, as I did then, over this statement. I ignored it and went on my merry way to Charles University in Prague, one of the oldest institutions of higher learning in Europe. I did not stop to think that my rights were being invaded. I only thought my father was old-fashioned.

It was a windy day in March 1939 when the Nazi war machine rolled into Prague. The previous fall the long-trusted democracies—Great Britain and France—had sold Czechoslovakia down the river at Munich. In the bitter poetry of the Czechs, new epithets described them as 'perfidious Albion' and the ironical 'la douce France.' The formerly protective Western allies had allowed Hitler to denude Czechoslovakia of its western defenses by carving out the Sudetenland. The Hungarians laid claim to the southern portion of Slovakia, and Poland took a small part of Silesia.

Czechs from the occupied territories had been evacuated, and so I had moved to Prague. I stood on the sidewalk looking at the German tanks rolling in. People with tears streaming down their cheeks watched the Nazis parading under the statue of St. Wenceslas, patron saint of the Czechs. It seemed like a sacrilege. But the gallows humor of the Czechs flared up when a Nazi vehicle broke down. Then there was loud applause. Otherwise the invaders rolled in amidst deadly silence.

Soon there were demonstrations against the Nazi presence. Arrests and executions followed. Students began circulating anti-Nazi leaflets. During the demonstrations of October 28 (the equivalent of the American Fourth of July), a medical student was shot and later died. At his funeral on November 17, 1939, there were more demonstrations and more reprisals. As a result, all institutions of higher learning were permanently shut down. All student government leaders were summarily shot; over a thousand students were taken to the concentration camp of Sachsenhausen in Oranienburg, near Berlin. All Czech universities remained closed for the duration of the war to prevent the rebellious Czechs from gathering together and conspiring against the Reich and to prevent the education of defiant intellectuals.

I am often asked if I joined the Resistance under the auspices of a political party. Nothing could be further from the truth. First of all, I never had been a member of any political party. I did not join the Resistance as one would join a club. I became involved because my deepest beliefs, my moral and patriotic values, directed me to resist evil. I could not sit on the sidelines and play possum, pretending that I did not see the outrages committed all around me. I reached this conclusion instinctively, before even rationalizing it. It was the only way to act if I cared to maintain and protect a world that seemed to me to have been arranged according to some divine justice.

A few days before that fateful November 17, a fellow student stuck a bunch of leaflets into my hands in the hallway of my college with a short admonition: 'Hide and distribute!' The stack of papers was bulky, and the purple mimeograph ink stained my fingers as I stuffed them into my briefcase. It was so full that I could not close it. I went to my assigned desk and left half of the leaflets inside it, luckily under lock. Then I inspected one of the leaflets, actually a four-page brochure. It contained the latest news broadcast from the BBC in London about what was going on in occupied Prague and its environs. It also had a patriotic poem, a few quotations from Masaryk displayed under the emblem of the Czechoslovak Republic and its motto: TRUTH SHALL PREVAIL. Typically for the nation of Schweik, it also contained about half a dozen political jokes, all aimed at the Nazis, of course.* That was the last time I was at that desk. I took the remaining half of the leaflets and distributed them into mailboxes and left them on tables in the student cafeteria.

Clashes between Czechs and the Nazis were a daily event. In movie houses, newsreels of German armies were greeted with boos, and minutes later the Gestapo would clear the theater, arresting anyone who looked suspicious to them. I recall seeing a newsreel of Hitler looking out of a window of Hradchin Castle, the seat of ancient Bohemian kings, and it turned my stomach. I do not know if it was my budding sense of history or my patriotism, but I felt

*Jaroslav Hasek's *The Good Soldier Schweik* reveals that the Czech people have a history of flaunting authority with humor and a keen sense of independence. It is a fictional account of the Czech response to the Austro-Hungarian empire.

physically the sacrilege perpetrated on sacred ground by that nobody.

When I heard of the closing of all institutions of higher learning on November 17, I rushed to the college to retrieve the illegal leaflets from my desk. I was too late. There were SS guards in front of every school. A few days later, returning to my room, I met two plainclothesmen walking up the stairs toward my apartment and asking me where Vera Oravec lived. I was able to remain calm and to direct them to the fourth floor. I lived on the second. I gained a few minutes of precious time. Naturally, I never returned to that place. I refused to live in constant fear. A few weeks later I left the country illegally, walking across several borders during the night.

My adventures started on a freezing January night in 1940 when I accompanied a family friend who was a high-ranking officer of the army and who was fleeing for his life. We were to cross several borders illegally on our way to Budapest. I was his camouflage. A couple traveling together was considered less suspicious than a single man of military bearing, especially since our train was headed toward the border. In a way, I had to be camouflaged too, for I was a teenager, looking just a bit too young to be huddled lovingly against my 'husband.' I had to wear makeup, which I then considered quite a sacrifice. I was dressed rather elegantly with a wide fur collar on my coat and a hat on my newly acquired curls. Leather gloves were 'de rigueur,' as was a rather large alligator-skin handbag.

We managed to get safely to the city of Olomouc, where we found the safe house. Although neither of us had ever been in that city, we had been given a detailed map of the way from the station to the safe house, and we committed it to memory. By midnight, we stood in front of the house. We were petrified. The building was the seat of a Gestapo office! Were we directed to a trap? We just could not believe that. We climbed to the third floor, pressed the doorbell, and when the door was opened we asked the prearranged passwords:

'Do you still have the old rocking horse?'

The woman showed no recognition of the password.

'What rocking horse?' she replied. 'You must have the wrong place.'

By this time a man joined her, shuffling to the door in worn house slippers. As the officer and I stood helplessly outside and the woman was getting ready to slam the door in our faces, the man said:

'Wait a minute, Maria.' He turned to us and asked: 'Who sent you?' We explained our situation and were ushered into the apartment, to the great relief of all four of us.

We had barely fallen asleep when the doorbell began to ring insistently. Knowing that the Gestapo offices were just below, we woke with a start. We had slept fully clothed, and now we headed for the back door as our landlord had instructed us to do in case of danger. But we did not have to face the night and the cold, for the man entered our room and calmed us. It was the messenger with the password about the rocking horse. He was delayed because he had a flat on his bicycle. After that we did get a good night's sleep and a hearty breakfast the next morning.

A local train took us even closer to the border. We were met at a small village and given instructions on how to reach a forester's cottage in the mountains. We had a jolly time at the forester's. He was a character straight out of Dickens, brimming with energy and with many stories to tell. By nightfall he had pumped us full of home-brewed *slivovitz*, 'to keep us warm' on the next leg of our adventure.

Accompanied by his wife and dog, he led us to the border between the Nazi-established protectorate (Bohemia and Moravia) and the newly established Nazi puppet state of Slovakia. His wife was his alibi in case we would run into German patrols. We were supposed to evaporate into thin air in that eventuality, and he was supposed to be 'just out for a stroll with the wife.' Luckily, we did not have to test his theory.

We had an encounter on the border that night that fitted a Hollywood horror movie. As the forester at the head of our Indian file whistled, we all ducked off the trail among the snow-covered trees. We were quiet as mice when the cat shows up! Above us came two figures in dark coats, hats pulled down almost to their noses, hands in their pockets, swiftly advancing in the opposite direction. The apparitions emerged and disappeared into the night like ghosts. 'Smugglers,' the forester explained with a contemptuous wave of his hand.

We ran into a few other unexpected problems on our way. The safe house over the border in Slovakia became quite unsafe. A messenger intercepted us in the forest with the warning that there was a rip-roaring birthday party going on there, with all the border guards present. We lost the place for our overnight rest, but our crossing became easier, knowing that the Slovak border was temporarily unattended.

On the next border, from Slovakia to Hungary, a small boy of about twelve was our guide. At times he just about disappeared among the dry stalks of the grapevines. Finally, we were safe on the Hungarian side. My officer companion unceremoniously hid in the toilet while I purchased our tickets and engaged a curious gentleman in conversation in Hungarian. He might have been a police agent. After all, this was a border town. Evidently he was satisfied with my tale of visiting relatives and returning to Budapest. He did not ask for papers. Maybe he just liked my hat. But he prevented me from alerting my friend that the train was coming. He ran out from his hiding place and jumped into the first car near him.

Unfortunately, since my friend did not speak a word of Hungarian, he did not notice that this was the car coming directly from Slovakia and hence subject to passport control. Sure enough, he got picked up by the police. He told them he was from Yugoslavia, so he was deposited at the Yugoslav consulate. With one day's delay, we met again in Budapest.

In Budapest, our ways parted. I stayed on, and he left with the next group of Czech and Slovak men via Yugoslavia and Greece to Beirut in Lebanon. From there they boarded a ship for Agde in France, where the military training of the Czech troops took place. The Free Czechoslovak forces fought alongside the Allies throughout the war. Later, I was happy to learn that my friend survived the war.

In Budapest, I could be useful because I spoke fluent Hungarian and also because I was female and hence less suspect. Our men needed lodging, clothes, food, and medical care. Since they did not speak Hungarian, their needs were taken care of by messengers like me who could move around rather easily as long as we did not get into trouble with the police. In 1940, Hungary was seemingly far removed from the war, even from the daily irritations of the Nazis. A well-dressed woman could move around freely and without much fear.

Sometimes our rage against the Nazis turned us into pranksters. My fondest recollection of a dangerous situation in Budapest that turned into a farce is the day when my Czech boys in a particular apartment greeted me with: 'Trouble! The landlady wants to hear the Polish anthem.' Because of the sympathies between Hungary and Poland, the men were introduced to the landlady as Poles. Nobody knew the Polish anthem. Would this small technicality stop us? No way! I suggested that we all sing a popular Czech song about young love. There we stood and with solemn faces sang this ridiculous song in a funereal tempo. The landlady was close to tears. We were close to an outbreak of hilarity.

At times I also purchased the train tickets for the men and even accompanied them to the southernmost city in Hungary, Szeged. It was at Szeged where, one evening as we arrived, we faced an entire cordon of police agents. We were surrounded, herded into police wagons, and taken to the infamous Csillag (Star) Prison. I managed to talk myself out of the compromising situation. Only a female could have done that.

I was then taken back to Budapest under police escort. On the way, I told the policeman that I had to go to the bathroom. While he was waiting for me outside of the door, I was crawling out of the window to safety. I wondered how he failed to see through such a transparent ruse. But now my usefulness in Budapest was ended, and I moved on with the next transport to Yugoslavia.

Belgrade was an important center of the Czechoslovak underground. It was here, in Czechoslovak House, where the start of the long road to the West was centrally organized. The men and a few women flocked to this place from all over. The men swore military allegiance in Belgrade. They were housed and fed for several days. Twice a week about fifty or sixty of them moved on to join the war in active service. Many of us wept as, after a brief ceremony, the boys departed.

The Yugoslavs had a special fondness for their 'brother Czechs.' Many had happy memories of their university days in Prague; the two countries belonged to the Little Entente. I stayed in Belgrade for over a year, helping out at Czechoslovak House, welcoming and sending off our boys. As a cover, I also registered at the University of Belgrade without any proper papers or credentials. The dean was a great friend of Czechoslovakia and provided many of us with university identification cards. The police also helped us, often warning us when a raid was in the offing.

Professor Kozak was also in exile at this time, teaching at Oberlin College. He wrote to me that I should immediately come to America and he would help me get a scholarship at Oberlin. Had I done so, I might have saved myself a lot of grief. But in a moment of patriotism, a friend of mine had removed the overlaid label, 'Protectorate of Bohemia and Moravia' from my originally Czech passport, thus making it legally invalid in the eyes of the American authorities!

I confess that I was not too chagrined by that. I instinctively felt that if I could not join my fellow patriots in Great Britain or

America, I should stay where I was, making myself as useful as possible in the war effort. As much as I loved studying, nothing was more important at that time than ridding the world of the Nazi führer. I thought of those days after the universities were closed in Czechoslovakia when many of my close friends were sent to the concentration camp of Sachsenhausen in Germany and when the members of the student government were all executed. As did Masaryk, I disagreed with Leo Tolstoy about turning the other cheek, an angelic theory but one that would lead only to further subjugation. If persecuted and oppressed, one should fight back. Liberty, the greatest human value, includes responsibilities. Thus, I carried on until yet another drastic intervention by the Nazis forced me to change directions.

On April 6, 1941, the open city of Belgrade was subjected to one of the most devastating carpet bombings of World War II. With a group of friends I fled the city with bombs raining all around us. The pictures that remain in my mind of that morning can be compared to Dante's Inferno. A bomb shaved off the front of a house. In an upstairs room, as if on a stage, a woman in her nightgown was playing the harp, emitting incomprehensible shrieks to the people running by. Limbs torn from bodies and headless torsos were lying all over the place. Mothers were shouting for their children, and children were crying for their mothers. A father was cursing his youngster, who would not let go of his bicycle although both its tires were flat from the sea of glass on the streets.

The panic around us was total. The physical destruction, the cries of separated families, the screaming of men, women, and children all contributed to a feeling of doom. On top of it all, a second wave of German Stuka planes attacked not only the burning Belgrade but also the streams of people trying to flee from the inferno. Bombs were falling in front of us and behind us. At one point we hid in a crater left by one of the bombs, because bombs are never supposed to fall on the same spot. In our case, it proved to be true.

We walked the entire day, until we came to a village about twenty kilometers from Belgrade. We simply could not go any farther. Our feet just would not carry us. So we bedded down in a barn, thanks to the goodwill of a farmer. We were hungry, thirsty, and covered with dust. Among the few possessions that we had grabbed as the first bombs fell on Belgrade was a strange conglomeration of things. I had dumped my identification papers into a large handbag. The only thing I could lay my hands on as I ran from my room was a fat English-Czech and Czech-English dictionary. I never thought of a toothbrush or a first-aid kit. I also lugged a heavy winter coat, just because it was on my way to the door. I had no use for it, but it did come in handy when we exchanged it for a week's food supply for three people.

The first night outside Belgrade was lit up with the reflection of red and orange flames on the horizon: Belgrade was burning! The indignation of the refugees was deep. They could not comprehend how it was possible that Belgrade, declared an 'open city,' had been violated by the Nazi bombers. It was just a foretaste of many other atrocities I was to experience at the hands of the Nazis. There had not been a single soldier in Belgrade. As a matter of fact, the last days before the bombing that Easter Sunday, thousands of women and children came into Belgrade seeking refuge because it was an 'open city.' The Nazi aggressors had no respect for international law.

After a few days of respite in that village, I managed to escape to the north to a former Slovak town that was now under Hungarian occupation. This was in southeastern Czechoslovakia, before Munich and the equally unfair Vienna *arbitrage*. Munich detached the Sudetenland, and the Vienna decision detached part of southern Slovakia from the Czechoslovak Republic. So now the former Czechoslovak town was under Hungarian rule. That meant that the border had shifted northward, yet the old border was still not open. Both Slovak and Hungarian border guards were patrolling both frontiers. The town itself had not changed much since I had known it in my earlier years. While many people had fled, most of the population had stayed. Among them were numerous friends of mine. There was a new group of people, those who were commandeered from Hungary, some officials and army personnel among them.

Since I needed to feed and house myself, I started giving language lessons. The most popular demand among the Hungarian military and bureaucrats was for German. So, with a feeling of disgust, I started teaching German to the children of Hungarians from the Motherland. As it turned out, this was not such a bad idea. Most of the children learned very slowly, which suited me fine. Many of the parents were decent people with proper manners who would invite me for tea or a snack. As time went by, I realized that I could learn a lot from these occupation officials and their wives. Gradually, I started reporting bits of useful information to the underground.

Just as I had anticipated, soon after my arrival ir town, I was contacted by the Resistance. If my intellectual upbringing supplied the moral justification for becoming part of the Resistance, my predilection for sports brought about the chance that provided the opportunity. One day, a friend in the swimming club mentioned casually that there were some French prisoners of war who had escaped from Nazi camps in Poland. They were hiding in Slovakia and would like to get to Hungary as a first leg on their way to freedom. Would I like to join in guiding them through the mountains from Slovakia to Hungary?

I knew what was the right thing to do, the humane thing to do. I did not philosophize about human rights or civil rights. Of course, I knew that the undertaking was dangerous and that I could land in jail or a concentration camp. But I felt that I could never look at myself in the mirror if I did not lend a helping hand.

The odds were favorable, or so it seemed to our teenage minds. We were up against inexperienced border guards. In the winter they were useless on their skis. In the summer they got lost among the hundreds of trails. We were expert skiers. Some of us were school champions and we knew every nook and cranny of the woods. So we started with the Pierres; every Frenchman was Pierre to us. Later, we expanded and guided Jews fleeing persecution in Slovakia while Hungary was still not under the direct Nazi boot. [Adolf] Eichmann would arrive in Hungary in the spring of 1944, relatively late in the course of the Final Solution.

Looking back on these people-smuggling days of my life, I can see more clearly the dangers we subjected ourselves to. At the same time, I can also see the tremendous luck we had in our undertakings. We carried forged identification papers—in the right pocket from Slovakia, in the left pocket from Hungary. We were stopped a couple of times during the day as we were returning alone from a trip with our charges safely delivered to their destination.

The border guards were mostly simple peasant boys, who most of the time had no idea where the borderline was. Their intelligence did not match ours, and their resistance to a few cigarettes or a piece of chocolate was minimal. We were seldom confronted with border guards during the night, when we guided our passengers through the mountains. I wonder if the border guards stayed in at night because they had heard the tales of vicious boars and wolves, rumors that we propagated among them on our more innocent outings.

The Frenchmen were easy to bring across. They were young and tough. They also knew that the worst that could happen to them as prisoners of war was to be returned to their camps, although that was not necessarily what happened in every case. As civilians, the Jews were less disciplined and also less tolerant of hardships. Many insisted on bringing luggage that they could not carry for more than an hour. I recall a lady who arrived in high-heeled shoes, or a couple who would not budge without their silver candelabra. We dealt with all of these minor emergencies. We learned with experience that children must get aspirin to make them drowsy, that older people must carry a cane, and that all must go to the bathroom before we started out.

I was not the only girl in the Resistance. There were girls and women in the resistance movements in every single country occupied by the Nazis, from Norway to Italy, from the Soviet Union to France, and even in Great Britain. Many British women were members of the Special Operations Executive and were parachuted or flown into occupied Europe for resistance work. There was also a sprinkling of American women in the Resistance.

Mine is only one girl's story. There were many of us, and while each of us has her own story to tell, we were held together by a common bond in those terrible years. It still binds us now. Many women paid with their lives for their altruistic deeds. Some were captured, tortured, and executed. Some perished in Auschwitz in the gas chambers or of typhus. Others were experimented on in Ravensbruck, the infamous women's concentration camp for political prisoners.

I was somewhere in the middle in my fate. I was lucky to have had the chance to fight Nazism for several years. Betrayed by an unknown person, I landed in Auschwitz. I marched out of there on my birthday because I had the fixed idea that few people ever die on their birthdays; hence, I volunteered for a transport. With a fifty-fifty chance, my transport would not 'go up the chimney.' It truly was a transport out of overcrowded Auschwitz.

I also graduated from Gross-Rosen and from Dora-Nordhausen concentration camps. My life in these extermination camps does not belong to this story. Suffice it to say that on a hunger march from Nordhausen in the spring of 1945, I took advantage of a great confusion over some boiled potatoes and jumped over a fence to freedom. I knew when I landed on a heap of manure that I was in luck!

I hid for four and a half days in a hayloft, barely daring to move; straw can make a hellish racket when you are afraid of every sound. Meanwhile, the front somehow passed over me. On the fifth day I clambered down from the hayloft and received the first food in about a week from a Ukrainian forced laborer on the farm. He shared with me the best news I had ever heard in my life: 'Hitler kaput. War kaput.'

During our brief Czecho-Russian conversation he also confided in me that Stalin was a son of a bitch and that he would not go back to the Soviet Union. That absolutely floored me, but that is another story.

The Americans were just outside the village. They almost shot me with a machine gun when I emerged into view with my hair about one inch long, straw sticking to my clothes, filthy dirty, and I am sure emanating odors that were quite different from Chanel No. 5. In instinctive self-defense, I collapsed. Then they approached, and I saw one man eating a most beautiful, a most red apple. I grabbed it from his mouth and devoured it. Never before or since did food taste as good.”

Notes

1. Vera Laska, ed., *Women in the Resistance and in the Holocaust: The Voices of Eyewitnesses* (Westport, CT: Greenwood Press, 1983), 53.
2. Ibid., 79.
3. Ibid., 169.
4. Ibid., 301.

2 / Eva Brantley

EVA BRANTLEY IS A PETITE WOMAN whose delicate beauty and charm belie a dynamism and intensity that has served her well in human rights work. She is driven by a commitment that often keeps her working around the clock and thinking ahead to the next situation while completing a current project. Eva brings to her work a strong sense of ethics, rigorous standards in documenting abuses, and an unusual sensitivity to the needs and culture of the people she serves. Much of her work involves travel to war-torn areas of the world where there is a need for either legal assistance or help in documenting abuses of dignity. Most recently she has worked in Kosovo, and in former Yugoslav republics such as Bosnia, where her language skills and her warmth have earned her the love of those she has served. Eva never forgets that those who suffer violations of their rights are human beings, and she brings not only professional skills but also her kindness and understanding wherever she goes. This combination of qualities stems from her ability to remain an activist while enjoying the more private side of life. Although continually immersed in researching human rights issues and preparing testimony, Eva knows how to savor quiet moments, and she radiates inner joy. These traits have enabled her to transcend serious health problems as well as her blindness. They have also taught her how precious life is.

Eva Brantley was born in England in 1949, the daughter of Polish exiles who were active in the Resistance against National Socialism and who each under terrible circumstances during World War II suffered the loss of a spouse, and in her mother's case her babies. Her family history and her own personal experiences inspired her to become involved in human rights work at an early age, to study law at Surrey University, and in 1978 to acquire a doctorate in international human rights law at Harvard University.

The household in which Eva grew up and her survival of repeated bouts with serious illnesses have given her strength of purpose and character. During an operation for a problem connected with rheumatoid arthritis, the surgeon mistakenly severed her optic nerve, and Eva lost her vision at the age of nineteen when she was working toward a degree in music. As a result, she discontinued her study of the piano at the Royal Academy of Music and turned to languages, an endeavor that indirectly propelled her into the defense of human rights. Her career in human rights work began in 1968, shortly after the loss of her eyesight. On a visit with family in Poland during a semester break from teaching languages, Eva was arrested for participating in a demonstration. While in prison, she met people who would become leading figures in the human rights movement and in the trade union Solidarity.

When Eva returned to London after her release from prison, she joined Amnesty International and began working with one of the groups that adopted prisoners of conscience. She also joined groups in other countries that were working toward human rights, such as the precursor of Charter 77, a group formed by artists and intellectuals in Communist Czechoslovakia to monitor the Helsinki Accords' provisions for human rights. As a member, she received and circulated information about human rights violations in that country and also monitored the use of psychiatric means against prisoners in the former Soviet Union, where her language skills proved very useful.

After receiving her doctorate in human rights law, Eva began a career in teaching and simultaneously recommenced her human rights work. Her first big project was to work against the castration and sterilization enforced by Indira Gandhi as a means of achieving birth control. She attempted to alert public opinion to the brutality of this campaign, which often involved pulling men off trains and dragging them into station rest rooms to enforce castration without any medical care. Eva was successful in bringing this issue to the attention of the Canadian parliament and, ultimately, to the United Nations. The campaign resulted in a policy of tying foreign aid to India to an improvement in human rights. However, Eva does not believe that this type of connection is a useful tool in the long term and looks forward to the time when other means will be found to pressure governments that abuse the rights of their citizens.

In the late 1970s, as a result of the contacts she had made in prison in 1968, Eva became involved with Solidarity, serving as a legal counsel to Lech Walesa. That movement was born in the early seventies and erupted into a general strike at the Gdansk Shipyards in December 1980, ultimately threatening the rule of the Polish Communist Party and leading to the imposition of martial law in 1982.

Witnessing the key role played by women, both leading up to the strike and during the uprising, transformed Eva's perspectives on human rights. She found that the women involved in Solidarity spoke with a different voice and espoused broader goals than those traditionally associated with human rights. While the men were concerned with trade union rights and free elections, the women were working toward adequate health care, social support, and economic security as well as local autonomy in the workplace. Eva has adopted this approach in her own work, stressing that all prerogatives are interconnected and that one cannot violate economic rights, for example, without impinging upon dignity or freedom of expression. She believes that the best guarantor of these just claims is a sense of mutual responsibility between individuals and among various social and ethnic groups within a democratic system that respects pluralism at all levels.

Eva continues to teach seminars on human rights around the world while maintaining active involvement in the field. However, the work she finds the most rewarding is her efforts at the grassroots level because she believes that that is where human dignity begins. She has dedicated herself to helping local people gather and formulate information about abuses so that the knowledge gained can be used in international forums and also so that these people can retain control over it. One of her most gratifying efforts has been helping to organize a labor union for indentured children in India based upon the children's own demands and requirements.

Because Eva is known internationally for her achievements, she is frequently contacted through intermediaries by local groups around the world such as the Karin minority in Burma, which is subjected to forced labor by the Burmese army. She helped the Karins formulate their complaints, drawing upon standards established by the International Labor Organization. Eva is also lending her expertise to the Mothers of Russian Soldiers Committee, whose members she met during a conference sponsored by the Organization of European Security and Cooperation. The Mothers Committee is seeking to end the conflict between Russia and the republic of Chechnya and to protect conscripts of both nationalities.

One of Eva's most recent efforts is the result of a dream she conceived while working in St. Petersburg, Russia, at a conference on minority rights. She imagined the Trans-Siberian Express traveling throughout the former Soviet republics and Eastern Europe, picking up women's groups along the way so that they could exchange information and help each other resolve problems. During an interview with the Polish press the following year, Eva spelled out her idea, which was immediately picked up by many nongovernmental organizations involved in human rights as well as the German and Scandinavian governments. That dream became a reality for the Fourth World Conference on Women, held in Beijing in September 1995, when two trains began their journey from Warsaw and Berlin, respectively, ten days before the conference of nongovernmental organizations, gathering activist groups at each stopping point. During the train ride the various organizations were able to discuss their issues and goals through workshops and seminars and to communicate with conference members via a satellite dish. They were thus able to participate in the strategizing on the text of the official document produced by the conference before arriving in Beijing, where, unfortunately, their working conditions were hampered by the Chinese government. Eva, however, was denied a visa to attend the conference, with the Chinese government claiming that it was for her own safety. In actuality, Eva's lobbying on behalf of the Coalition for Democracy, operating in China and abroad, before the Human Rights Commission in Geneva was the reason for her inability to enter China. She had begun this lobbying activity in 1989, gathering more votes against the Chinese government with each passing year. The vote in 1995 came the closest to condemning China because Eva was instrumental in gaining the support of the Central European countries. Only a last-minute defection by the Russian Republic prevented the resolution criticizing China from passing.

Eva's blindness has not been an obstacle in her work. For example, she journeyed through Afghanistan on a donkey with her voice-activated computer during the war between that country and the former Soviet Union in the 1980s, gathering testimony on the Soviet practice of dropping explosive toys that mutilated and killed many Afghan children. She since has noted that her work on this issue revealed the differences between women and men who act on behalf of human rights. While she observed that the men went straight in and began interviewing people and collecting data, women would sit with the victims and wait until they were ready to speak. They would then touch them and hug them, thus taking part in the experience of the violation. She has admitted that one of the most difficult tasks she has ever performed was to testify about these children who had been so badly injured.

Eva has testified before the UN Human Rights Commission since 1982, often confounding ambassadors who seek to discredit her work because of her blindness. In fact, Eva is so adept at listening and in the gestures of responding that it is sometimes difficult to realize that she is sightless, as one African ambassador discovered at a meeting of the Human Rights Commission in Geneva in 1983. He told her that he did not believe that she was really blind, to which she responded by removing one of her glass eyes. The ambassador promptly fainted. "One shouldn't ask questions one doesn't want answered," she later commented, laughing.

Eva has struggled very hard to develop a code within the European Community for the protection of the blind and to ensure them access to public places such as museums and churches. In 1993 she sued the British government for refusing to allow her to bring her guide dog into the country while visiting her ailing father. It is ironic that while working toward human rights for others, she also must struggle to achieve her prerogatives as a blind person.

The "self-employed troublemaker," as her husband calls her, or "the blind subversive," as the former Communist government of Poland referred to her, is continually at work in trouble spots around the world, operating on the basis of grants or dipping into her own modest financial resources in order to carry out her projects. She sees her work as helping grass-roots organizations develop the tools to carry out their own human rights programs and, also, as educating government officials about the violation of rights. She is most concerned about early intervention to prevent abuses. In this connection, she prepared documents for the European Commission of the European Economic Community on how to deal with the situation in the former Yugoslav republics. Her vocabulary does not include the word "obstacle."

EVA SPEAKS

I don't see my work as a "role." That's just too big. I'm not that size of a person. I'm just somebody who cares and if I can help, then I'll try and help. That's the way I see human rights work in general. I am my brother's keeper in the sense that I have to care if I want people to care about me.

"I'd had rheumatoid arthritis as a child, and it was effectively under control. I went into the hospital for some cosmetic surgery, but during the operation the surgeon severed the optic nerve, and at the same time I got an infection in the other eye that destroyed it. It was my nineteenth birthday. I was in the Royal Academy of Music at the time, studying concert piano, with the organ as my second instrument. After the operation, I played my first and last concert in St. Martin's in the Field. I was playing the Bach G Minor, and Her Majesty was there.

The surgeon told me that if I went to an ordinary rehabilitation program I would go crazy. He asked me which language I didn't speak, and I answered that I didn't speak German. He assured me that I would soon have a job in Germany, dialed the German consulate, and handed the phone to me. Within two weeks I was in Germany doing English conversation in a German boarding school.

During the semester break, I went to Poland to visit family and participated in my first demonstration. I had gone to visit some friends, and they were going to an anticensorship demonstration. The authorities had closed down a play written by the most famous Polish playwright. This particular play had been written to oppose the czar and authoritarianism—dictatorship, denial of rights, especially freedom of expression. The playwright also happens to be the mascot of all students; there's always a ceremony on his birthday where students crown his statues with flowers and everyone gets roaring drunk. The demonstration was against censorship, but the students also considered shutting down the play as a slight against them and demanded freedom of expression, more rights on campus, and better living conditions.

During the rally one of the student leaders got on a podium and read one of the speeches that Prime Minister [Wladyslaw] Gomulka had given against [Nikita] Khrushchev, word for word. The student was arrested, beaten, and subsequently sentenced to fifteen years in prison. It was interesting that under Gomulka's leadership, a speech that Gomulka himself had made would cost a student that much time in prison.

The police began attacking us with water cannons and night-sticks, so we tried to run away. I was arrested and charged with hooliganism and attacking a police officer with a lethal weapon, namely, my white cane. I was questioned for about an hour and a half and then brought before a judge in summary proceedings. I asked for a lawyer and was told, 'This is Poland,' which I already knew. I wasn't allowed to put forth my side of the situation, and that was it. I was sentenced to two years in prison in the space of less than five minutes. I spent just over a month and a half in prison. There was an appeal by well-situated persons, but that is a story that I don't want to repeat because people could be hurt.

Prison was educational, depressing, and inspiring. It was more kaleidoscopic than one normally thinks. Prisoners were subjected to continual humiliations; the physical conditions were intended to degrade in terms of hygiene, exercise, lighting, when you could talk and whom you could talk to, what you could read. On the other hand, there was this Morse code that developed between us women, and we communicated and told jokes to each other. It was almost like a Samizdat press going on via the bars and the walls. That was very inspiring because the prisoners were young women. Some of the women in the various cells subsequently became very instrumental in creating Solidarity. I kept in touch with them. A few of them, unfortunately, have changed their position in terms of how they treat other people. Others are still wonderful and are in the opposition under the new government to ensure that standards are observed.

There were ups and downs in prison and there were jokes. What I learned from it was that there could never be a situation one could not find a way of living through. For example, we realized the importance of talking to one another about living through the types of humiliation and abuse that one was subjected to. We talked to one another before abuse happened, not with a view to scaring people but to try to help each other live through that moment, and the next.

There were ten of us in the cell, four of whom had been tried for prostitution. They were the ones who taught us how to deal with the guards. They were incensed for us and had actually started a sort of reform movement to improve prison conditions because they had learned from prisoners who had served almost their full time how to negotiate for things and how to read and write. All these women joined together and started canvassing for better prison conditions. They got internal prison documents which spelled out how one could discipline people and they did quite a lot initially to improve prison conditions.

I was in prison not only in Poland but later in Serbia and in Lithuania. When you are arrested as a woman, no matter where you are, your first fear is that you will be raped, especially if you are being questioned by more than one person. In a way that is worse than being physically attacked. The first thing that the police did in each case was to tell the women to strip, although not many men were stripped during questioning. When you had to strip, you tried to do it on your own, not with the 'assistance of a police officer.' Both in Poland and Lithuania this was done prior to a trial, if you could even call it a trial, by usually four or five soldiers that stood in front and behind you and under glaring lights. At that point it was so difficult not to say: 'Let me put my clothes back on, and I'll tell you everything.' It was not that you were necessarily physically intimidated, but that you were told to strip in the presence of five policemen making comments about it. That was very, very scary. The beatings were not very pleasant: rubber truncheons and wet towels on the soles of your feet, and you're praying to lose consciousness, and it's really quite a blessing when you do. The hygienic conditions were terrible, with latrines that were basically holes in the floor, in Poland, Lithuania, and Serbia. The guards would come and watch you when you wanted to relieve yourself, and they were usually male guards although the women guards could be fairly brutal as well. If you were lucky, you would get to have a bath every third week and wash your hair; and, as a result, there were problems with lice, fleas, and dysentery. These conditions were a way of intimidating you and stripping you of any dignity. Women who had babies in the prison had no diapers or facilities to change their children or to wash them properly.

It's funny how similar prisons are, not just criminal prisons but political prisons, in all the places where I've been. The physical plant of the prison, the fact that you constantly fear you are going to be raped and beaten, that you have no privacy, that there's no space for you, was similar in all the prisons I've experienced. I mean, some prisons are more slummy than others, some are more crowded. In Lithuania (it was immediately after the Russian army had surrounded the parliament in 1992), there were twenty of us in a space which was marked off as being three feet by four feet, so there wasn't anywhere where you could lie down. You had to sort of take shifts in order to sit or lie down at any given point in time. In that particular cell, there weren't any facilities, and if you had an accident there was nothing you could do about it. It was used to demean you, to take away your dignity. I can tell you something about being in prison as a woman. The latrines are definitely designed for the men and not women.

When I got out of prison in Poland, I made the decision to go to law school. I was really angry at the way I had been treated and thought I would do something about it. I applied to law school, but I thought I'd be bored just doing law so I did a triple major, taking German and French at the same time. I studied at the University of Surrey, which was a very modern university at the time, called a glass university in comparison to the traditional brick universities. I don't know how I did it. I don't think I'd have the energy to do it now.

I was given a scholarship to Harvard after that. I didn't apply for it. I wanted to do a Ph.D. in European Community law. The person for whom I wrote my thesis just got hold of the forms for the Knox fellowship and copied the information on the form I had written for the Ph.D. application and sent it off to the scholarship committee. He didn't think I would apply, and he was right. In January I got a phone call asking would I come to an interview, and I refused. My brother came up to Surrey. He is 6'4" and my professor was 6'8", and there's not much you could do with two giants. My brother came home with me and pulled out what I should wear for an interview because he'd seen me go to another interview and just laid it on the bed. So I got marched into this interview. I had my first guide dog at the time.

My interviewers started talking about what was on the form and what I liked about European Community law. I wanted to deal with aspects of European Community law that dealt with social and economic rights, the ramifications of freedom of movement, the interplay between the European Community and human rights documents. At that point they had fifteen thousand applications because it was a full Commonwealth, not just a British, scholarship. They had whittled the applicants down to twenty-five for interviews; and five people, including myself, were accepted. So I came to Harvard in 1973, graduated with my master's in 1974, and received my Ph.D. in international human rights law in 1979. While I was doing my doctorate I was teaching at McGill: contract law, legal history, legal philosophy, legal writing, international law.

My initial forays into international human rights were writing documents and advising, as, for example, when what eventually became Solidarity began getting off the ground. There was a big strike in 1970 that was brutally put down, and a lot of people were killed. At the time, the strikes were limited to Gdansk, and the negotiations were done internally.

In 1976 the next round of strikes and negotiations came up. People who shared the prison experience I mentioned and who had subsequently graduated in law in Poland, and myself, had decided that the next time that there were going to be big demonstrations and people were tried for taking part in demonstrations, lawyers would offer their services. That was the beginning of the formation of KOR [Komitet Oberony Robonikow] (Committee for Self-Defense). KOR's goal was to use legal documents to help promote civil, political, and economic rights and to get this information out to international forums. One of the things I was asked to do was to work with the people of KOR using ILO (International Labor Organization) standards to formulate a charter of workers' rights, which was then submitted to the government. This was the early stage of the formation of the trade union. At that point it was still very much on paper.

KOR started as a group of concerned intellectuals, but if one was going to succeed in promoting rights before the government, one couldn't work for just intellectual rights or workers' rights. Everyone had to join together and effectively form a sort of civil society, an alternative society to the government. That society would help protect rights and would try to influence the government toward change by isolating it. KOR had various modes of action, and one was developing a charter of rights and having that disseminated to workers—in other words, teaching negotiating skills. What had happened in 1970 was that, given the structure of the Polish language, when the workers were talking to the government and to the directors of the factory, they were speaking different languages. The Polish language is very much like Latin. While the directors and the government officials would use the third person plural, workers would be using the second person plural as a mode of esteem. The point is that when you structure an argument or a thought, you use verbs in the one case and nouns and adverbs in the other. Therefore, the workers and directors were talking past each other.

It was very clear in looking at the documents that the government had been very consciously avoiding the workers by using abstract as opposed to concrete types of proposals. The workers would say to the government, for example: 'You will give us doctors in the workplace.' This was actually translated by the government as: 'There will be medical assistance in the workplace.' That's not the best example, but there was a big disparity in terms of what the workers said they wanted and what they were given. The workers didn't necessarily understand what had happened, not because they were stupid but because they were just not used to formulating their thoughts in a very abstract manner. One of the things that was done to avoid this and to help the workers conduct their own negotiations was to give them language and grammar lessons, and to role play negotiations with the people who eventually became Solidarity and student leaders.

The third thing KOR accomplished was gathering information because that is the biggest weapon a government has, information about what it's doing and what is going on. A network was set up for sending information to an office, having that information processed and published illegally in Samizdat, and then sent back through very primitive ways of reproduction. There were no Xerox machines or anything. People would cut stencils, and then they would scour ovens and scrape the soot that had accumulated when people burned food, and that was the basis for the ink. The original Samizdat stencils provided information about people who had been arrested or thrown out of their jobs, or whose children were denied access to school or medical treatment, or who had been imprisoned because they had made some type of worker complaint or had taken part in a demonstration. The information was sent almost through a relay, a bush telegraph because lots of people's telephones were tapped, to this central place which moved around the whole time so as not to be caught. It would then get written up, be reproduced in this fashion, and be sent back to workplaces and other locations. There would be one copy that would be read by five hundred or six hundred people a week because it would be handed down, and there was a whole rota for handing it down.

At the same time, this information was then passed off to Radio Free Europe through various mechanisms that were developed so that the workers could contact the outside world. Radio Free Europe rebroadcast that information back into Poland for the people who were outside the workers' group or who may have had shortwave radios, which were very popular at the time. The information that was rebroadcast into Poland was then passed on by word of mouth at cocktail parties. That was the very crude or primitive way things were done. They're both in a sense very negative words, but they're not negative, they just mean simple fashions. What I was doing was trying to formulate the information so that one could bring a case before the International Labor Organization.

Most of the information was gotten out through Radio Free Europe, and it was done on a need-to-know basis because you never knew when you could unwittingly say something and hurt somebody in the process. So the information I received was smuggled out from these sources through Radio Free Europe.

In 1976 I was taking an advanced course on comparative labor law in Trieste, and one of the professors there was Polish. He had heard about me and I knew about him, and that's how I began my involvement with this project. I was the only person who could speak Polish, and we were talking about how to make labor standards a reality as opposed to something nice on paper, and we just started talking about how it could happen. It was basically kinetic: I sort of volunteered, and it was intimated that it would be nice if I did volunteer. That's how Solidarity developed. It was very much of a hands reaching up, hands reaching down, hands reaching around type of movement. When Solidarity was actually formed, the logo was designed by an artist who was outside the shipyard. What struck him was that there were little children, old ladies, young men, old men, even police officers, all leaning against each other in support of the strike, hoping that it would succeed. It was reaching out and reaching down in different sizes. That's why the Solidarity logo is made of letters leaning against each other in all different sizes, because of the vision this artist had looking at the mass of people interacting with the strikers and even trying to interact wherever possible with the police.

I was involved with Solidarity from the very beginning. Already, at the negotiation stage and contrary to mythology, Lech Walesa was not the driving force in Solidarity. Walesa joined the strike five days after it had started. He wasn't even near the shipyard at the time. The strike was called by the women workers of the shipyard in support of a wonderful crane operator whose name was Anna Walentynowicz. Anna Walentynowicz was kicked out of her job one day before she was to retire, which meant that she wouldn't get any social security or medical help. She had breast cancer at the time and would therefore have been denied treatment. The strike was organized to guarantee social security and economic rights for people who were trying to establish a dialogue with the shipowners. Before the strikes, there were already very many informal trade unions in the shipyard, not only in the shipyard but in the coal mines throughout Poland.

The whole trade union movement started in the seventies, not at the time of the strikes of 1976. The organizing had been largely done by women who were asking for crèches [day nurseries] for children, for equal pay, for maternity leave, for freedom of expression to be able to talk about the demands that they wanted, for the right of men to organize so that they could feel empowered.

Most of the original work that was done in the nineteen seventies, and even the initial negotiations that occurred then, was done by women. They didn't go and confront the management and say they were going to start a strike but just started setting up crèches and then asked the management to pay for them, and doing much the same thing in the medical field. They went around and interviewed gynecologists, pediatricians, and different specialists such as those in work medicine and asked them to come and set up a voluntary clinic in the shipyards. When the clinic had started, they went to the management and asked them for financial support. As a result, this type of action—very practical, concrete action, creating a space for their needs, trying to get security in the broadest sense—served as the basis for the more comprehensive rights then being tacked on to the right to organize. The intention was to have these rights effectively protected not just in one workplace but throughout Poland and then throughout Eastern Europe.

The strike that was organized was first of all to prevent Anna Walentynowicz from being fired, to establish some mechanism of protection, and to change the labor law so that a person who was asking for higher wages and better working conditions wouldn't be summarily fired and left with nothing. It was a problem not just for the women but also for the men. So the women went to the heads of the departments and asked them to join in. The night before the strike broke out in the middle of August, the women were making placards and posters, they were sewing strike arm bands, and they were holding a competition for Solidarity's logo. They were convinced that they would win, that there would be a trade union, and that it would go beyond the shipyard.

When the strike started, it was pretty intense and it wasn't covered by the press here. I was asked to come and to leave my dog behind because it was a bit of an identifier, so I got on a Swedish trawler and crossed the Baltic Sea. I wore a black wig, and, since my eyes are artificial, I changed my eyes to blue. We walked into the shipyard and started negotiating with the government. What the government was trying to do was to try to persuade the original leaders, including Lech Walesa, that it was enough to have a trade union, that wages were secure in the shipyard, and that therefore they should break up the strike. It promised the trade union leaders that if they broke off the strike, the military that was surrounding the shipyard would withdraw, press censorship would be dropped, and everyone would be safe. They would guarantee that nobody would be imprisoned within a month.

What Anna Walentynowicz did, along with a colleague of hers who was a nurse at the shipyard, was to go out to the main gates leading out to the shipyard where the military had asked all the workers to exit. Using bullhorns, these women asked all the workers to turn back, telling them that they shouldn't leave the shipyard until they had secured for every working man and every working woman the same rights that they had. By the sheer force of their presence and the respect these women had earned by trying to find practical solutions not just for the women but for the men, the shipyard workers went back into the factory. The conditions there were incredible. You slept in shifts because there were people around the walls trying to see what the military was doing. Food had to be brought in from the city, so there were days when you didn't have any food and you didn't have any coffee and the level of fear was really intense. Yet these two women said that it was not enough for them to have rights if everybody didn't share them. Through their efforts, they managed to have the rights that were originally negotiated for the shipyard extended to all enterprises in Poland.

What the news covered is perhaps what men wanted covered, the right to organize. But that was only one of the demands that was acceded to at the Gdansk strike. One of the other demands was for freedom of expression. There was also the demand for health care, that it couldn't be tied to a job, it had to be universal, and it had to be secured. The demands dealt with working conditions; that the standards of the International Labor Organization in each and every enterprise had to be acceded to and implemented, that there had to be a body of workers in each enterprise to sit on a board together with government specialists and government officials making sure that the minimal working conditions were acceded to, that if there were accidents at work or any health problems that arose after that, this would be taken care of. It was the women who created Solidarity and served as the force behind that movement, largely through the martial law period and even during the negotiations.

The follow-on negotiations to end martial law and that resulted in the roundtable agreement were conducted by the figureheads of the movement, people who did earn their place in the sun but who are now, unfortunately, betraying what they had fought for. These figureheads demanded a change in the political system, free elections to the parliament, and changes in the police, but the women who were on the so-called lesser commissions asked for democracy not only on the national level but in local government and in the schools. The women asked that there be justice before the law, asserting that everybody should be given legal counsel, not just if they were accused of a political crime or if they were well known, but everybody by definition should be given the right to legal counsel not only in criminal courts but also in labor tribunals.

Many other things that were considered to be of less importance by the leaders but which are crucial to the functioning of democracy were put forward by and negotiated by the women. They were negotiated by the women members of the team precisely because, in a way, they were the most threatening things that had to be negotiated. The government could always win in a parliamentary election because it drafted the electoral laws. The government could always back out from a promise because it made the promise, and there was no machinery for making the government implement the promises. The government could change the labor laws, but those labor laws didn't have to be implemented. What the women did was to negotiate things that went to the very core of democracy. The women looked at democracy not as a system that goes from the top down but in the sense of popular sovereignty, that everyone be given the right to speak. So while the top echelons of Solidarity were negotiating parliamentary elections, the women were negotiating how local elections and, from thence on, parliamentary elections would be conducted. They were making sure that everyone would be given economic security under the changing system, and, what was most important of all, they made sure that in the final text the statement was made that democracy means that we each have to look after each other, that we have a responsibility for each other, and that we must respect differences. Democracy thrives on diversity, not on uniformity.

The women of Solidarity were instrumental in creating Solidarity and in making sure that there was space for democracy to flourish, and space and a fixed secure income for the women and everybody else to survive, so that they could accomplish whatever they wished to do. The women gave the men courage, and they showed that fear did not have to be a negative force but that fear could be made to move mountains. Yes, the men were afraid leaving the shipyard, but by dealing with their fear, and using it positively, they achieved a lot.

I continued working throughout the strike and beyond until the roundtable discussion with the government. At that time I ended my contribution in Poland because I felt that the future had to be dealt with by the people living there. They had to find their own solutions; it would have been almost colonialistic of me to talk about possibilities from the outside. I never formally resigned or was asked to. It tapered out, basically.

At the same time, I got involved with the Jazz Section in Czechoslovakia through a musical contact I had through the Royal Academy. It was basically reaching out to young people through jazz music. All the Jazz Section did in Czechoslovakia was to parody the Czech politicians and give musical skits as a form of dissent. Lots of people would come from all over to hear them. Later on, members of the Jazz Section were imprisoned for spreading information that was harmful to public order even though the group was recognized by UNESCO. I was involved in making their case known internationally and before that with making people around the world aware of the Jazz Section and of Charter 77, a group of dissident artists and intellectuals. When these people were tried, I made sure that observers went to the trials. I filed amicus curiae (friends of the court) briefs.

Later on I was involved in a peace seminar in East Germany, called the Jena Peace Seminar, that was an offshoot of the Lutheran Church. The seminar gathered together young people who were beginning to demonstrate against nuclear weapons and on behalf of the environment. Vigils were also held and assembled by word of mouth on the anniversaries of people who had been killed trying to scale the Berlin Wall. These peaceful demonstrations kept growing even though the participants were brutalized by the police. Ultimately, they were aimed against the state security forces, the Stasi, claiming that the forces were being used against rather than on behalf of the East German people. As the vigils grew to include many thousands of participants, they began to protest against the entire government. It was these mushrooming demonstrations that had a significant impact on toppling the East German government. Then

I was asked to get involved in Tibet, and I'm still working on that. I was asked in 1984 by a friend who is active in Tibetan affairs and whom I met at the Human Rights Commission in Geneva. We were both preparing our speeches, and we started talking about what one could say in presentations and whether we could include jokes. My friend wondered what one could do more concretely other than give speeches, and we both started questioning the information the Chinese government had sent to the Human Rights Commission regarding how a demonstration had been put down in Lhasa. The government had said that Tibetan monks were using karate techniques to jump the height of a three-story building and thereby threatening the soldiers who had automatic weapons and were firing on the Tibetan monks. We managed to get the information questioned by the UN officials and new queries sent out to the Chinese government. That was a first in UN procedure. Afterward, I showed my friend how to use the information which he had received and which other people in Tibet were sending out, how they could access and send this information to the United Nations to make it more broadly effective, and how to contact journalists and write articles, that sort of thing.

My work is all interrelated. It all deals with the same types of violations. Basically, if you are lobbying for one situation, you can lobby for two situations and you can still insert information about another country when you are writing letters. I can write one letter covering several problems.

I started testifying at the UN Human Rights Commission in Geneva in 1982, immediately after the declaration of martial law in Poland. (Before 1978 nongovernmental organizations could not address the Commission.) Since then, I've gone every year. Nineteen ninety-two was the only year I missed because my mother was dying, and also my guide dog, Waldo, died. I needed to be available for them.

I was once addressing the Human Rights Commission on the subject of Tibet when a funny incident occurred. It was when I was taking information about the people who had ostensibly jumped three stories high to attack the Chinese soldiers. After my speech, some people wondered how I could know anything since I was blind. I then pulled out all the photographs that had been smuggled out and held them in front of the Commission. I showed them to the Chinese officials who were there and to the UN officials to counteract those allegations. You could see very clearly from the photographs that the police were firing on people who were in no way levitating from the ground, many of whom were women and children.

I have taught human rights in different settings, both at universities and in workshops for grass-roots organizations. I've taught leaders of these organizations in the places where human rights violations were occurring or outside the countries where violations were taking place. They are different experiences, and you teach them in different ways.

I have taught in India, in Kosovo, in Poland, in Leningrad, in Vilnius, Alma-Ata, Kazakhstan, and Bucharest on a regular basis. I'm generally contacted. Sometimes there's a restriction of money, so I have to do grant proposals because the travel is expensive. If I have the money, I pay for it myself. I'm about to teach a course in Nova Scotia, sponsored by the Canadian Human Rights Commission, for leaders of human rights groups from countries all over Eastern Europe. I traveled to these countries to select the participants with the help of the Canadian embassies there.

The workshop I gave in Kosovo was intended to help the people more effectively and accurately document violations that occurred. Part of the course covered how to do fact finding and how to develop a questionnaire for distribution and completion by the people who took part in demonstrations. For example, there was a demonstration by students who wanted the primary schools to be opened, and the police fired on them with live ammunition and water cannons. The demonstrators were mainly children between seven and thirteen, along with their parents. The federal government had promised that schools would be opened after two years of closings, and they had not fulfilled this promise for what were ostensibly technical reasons but were probably not technical reasons. I helped develop a questionnaire so that the information gathered could serve as a basis for a report to the United Nations on the illegal use of force and at the same time allow for cross-checking the information, to make sure that the government couldn't claim that violations had not occurred. I helped them develop a questionnaire that was appropriate to their psychology and yet reflected the principles that exist in international law.

Working with grass-roots organizations is the one activity that gives me the most satisfaction and is where I put much of my effort. It is work that bears fruit. If it works for one grass-roots organization, then the people involved pass the information on, so it's a very effective use of my time. It's important for grass-roots organizations to feel that they can help the people they are trying to serve, and thereby the larger community. That feeling is often lost if the information is sent to a group like Amnesty International, which does fantastic work, but somehow the link to the local organization is dropped.

For example, in India, Amnesty International gets lots of information from the PCLU (People's Civil Liberties Union), most of whose members are high-ranking lawyers who get the data from the field. However, the people in the field don't know what's happened to the information once they've given it. They have no trickle down, don't know whether any action was taken as a result of their details, whether the information they gave was effective or what happened to it. Somehow it no longer becomes their data or their suffering; and what, if anything, is done to help them is not theirs. I think it's important that it remain theirs in even the smallest ways, such as having a well installed in a village, for example. It's important that villagers know that it was their gathering of information about hygienic conditions and then passing it along that helped them get the well. It's important that they be shown what information in that situation they need to gather. It's not that they don't have the data, but often it's a question of how to formulate it. A lot of information is lost because of the inability to present it.

It's important that people in India and Africa and Asia can link this type of demand together with literacy programs so that it becomes a web. Human rights is not just civil or political or not just economic or social; they're all interconnected. You can't violate the rights of a campesino in El Salvador in terms of his right to the land without violating his right to life and liberty and dignity and self-expression. So grass-roots organizations both identify their own rights, ask for them in their own national and international context, and use that material to develop literacy programs or hygiene programs in villages and to get everybody involved in helping each other. This work is major for me in the sense that I think it's both the most satisfying and is an effective way of spreading information about human dignity—not just human dignity, every thing's dignity. I think one should refer to dignity rights and not human rights. It also is a way of hopefully having everybody take responsibility for each other and to avoid feeling abandoned.

I think that one of the biggest violations of human rights is that of instilling fear, not that people accept the violations but that they are afraid of doing anything about the violations. This is in and of itself a violation by the government. It doesn't have a specific effect in terms of a right violated or in terms of having a specific victim or group of victims being violated. I think that one can turn fear around by using fear, and transform it into a collective courage by turning around and facing it. I hate to use the analogy of a boar, but if you look at a mother defending her children in the wild, often the mother will turn around and face the predator, and in some cases the predator will back down just because an animal has moved to face it. I think that if people marshal themselves to face the fear, then the government or the group of people or the system that's instilling the fear will back down or will begin seeing its actions in a different light.”

3 / Annette Lu Hsiu-Lien

CHINESE FORTUNE-TELLERS USE EIGHT characters to read a person's destiny, two each for the time of birth, the day, the month, and the year. When a friend of Annette Lu Hsiu-Lien brought these statistics to a fortune-teller without mentioning her name, the seer predicted that Hsiu-Lien would be imprisoned at the age of thirty-six. Sure enough, she was imprisoned under martial law between 1979 and 1984. However, this experience was only one aspect of her many-faceted life, which encompasses roles as a prominent human rights activist against an authoritarian government as well as the founder of the women's movement in Taiwan. Today, Hsiu-Lien is a senator representing the opposition Democratic Progressive Party in the Legislative Assembly with a seat on the foreign affairs committee, as she pursues UN membership for her country.

Maintaining her concern for the status of women, she continues to be a leader of the feminist movement in Taiwan, and, in February 1994, Hsiu-Lien hosted the Global Summit of Women in Taipei with four thousand participants from over seventy nations. She is also the author of thirteen books and numerous articles on feminism and human rights.

On March 8, 1995, International Women's Day, Hsiu-Lien made public her intention to seek the nomination for vice president from her party for the first popular democratic presidential and vice presidential election, scheduled for March 1996. Explaining her candidacy, she reminded the Taiwanese that women must have an active role in the new democratic society and that, as someone who has struggled for justice for more than twenty-four years, she was well qualified to lead her country.

I first met Annette Lu Hsiu-Lien shortly after her release from prison as the result of Amnesty International's efforts. Although still frail from a long bout with cancer and her incarceration, she immediately recommenced her human rights activity in the United States. She organized the Taiwanese community abroad on behalf of political change and spoke throughout the country on her passion for achieving democracy and equality for women in her country. While a charismatic speaker and leader, she is disarmingly humble about her achievements. Her struggles have made her acutely sensitive to other people's difficulties, and she is quick to express concern not only for her friends but for all those who cross her path. Her overflowing generosity included compassion for her jailors and a desire to educate them during her time in prison. She typically takes great joy in giving gifts and mementos of her country to her friends and acquaintances. However, the greatest gift of all is the one of self, which she pours out without measure or thought of recompense.

Hsiu-Lien was born on D-Day, June 6, 1945, the youngest of five children. Although her father was disappointed that she was not a boy, he nevertheless nourished high expectations for her and encouraged her to study law. She graduated with honors from the Law Department of the National University of Taiwan in 1967 and ranked first in the university's Graduate School of Law the following year, an unusual achievement for a woman in a traditional society. She subsequently received her master's degree in comparative law in 1971 from the University of Illinois, where she was deeply influenced by the women's movement. On returning to Taiwan she spent four years working in various capacities in the executive cabinet within the Kuomintang government, formulating laws for health care and pollution, and serving as an ambitious and capable government official.

At the same time, she devoted her weekends and evenings to developing a women's movement in Taiwan, writing articles criticizing traditional sexual roles, giving talks in various universities, creating a feminist press—Pioneer Press—and establishing women's hotline services in Taipei and Kaohsiung. These were remarkable accomplishments in a society heavily influenced by Confucianism and by the Japanese occupation, under which women were socialized to a life under male domination and relegated to the household. Hsiu-Lien's views on women were so far ahead of her time that a long-term relationship foundered when her partner made it clear that he did not want to marry a strong-minded person. She realized then the painful gap between being a woman and a person in Taiwanese society.

From January to September 1975, Hsiu-Lien visited the United States, Korea, and Japan, seeking to learn from the women's movements in these countries. That same year, she represented Taiwan at the World Conference of the International Women's Year in Mexico, but, due to pressure from China, was forced to return to Taiwan midway through the proceedings. Upon her return, she resigned from her government position in order to devote all of her energy to the women's movement and published a number of books on feminism. She sponsored symposia for middle-class women and also sought to spread the movement to lower-class women, many of whom worked for very low wages or served as prostitutes for tourists, thereby providing one of the main sources of foreign currency.

Her feminist activities did not go unnoticed by the Kuomintang government: Hsiu-Lien was subjected to intense political harassment. Her books were banned, security agents intimidated volunteers in the women's organizations she founded, and she was denounced in the government-controlled press. Until martial law was lifted in 1987, freedom of expression, assembly, and the press was proscribed, and education was carefully controlled to prevent independent thinking. Anyone who dared express differing ideas or address taboo topics such as democracy or feminism was subjected to political harassment, arrest, torture, imprisonment, and even execution. Hsiu-Lien's increasing vulnerability to these measures prompted her decision to leave the country in 1977 and attend Harvard Law School to acquire a master's degree.

While at Harvard, Hsiu-Lien wrote her thesis on the legal status of women in Taiwan and earned the respect of her professors for her scholarship and her expertise in various aspects of the law. When her studies were completed, she was urged by the Taiwanese community abroad to remain in the United States in order to mobilize American public opinion to pressure the Taiwanese government for political reforms. However, despite previous bouts with censors and the security police, Hsiu-Lien decided to return to her country and enter politics in order to promote democratic values, feminist views, and the rule of law. She would prove to be singularly focused on these goals throughout her long and dangerous career on behalf of justice.

Starting in the 1970s, a struggle for democratization had been taking shape in Taiwan. As the island's prosperity and involvement with the world increased, the country seemed to be evolving toward openness. During the November 1977 election, a fledgling opposition emerged, and there were local outbursts against the government's denial of human rights. Hsiu-Lien wanted to be part of the efforts to create a more just society and, shortly after returning, became a candidate for the National Assembly in an election scheduled for December 1978. She announced her candidacy on October 6, speaking in formal Mandarin Chinese rather than in her native Taiwanese. Her speech riveted the audience with her plea for overcoming the mainlander/native Taiwanese split, broadening the appeal of the democratic movement and transforming the anger of the Taiwanese over oppression at the hands of a mainlander ruling class into hope for an integrated future. Moreover, she endorsed the platform of the newly formed Opposition Candidates Campaign Coalition, which demanded the end of martial law and the restoration of civil liberties and human rights.[1]

The election was postponed following President Jimmy Carter's recognition of the People's Republic of China as the legitimate government of China. The effect of that decision was like a bombshell, heightening tension on the island, postponing the development of a greater political openness, and leading to a number of arrests of opposition candidates. Despite the negative atmosphere, the democratic movement chose to demonstrate publicly against the arrests and governmental harassment of the opposition. Hsiu-Lien was a primary speaker at many of these gatherings.

Denied access to legitimate political activity, Hsiu-Lien turned to her writing and published a book, *Taiwan Past and Present*, which was soon banned. In 1979 she joined the Formosa Magazine Association (FMA), whose monthly publication was designed to provide an outlet for opposition opinion. That association, which created branch offices throughout Taiwan, acted as a substitute for the opposition party that the government no longer tolerated. Hsiu-Lien devoted herself to the magazine with her characteristic energy, contributing her own funds and decorating the office. A large banner was hung in the main room proclaiming "DEMOCRACY, UNITY, LOVE, TAIWAN." She also made certain to have a grating installed around the balcony adjoining the office to prevent the staff from "accidentally falling" over the railing in the event of clashes with the secret police.[2]

The differences between the way women and men operated within the opposition has been noted by Linda Gail Arrigo, the wife of Shih Ming-Teh, a prominent leader of the FMA movement. While the men spent countless hours discussing strategy, the women were deftly preparing the signs for protest rallies. Further, while a certain secrecy was necessary given the government surveillance, the core opposition group made decisions in an autocratic fashion, failing to engage the activists in discussions. However, Hsiu-Lien scheduled frequent group discussions and delegated responsibility. She established forums that were notable for broad participation, a sense of community, and free expression, in contrast to most opposition events where well-known male figures delivered rhetorical speeches on the oppressive government.[3]

Throughout the latter part of 1979 the FMA made great strides, sponsoring political gatherings of thousands of people even when surrounded by riot troops and tanks. These confrontations with government troops continued on an escalating scale with snowballing popular support for the democracy movement, on the one hand, and an increased show of force by the government, on the other. Despite the implications for their personal safety, the leaders of the FMA decided to hold a rally and parade on December 10 to commemorate World Human Rights Day. The police agreed to a rally but not to a march. Nevertheless, Hsiu-Lien set out with placards calling for the return to democracy, with the abolition of martial law and censorship, and, as deputy director of the FMA, was a key speaker at the gathering. When the unarmed marchers encountered a police blockade, they charged and a riot ensued. A few days later there were widespread arrests, and eight members of the opposition leadership, including Hsiu-Lien, were prosecuted for sedition before a military tribunal under a special statute against rebellion that suspends the constitutional guarantee of a civilian trial. She was sentenced to twelve years' imprisonment.

While in prison, Hsiu-Lien endured psychological as well as physical harassment. Promises of release were mingled with threats of her family's arrest and her own execution. She experienced renewed symptoms of a thyroid cancer she had suffered several years previously. Although she endured severe pain, suffered strangling attacks at night from difficulty in breathing, and vomited blood, her jailers refused to allow her medical attention until Amnesty International adopted her as a prisoner of conscience and began working for her release. Despite these harrowing circumstances, Hsiu-Lien wrote two novels and two nonfiction works. She also studied philosophy, aided by a university professor whose weekly sessions with her were arranged by Amnesty International's New Mexico chapter. The result was a substantial manuscript comparing the philosophies behind human rights in Eastern and Western cultures.

Because of her medical problems and her failing health, Hsiu-Lien was granted an early release in 1984. Returning to the United States the following year, she entered a program on human rights sponsored by Harvard Law School. Among the mementos she brought with her was a pair of slippers that she had embroidered while in prison, the word FREEDOM boldly stitched across the tops.

Hsiu-Lien received the Human and Civil Rights Award from the Massachusetts Teachers Association in 1987 and traveled widely on behalf of Amnesty International before returning to Taiwan in 1988 and immediately plunging into political activity. In 1990 she established the Coalition for Democracy to promote democratic and constitutional reforms in Taiwan, and she participated in the Democratic Progressive Party's Constitution Committee drafting of the Magna Carta for Democracy. Two years later she was elected to parliament, all the while continuing her work on behalf of women's rights around the world.

HSUI-LIEN SPEAKS

To crow at dawn is the natural duty of a cock. To participate in affairs outside the home is traditionally none of women's business. The Chinese expression, "A hen crowing at dawn, pin-chih-shih-chieng" is intended to ridicule a woman who dares to engage in politics.

Nevertheless, according to feminism, when a cock fails to discharge his duty, why can't a hen crow at dawn?

"In 1978 I was granted a research fellowship to work at the East Asian Legal Studies Center of Harvard Law School, where I had just graduated with an LL.M. degree. But that summer I decided to return to Taiwan and run for Congress. I made this decision not to become a celebrity but rather because I felt morally obligated to do something for my country before it was too late.

For people living in a democracy, freedom is like the air and water which sustains life. Yet, for those who have been living under long-term martial law, to reveal something which the government has concealed from the public is to risk one's liberty, if not one's very life. But what did the government of Taiwan conceal from the people? Quite a few things: the whereabouts of the enormous amount of foreign exchange earned by Taiwanese from the brisk foreign trade, and the large-scale immigration of the top leaders to the United States, along with property taken from Taiwan, were just some instances. What I attempted to reveal to my fellow Taiwanese at that time was the imminent crisis of the derecognition by the United States of the Nationalist Chinese regime (the Kuomintang, or KMT).

This was to be a dramatic crisis for Taiwan. Despite its miraculous economic achievements, Taiwan lost its diplomatic relations with the majority of nations due to the policies of the Kuomintang, which, led by Generalissimo Chiang Kai-shek, had fled to Taiwan after being defeated by Communist China in 1949. In order to maintain itself in power, it immediately began the world's longest period of martial law. It also claimed to be the sole legitimate representative of China. While martial law infringes on most of the human rights protected by the constitution, the claim to sole representation of the Chinese people caused the nations of the world to switch their diplomatic recognition from the Republic of China (ROC) in Taipei to the People's Republic of China (PRC) in Beijing. As a result, only twenty-two nations still recognized the ROC, and the only Great Power among these was the United States.

Yet Washington had been eager to break the impasse with the PRC ever since President Richard Nixon sent a ping-pong team to knock on China's door. In the summer of 1987, rumors of the negotiation for U.S. normalization of relations with the PRC were spreading. In Taiwan, however, the Kuomintang maintained silence and acted as if nothing unusual was afoot. There was no sign of the impending political storm. In Congress, the minister of foreign affairs even refused to answer any questions regarding the possibility of the U.S. de-recognition of the ROC.

I was haunted by the tragic scenes shown on television after the collapse of South Vietnam in 1975. I speculated that a similar tragedy might occur in my country when its most reliable friend would abandon her. The best opportunity to alert my fellow citizens to such a crisis seemed to be the campaign platform. Under martial law, freedom of expression was curbed except during election time, and that period was called 'holidays for democracy.'

I went to consult with my advisor, Professor Jerome Cohen, the assistant dean of Harvard Law School. I felt uneasy about giving up the research fellowship he had just granted me.

'Why not? You are nobody here. But you can be somebody at home.' Instead of expressing displeasure at my plans, he firmly stated, 'I am totally behind your decision.'

'But I might be imprisoned if I did what I would like to do,' I responded, half joking, half serious.

'Then I will wave the flag for you in Taipei.' He raised his right hand and waved it.

The next time we met was seven years later in the Taipei Armed Forces Hospital, under secret arrangement by the Taiwan Garrison Command, after I had been in prison for five and a quarter years. 'I have been so upset that I was unable to help you out in the past years,' he said, pulling a handkerchief from his pocket. It was astonishing to see the tears streaming down his face. His tears meant so much! Tears shed on behalf of justice and human dignity are the diamonds of God's crown.

~

A few minutes after nine o'clock on the morning of December 16, 1978, I was woken up from the soundest sleep I had had since the campaign started. I had to attend two or three official platform appearances sponsored by the Election Office in different towns during the day, while in the evenings I delivered two or more speeches nonofficially. The only exception was today, when there would be no official campaigning. I was advised to take a complete rest so that I could gather my strength for the next half of the battle. I was right in the middle of the campaign. It had begun on December 8 and would end on December 23, election day.

My campaign manager was waiting anxiously for me downstairs. At the sight of his pale face, I became wide awake. 'The United States announced the normalization of relations with the PRC today! It was just broadcast over the radio.'

'What?! The normalization? Damn it! How could that happen at this crucial moment? There were two more months before the New Year. Damn Uncle Sam! What will the KMT do now?'

A few minutes later, my campaign staff filed into my house, asking me what they should do. 'Tear off all the provocative banners on the Wall of Democracy. End the soundtruck broadcasting. There will be no further campaign activities until we hear from the Opposition Candidates Coordination Committee,' I ordered.

It had finally come. I had been predicting this event throughout my campaign, how it would occur, and even when. I thought it would be likely around the New Year. I urged my audiences to be prepared for it from the beginning of my campaign until the last speech I gave the night before. All of my predictions had come true except for the timing. I had researched the issue and interviewed some China experts in the United States before I went home for the election. What I had miscalculated was the New Year. Subconsciously, I had thought the recognition of the PRC would take place during the Chinese Lunar New Year, which would not come until February. In fact, the Americans celebrate the Western New Year and not the Lunar New Year. I must have been too busy and too exhausted to realize this.

Just because of this slight mistake, my destiny and that of democracy in Taiwan was profoundly altered. Like most of the other opposition candidates, I would have won the election if the campaign had not been canceled under an emergency decree proclaimed by President Chiang Ching-kuo. By announcing the breaking of diplomatic relations two weeks in advance, the United States actually helped the KMT avoid defeat by the opposition.

I would have won the election overwhelmingly because my campaign was miraculously successful. It was a difficult battle, not only because I didn't begin until early November but also because the conservative constituents in my hometown of Taoan were unsympathetic to the feminist movement, which I had founded and which I was leading. I had been defamed by my opponents as a sexual liberal and a destroyer of social harmony. Nevertheless, I had earned the respect and support of men and women, old and young, in just one and a half months of campaigning.

How did I achieve this success? It was simple. Once I had made the decision to run, I spent three months at Harvard studying and writing instead of going home to visit and to shake hands with my constituents. I published a book called *The Past and Future of Taiwan* before the campaign started. Under the KMT's colonial rule, people had not been allowed to learn about the country where they lived nor to speak of the right of self-determination for the Taiwanese, a right which I demanded in my book. What I mentioned in my book and in my speeches was almost unheard of. No wonder the public was so eager to listen to me. Wherever I went there was a huge crowd, and whenever I spoke there was great applause.

When the news came out of the U.S. recognition of the PRC, people were amazed at the accuracy of my predictions, and some even called me a prophetess. On the other hand, KMT authorities became suspicious of my popularity. Rumors began to spread that I was an agent of the CIA, and by late afternoon that day there were even rumors that I had been arrested.

Worse than that, my family was subjected to threatening calls. Some of these calls threatened murder or arson. After being harassed with calls for a week, everyone in my family felt as if they were living in a hell on earth. As for me, I was almost sure of my destiny, that I would be the hen crowing at dawn, and that I was moving inexorably toward this goal like a moth flying toward a lamp.

~

'My dear fellow Taiwanese, all of you people with a conscience and with compassion: Today, December 10, 1979, is International Human Rights Day. For hundreds of years, we Taiwanese have never had a chance like the one we have today. Today, we have a chance to give resounding expression to our burning desire for justice, to cry out our demand for human rights.'

That chilly winter evening on the street of Kaohsiung, the second largest city in Taiwan, I was standing on the platform above the truck, facing some tens of thousands of men and women. They raised their heads, listening quietly and with concentration. It seemed as if the fierceness of the violent confrontation which had taken place minutes ago was forgotten and as if the heavily equipped antiriot troops and trucks surrounding them did not intimidate them. 'We came for speeches!' they shouted, when an order to disperse was made. I then spoke: 'Dear members of the security police, you are all human beings with blood and tears. Don't you feel ashamed of what you are doing today? Your behavior has been very violent.

'Dear members of the security forces, you are wearing helmets and uniforms. But I know that without your helmets and uniforms, your hearts are the same as ours, your blood is the same as ours. Please, remove your helmets, forget your uniforms and be Taiwanese too. I can see inside your hearts today. Perhaps you are doing this willingly. Perhaps you are doing what you do not want to do. Perhaps you are being deceived. It doesn't matter. The taxes of eighteen million Taiwanese should not be used to trample our people, but rather against those on the other side of the Taiwan Strait.'

It was an outdoor public rally to commemorate the thirty-first anniversary of the proclamation of the Universal Declaration of Human Rights. It was a peaceful human rights rally sponsored by the Formosa Magazine Association, the opposition Taiwanese. But how had it become a fierce confrontation? Glancing over the antiriot troops and trucks, I couldn't believe the brutality of the KMT. They had given permission for the rally, so how could they send antiriot troops and trucks to spray tear gas on a peaceful audience? It was at this point that the confrontation between the unarmed public and security forces started. I hated to see violence among my countrymen. I had to say something to raise their consciousness, to educate them about democracy and human rights.

'This has been a very exciting year in the international arena: dictators all over the world have fallen. They have been toppled, exiled, and even assassinated. It has happened in Africa, in Asia, in Central and South America. It has also happened to President Park [Chung Hee] of South Korea who was considered a good friend by the KMT. One night his life was taken by the head of his secret police. It is sad that people should die, but these people were all notorious tyrants. We were not grief-stricken over their removal from office, but thankful.'

The crowd greeted this speech with loud applause. I continued to speak, imagining how President Chiang Ching-kuo would have felt if he had heard what I said and how furious the military and intelligence authorities, which supported the KMT's martial law regime, would feel. They would kill me, I supposed. I speculated that they were hatching a plot tonight. The night before this incident the police had captured and brutalized two volunteer members of the Formosa group who were broadcasting news of the rally.

The police brutality aroused the opposition forces across the island. They all came to join the rally, and they were all unarmed. But where did all those tough-looking people come from? Could they be thugs recruited to infiltrate the crowd in order to malign the image of the opposition? The KMT had used such tricks before. Nevertheless, I couldn't help but continue my speech.

'Look up at the sky, look down at the ground. Isn't this heaven and this earth the very place where our ancestors worked with pain and suffering in the hope that they could give it to us so that we, our children, and our grandchildren could live here forever in peace and prosperity? Have we ever known a time when we Formosans have been masters in our own house? Isn't it true that we have always been slaves, subject to the whims of others? We have never overcome! Yet we who are here today struggling for human rights must give our utmost for our homeland!'

All of a sudden, from the far end of the street, a line of riot trucks with searchlights and with clouds of smoke approached the center of the assembly, as loud as thunder. The dinosaurs are coming, I thought. I have never seen a dinosaur at all, but the frightening sight before me reminded me of something full of horror. At first, people were so frightened that they attempted to escape from the tear gas. But in a few minutes they were filled with indignation as they realized that it was the KMT. Instead of retreating, they began to counterattack the security forces with bamboo sticks, iron bars, bricks, whatever they could find on the spot. I stepped down from the truck, walking around the turmoil, which continued for three more hours until past midnight. 'A scene of antityranny,' I told myself.

A few days later, more than one hundred members of the active opposition, including myself, were arrested and held incommunicado. During the interrogation, I was compelled to confess to being the one fully responsible for the chaos. According to them, my speech was provocative and seditious. 'Your speech made us lose more than two hundred thousand ballots.' They even complimented the power of my speech, after having failed to deny its legitimacy. According to them, there were approximately sixty thousand people who attended the rally, each of whom would influence three other voters. For this twenty-minute speech, I was eventually sentenced to twelve years of imprisonment and a ten-year deprivation of civil rights which, together with an injunction to seize my property, made it one of the most costly speeches in the world.

Room No. 1 in the Military Court of the Taiwan Garrison Command on the outskirts of Taipei was the stage where the political comedy of the court-martial of the Formosa case unfolded. Unprecedentedly, the trial was open to 120 select persons. Among them were journalists whom I had known ever since I had begun my feminist activities. There were also fifteen young, prominent Taiwanese lawyers who stood up on behalf of the eight defendants.

'From the records available to us, there is no evidence probative nor corroborative to support the defendants' guilt of sedition except for their confessions.' Speaking in front of the five judges of the court was a slim, handsome man wearing silver-framed glasses. He was my defense lawyer. He was also my brother.

'According to criminal procedure, confession may be used as evidence only when it is made in the absence of violence, threats, inducement, fraud, illegal detention, or other improper means, and when it agrees with the facts. In this case, may I request Your Honor to investigate the legitimacy of the confessions made by Lu Hsiu-Lien. I have reasonable doubt to suspect it.' Turning his face toward me, he winked. I was reminded of the advice he had given me the day before yesterday.

'Every one of you will retract. Be prepared to denounce the wrongdoings of your interrogators to the court. Remember!'

I trusted him. He was my brother, after all. I never had thought that the lawyers would use this unusual relationship as a tactic to challenge the legitimacy of our confessions. According to them, we, the defendants, must have suffered so much from the stress of the interrogation that all of us had made incredibly self-incriminatory confessions that none of us would dare to disavow.

'Have you ever been tortured?' asked the chief judge presiding over the trial.

'No.'

'They didn't beat me,' I replied. In order to make my statement reliable, I would have to be very careful not to say one false word. My philosophy is that nobody except a genius is capable of telling lies. Once a lie is told, you will have to tell a lot more to cover it up. And so often you forget what you had lied about in the beginning. 'However, I have endured methods more sophisticated than physical torture and which my interrogators used for extracting the confessions.'

I couldn't help remembering what a miserable and humiliating experience the interrogation was. After two and a half months of suffering and surrender, I couldn't even help bursting into tears. Suddenly, I felt the court become as quiet as if it were midnight. I paused a while until I had regained enough calm to speak.

'For instance, they applied the psychological approach of "destruction of personality" by . . .'

'Be careful about what you are saying, Lu Hsiu-Lien!' The chief judge was anxious to stop me from revealing any more. 'Don't use any abstract words to mislead our imaginations and to defame the image of the government.'

The word 'mislead' really misled the spectators. There was a ripple in the court as a result of the judge's order. I believed that my friends were all struck by my testimony. They probably expected to hear me give more details.

'Protest! Your Honor, the legitimacy of the confession is a matter that merits your attention. Please let her continue,' argued my brother.

'If it's a matter of the government's image, Your Honor, we better let her finish her statement. I am sure that our interrogators did nothing wrong.' Surprisingly enough, the quiet, timid Taiwanese chief military prosecutor gave his consent. With this assurance, the judge then nodded his head.

'They claimed I was an agent of the CIA, a member of the Overseas Taiwan Independence League, and so on. They therefore used any possible methods to compel me to admit . . .' I proceeded.

Indeed, during the past two months of absolute isolation, I had been subject to endless rounds of interrogation carried out by a group of two men and two women, each of whom acted as interrogator, guard, intimidator, or persuader. They forced me to write down the questions and answers. They then rearranged the wording or added their own words to distort the original meaning. Finally, they dictated it back to me for rewriting and signing. This procedure was repeated over and over again until the statement satisfied the interrogators. Sections were then glued together to fabricate the confession—that I had participated in the 'Formosa Magazine' with the intention of conspiring to subvert the government.

'Sometimes they kept haranguing me. Other times they threatened to arrest my brother or to apply physical brutality. They showed me a photograph of the bullet-riddled body of a recently executed spy. Then, they asked me to read a notice issued by the funeral parlor and requesting the family to collect the corpse of the executed, saying, "In a few days, a notice like this will be mailed to your family." They also composed an epitaph for me. In a word, to die would be easier than to go on living.'

There were other painful memories, such as being ordered to stand with high-heeled shoes for six hours, being deprived of food and water for the whole day, and being forced to swallow big pieces of paper which contained statements they found unsatisfactory. But I had said enough to embarrass the judges, to astonish the journalists, and to encourage the lawyers and other codefendants.

The next morning almost all the newspapers covered my testimony and condemned the illegitimacy of the interrogation and involuntary confessions. One of the pro-KMT newspapers, the *United Daily*, even made my story the headline on its front page. It was the watershed to turn people's support away from the KMT and toward the Formosa people.

~

For someone who has always enjoyed good health, the taste of illness is unimaginable. The experience of prison is as unimaginable to someone who has always enjoyed freedom. Unfortunately, I lost both my health and my freedom at the same time. I lost my health fighting for women's rights and my freedom fighting for human rights.

Like health, freedom is something you don't really value until it is gone. At first, you become furious at the loss of liberty. Gradually, you begin to feel powerless and without hope because everything you do is controlled by others. Once you become accustomed to the deprivation of freedom, you are grateful for even the slightest benevolence displayed by your captors. But, eventually, you develop a certain philosophy about freedom.

For instance, during the first two months of my detention I was not allowed to talk, to read, or to do anything besides enduring constant interrogation. I felt panic, fury, and frustration. On the day we became convicted, however, I was allowed to talk with another female codefendant. Both of us were so excited that we kept talking for days without sleeping as if there would never be another chance to talk. Another unforgettable taste of freedom was taking a bath. It was on June 10, 1980, six months after our arrest that I was allowed to have a bath outside the cell for the first time. Before that, I had had only a half gallon of hot water each day to wash within my small cell. Since there were four TV monitors at the corners of the cell, I had to bathe rapidly and carefully. I was thrilled to be able to have a private bath. Being alone, even in a small and dirty bathroom, was a wonderful experience.

When I became accustomed to doing everything according to rules and regulations, I began to experience another taste of freedom. One day I mistook some liquid medicine for eyedrops and, as a consequence, my left eye was severely burned. The doctor put bandages on both of my eyes, making me totally blind for three days. Without sight, I could do nothing but lie in bed thinking. Many ideas came to me during those days, including scenes for a novel. I then realized that there were many aspects of freedom, physical freedom and spiritual freedom, freedom in time and freedom in space. I then realized that what I had been deprived of was my physical freedom and spatial freedom. But I could enjoy freedom of the spirit and free time even more than other people.

I didn't waste my time during my imprisonment. I thought, read, wrote, and worked at crafts. I read hundreds of books and wrote four, including two novels. I crafted embroidery, wallhangings, handbags, slippers, and sweaters. Most of these pieces were auctioned off to support the democratic opposition movement. A sweater I knitted was sold in New York for $6,000 to celebrate the establishment of the first Taiwanese opposition party, the Democratic Progressive Party in February 1987.

One day I told my jailers while we were having an argument that the KMT had imprisoned the physical Hsiu-Lien, not the spiritual one. I had discovered that freedom existed inside oneself and could not be taken away by anyone or by any outside forces.

~

Tuesday was a special day for me. It was the day that my family was allowed to visit me. This Tuesday, in September of 1982, was even more special because, with her love, my sister brought me into the world beyond my cell. As usual, two jailers were sitting beside us, one with a pen to take down our conversation despite the TV monitor at the corner of the ceiling.

'A mayor from a city in New Mexico came to visit us. He brought you gifts and asked me to send you regards from your friends there.' Looking at my jailers' pen and paper, my sister said hesitantly, 'They are all very concerned about you.'

I did not recall having any friends in New Mexico, not to mention a mayor. What was my sister talking about? I was curious to know who they were but decided not to ask any questions. My sister was fearful that I might be punished for having connections abroad. Most dictators are resentful about foreign interference in their violation of human rights. I was not afraid of being punished, but I just didn't like to have the KMT intelligence agents know about my personal relations.

Instantly, the name Amnesty International came to my mind. Yes, it must have something to do with people from Amnesty International. At one time, during my year at Harvard, I had thought of joining them. All of a sudden I felt as if I were enjoying a sunbath in early spring. I saw blossoms everywhere, the blossoms of human love, and the green grass of justice. I had not been forgotten after all.

Later, when I was released and allowed to leave Taiwan, I learned about all the efforts made on my behalf by Amnesty International. Groups of Amnesty International in Albuquerque, New Mexico, and in Erlangen, West Germany, had adopted me as a prisoner of conscience. They had started a worldwide letter campaign to press for my release. They had written to demand that I be provided with medical attention during my illness and even the famous columnist Jack Anderson wrote about my story. The Albuquerque group wrote to the [U.S.] president suggesting that I be allowed to take correspondence courses with some American universities. Instead, the authorities arranged for a professor of philosophy to teach me three hours each week. We became friends, and with his help I was allowed to write my books.

After my release, I was allowed to visit the United States to help celebrate the twenty-fifth anniversary of Amnesty International and to give a speech at its national convention in Washington, DC. The following year I gave addresses at the national conventions of both the German section and the Dutch section of Amnesty. My most unforgettable experiences were the happy reunions with my two adoptive groups in Albuquerque and in Erlangen. Words could hardly express my profound gratitude to those who had helped me in the darkest years of my life and who had also made all the world one family.

~

The iron gate clanged. Knowing that lunch had arrived, I turned my face toward the wall and put the quilt over my head, pretending that I was sleeping. My stomach, which had been empty for four days, was uncomfortable when someone next to me was eating. The person eating would also feel uncomfortable because of the hunger of her cellmate.

It took my cellmate only half of the usual time to finish her lunch. She cleared away the dishes and bent over me to whisper in my ears: 'You'd better have some soup. According to the international standard, to have a drink or some soup is not against the spirit of a hunger strike. You need energy to carry on, after all!'

I remained unmoved and silent, only stretching out my left hand, as moving or talking would only consume my depleted energy. I had to preserve it so that I could have the opportunity to see my mother in the hospital before she passed away. My old, widowed mother had fainted at the shock of my arrest and had broken both of her legs. Ever since then she had been lying in bed, weeping and murmuring my name without being able to come and visit me. I felt a great regret for what I had brought upon her. As her youngest and as the only unmarried child, I had been cherished. During my imprisonment, I missed her so much that I often dreamed of her.

A couple of days ago, in the early morning, she had appeared in my dream, standing beside my bed, smiling and blessing me, dressed in a white Buddhist robe. She had then gradually ascended to heaven on smoky, white clouds. Strangely enough, right when I was watching her ascension, a loud crash of thunder broke, and I was suddenly woken up. Then, a heavy rain followed. According to Buddhist legend, it was the Buddha carrying her to paradise.

I knew I would never be able to see her again if I didn't take some action to get permission. For a person deprived of liberty, there's not much else to do except going on a hunger strike after having exhausted all the regular channels. I had no idea how many days one could last without any food. I remembered that a Northern Irish leader imprisoned by the British government died after fourteen days of a hunger strike. Since I had suffered from thyroid carcinoma since 1975, my physical condition was poor, and my metabolism was not quite normal. It became worse after I stopped taking synthyroid. And by the time of my fast, I had been told to stop taking synthyroid for two weeks in order to be able to have a nuclear scan. I knew I was risking my life, or at least my health, but what else could I do? I was even prepared to die if my request was ignored. My mother had given me my life, and if she should die, why would I mind dying? Of course, the KMT would not dare to let me die. Instead, they lied to me.

It was the fifth day of my fast when the deputy director of the Benevolence Rehabilitation Institute, where I was confined, came to visit me in my cell. Pretending to be as kind and considerate as possible, he showed me a piece of paper. A medical report with the signature of the president of the Chiang-kuun Hospital stated that my mother's health had improved and that her life was no longer in danger. However, after I was released, I was told that the hospital was forced to issue that false report by Garrison Command in order to stop my hunger strike.

'You shall feel better, Miss Lu, and you shall resume eating now.' The deputy director smiled. He then took out another piece of paper from his pocket, saying, 'Miss Lu, you are really a devoted daughter. This application for permission to see your mother was so well written that each one of us who read it was deeply moved. Miss Lu, as learned and famous as you are, you still have such a strong filial devotion. It is quite a virtue.'

He began to read the final part of my petition. Strange as it may seem, he read with tears rolling down his face. 'You know something, Miss Lu, I am going to make a copy of this for my children to read and memorize so that they will grow up with your traditional virtue. I have been telling people how wise you are.'

I was amazed at what I heard. I felt relieved that my mother would survive until I was able to see her. I, therefore, quit my hunger strike. And yet, she passed away only two months afterward. They even kept the news away from me until my sister came to visit me. Even worse, although the Law of Execution of Imprisonment provides that a prisoner shall be allowed a twenty-four-hour leave for a parent's funeral, I was allowed only two hours to go home, between midnight and 2:00 A.M. As a protest against their hypocrisy and inhumanity, I refused, letting all the journalists, friends, and relatives wait for me at the funeral home and later at the cemetery throughout the whole day.

~

Although it was past 10:00 P.M., when all the inmates were supposed to be in bed with the lights off, the television set was still on. We turned it down low so that the prison authorities couldn't hear us. I had a cellmate in this prison, which was built especially for us. Two jailers watched over us during the day and one at night. It took a lot of effort on my part to earn their friendship and cooperation.

During the first few months, they were very hostile toward us. It was not surprising, since we were all depicted as vicious, unpatriotic, and even violent by the KMT-controlled mass media. However, after being with us for months, they must have been puzzled by that image of us. One day, when my cellmate and I offered them food brought by our family, one of them said with embarrassment: 'I hope you don't mind my telling you this. We were so afraid of you at the beginning, worrying that you two might attack us at night. The authorities have accused you of being violent, you know.'

'Of course I know that, but do you still believe it?' I asked, laughing.

'No, not any more. Otherwise, I wouldn't be talking to you like this,' she said, blushing. 'You are really gracious and generous.'

Ever since then we had a friendly relationship. I told them that I wasn't going to blame them for keeping surveillance over us since someone would have to take that job. However, I reminded them that they should exercise their power in compliance with the law. Often, I pointed out to them that a prisoner was deprived of her liberty, but not of her dignity, and that our liberty was curbed under conditions stipulated by the law and not arbitrarily or unconditionally. I told them that if they honored the law, they would earn my respect. I sympathized with them. Since they couldn't find a better job than being prison guards, why should I dislike them? Besides, as a strong advocate of feminism, I emphasized sisterhood wherever I went.

At this time, the television reports were filled with announcements of the most recent election. It was election day for the Congress. The jailers were as anxious as we were to know the final results, except that we had opposite interests. They wanted the KMT's candidates to win, while we supported the opposition candidates.

In fact, we had made a bet the day before about the results of a certain race. It all came about over an argument about the reliability of the news reports. My jailers were loyal to the KMT, and their loyalty included a blind belief in whatever the KMT said. Since we were allowed to read only the *Central Daily*, the KMT's party newspaper, it was the only source of information available to us other than the television. Needless to say, the *Central Daily* reported successes for the KMT's candidates and losses for the opposition candidates.

'You opposition people are so mean and militant that you will all fail,' one of the jailers remarked one day when they were reading the *Central Daily*. Since they seemed to be in a cheerful mood, I decided it was time to educate them. 'Let me show you how to read the newspaper. Those who are the most severely criticized are the ones most likely to win.' I took a red pen to underline a couple of opposition candidates who had been strongly attacked by the *Central Daily*. 'Believe me or not, these people will be elected. Keep this week's papers and wait until election day to see whether I am right.'

So, we all watched the television reports together. Since the counting of ballots took a long time, we were awake throughout the night. It was a breach of regulations. If we had been caught, our jailers would have been punished more severely than ourselves. Fortunately we were not.

Even more fortunate, those whom I had circled with red pen got elected. Some of them were even the highest vote getters in their constituencies, and they were the ones most criticized by the *Central Daily*, including the wives of some of our codefendants! Ever since that time, when they would read something in the newspaper they had questions about, the jailers would come to me. This was just one of the many times that I succeeded in converting the KMT's secret agents from enemies into friends.

~

'Miss Lu, I am coming to bring you to the Armed Forces Hospital. Your family has filed an application on your behalf for medical parole. We are very much concerned about human rights. If the doctor says that it is necessary for your health, we will certainly consider it.' In the early morning of March 21, 1985, the director of political warfare of the Garrison Command came to my prison. I went to the hospital with him. The doctor who had taken care of me during the years of my imprisonment was sent in to explain the condition of my thyroid carcinoma to me.

My thyroid carcinoma was discovered in the summer of 1974, and I had had surgery when I was working for the Executive Yuan Cabinet of the Republic of China. It was also the third year of my vigorous activity on behalf of the feminist movement. I spent many hours after a full day of work giving lectures, counseling, and writing. I also taught law at a women's business college and wrote a column for two newspapers. The heavy workload, plus the pressure from the opponents of the feminist movement, resulted in my cancer. Ever since then I had had a metabolism problem and had not been feeling well. My illness worsened as a result of my imprisonment. I had suffered from fatigue, insomnia, and indigestion. On March 11, I was asked to take a heavy dose of 1-131, a powerful nuclear medicine. Apparently, there must have been something wrong with my thyroid.

'Please believe me that your carcinoma has been well controlled this time. I can guarantee that there isn't any possibility of a metastatic lesion. I don't think you really need a medical parole,' the doctor concluded. I was not surprised by this. How could I expect anything from the KMT? But then why should they bring me here today?

As soon as the doctor finished his comments, the director of the Garrison Command whispered to me: 'A professor from the United States wishes to see you. Would you like to see him? His name is. . . .'

'Jerome Cohen!'

Before he recalled the name, I instantly responded. I knew of his coming from the *Central Daily*, in which the story of Henry Liu's murder was released. Henry Liu, a Chinese-American writer who had written a critical biography of President Chiang Ching-kuo and was writing another piece concerning a scandal about Madame Chiang Kai-shek, was shot at his residence in Daly City, California, on October 15, 1984. The suspected murderers were chiefs of the Bamboo Gang, commanded by the KMT Military Intelligence Bureau. Professor Cohen came to attend the criminal trial held in Taipei as the attorney on behalf of the widow of Henry Liu. He was finally allowed to see me in the hospital because of the rule that no foreigners were allowed to visit the prison.

We met in the luxurious, carpet-covered visiting room of the president of the hospital, in the company of Ma Ying-jeou, the English secretary of President Chiang Ching-kuo. Ma and I had attended Harvard Law School together. At an informal meeting with the press in Taipei, Cohen had singled out his two former students in Taiwan: 'The one who was strongly for the government has received a high promotion, while the other one who was critical of the government is now in jail.'

In Ma's presence, he handed me a note, which he had written the night before, believing he would not be able to see me.

Dear Hsiu-Lien:

I was very moved by a visit from your family last night. It was good to see them, although their sadness because of your situation is understandably great. It was wonderful to hear from you, even if indirectly, and I appreciate your thought.

Please accept my best wishes for a speedy recovery of your health. I fervently hope that the authorities will release you in the near future and have frequently made this suggestion. Tonight I am meeting my former student, Y. J. Ma, deputy secretary general of the KMT to discuss your case and that of the others in the Kao-hsiung Group.

It is cruel and stupid for the authorities to continue to detain you. I will try to put pressure on them as soon as the Liu trial is over.

Please keep your spirits up. I hope to see you on my next trip. This time the authorities said I didn't give them enough notice. In principle I understand I will be allowed to see you because I was your teacher. I will always be proud to be known as your teacher.

Very best wishes from Joan, me, and your many other American friends.

Sincerely,

Jerome Cohen

As a matter of fact, the KMT had decided to release me before Cohen began to put pressure on them. Afterward, I learned that the authorities originally planned to release me on March 21. Because of his request for a visit, however, my release was postponed for another week. I believed this happened so that the authorities could 'save face.'

Was my early release 'a gift' for Professor Cohen, hoping that he would be less hard regarding the KMT's involvement with Liu's murder? Or was the recurrence of my thyroid carcinoma the true reason for the medical parole? The answer is still a riddle.

~

Standing there on the grass over the hilly cemetery, I looked at the people who came to worship their ancestors on this Taiwanese Memorial Day. I was amazed that I, who one short week ago had still been in the dark confinement of prison, was now able to be here. What is life all about, I asked myself? Was life a journey, with different encounters at each station? I felt that I had planned for and expected part of my journey, but that part of it was totally out of my control.

Standing there, in the forty-first year of my journey, my life flowed before me like a series of dreams. Some were beautiful, like blossoms shivering in the early spring wind; some were nightmares, full of horrible ghosts. Some were sweet, like the touch of a loving hand; and some were bitter, like the Taiwanese struggle against the KMT's martial law. However, it was time for me to go to the next station, and to the one after that. In this, my third life, I was not the same as I had been before. The worst had happened to me, and there remained nothing to be afraid of, even death itself. To know that was a kind of emancipation.

Standing there, I saw my mother's name written on a brand new, beautiful tomb. I burned the incense and worshipped her spirit, unable to control my tears. What could life have meant to her, I wondered? How could I begin to fathom her love for me, her dearest, youngest daughter, who had brought her so much anguish? What could that have meant for a simple woman whose whole life had been centered around her children? Standing there, looking at the endless rows of graves and the infinite expanse of the sky, I thought, 'some die, some are born; it is, after all, a cycle. The significance of a mother's life is not separated from that of her children's.'

And standing there I swore to myself that I would make her proud and, in my own way, give significance to her life.”

Notes

1. Linda Gail Arrigo, “Lu Hsiu-Lien: A Feminist in the Taiwan Democratic Movement” (unpublished paper, October 7, 1988), 1–15.
2. Ibid., 8.
3. Ibid., 11.

4 / Dai Qing

DAI QING IS ONE OF THE leading Chinese dissidents, whose efforts to unearth the secret past of the Communist Party through her independent historiography and her journalistic studies, endeavors that are tightly controlled in China, resulted in a critique of both the myths and the legitimacy of the political system. Like many critics in her country, she has lived through experiences that would crush most people, yet her eyes sparkle with defiance and she seems much younger than her years. However, despite her considerable accomplishments and her rebellious nature, she does not believe in glamorous public manifestations of dissent, but rather in difficult grass-roots efforts to achieve freedom of speech, human dignity, and environmental justice. Through her work, she has concluded that achieving genuine pluralism and a broad-based democracy animated by mutual responsibility would entail a complete transformation of Chinese society.

Dai Qing was born Fu Xiaoqing in Chongqing on August 24, 1941, to parents who were dedicated revolutionaries. Her father, a colleague of Chou En-lai working as a Comintern agent in China, was captured and presumably executed by the Japanese.[1] Her mother also worked for the Communist Party and was eventually imprisoned and tortured by Japanese occupiers. Shortly after the Japanese surrendered, Dai's mother, Feng, gave up her child in order to pursue her work for the Party, a not uncommon practice at a time when many Chinese sacrificed their whole lives for the revolution. Dai was raised by the late General Ye Jian-ying, who, until his death in 1986, was one of the most powerful men in the government. Her godmother is Deng Ying-chao, the widow of former Communist foreign minister Chou En-lai.

General Ye Jian-ying's household was loosely run, without a mistress and with the children left to their own devices in their free time. It was an atmosphere in which the future writer and dissident flourished. She could read for hours, pursue sports, and follow her inclinations. Dai grew up with all the opportunities of her position, including access to a top-level education.

During the Cultural Revolution, Dai was a Red Guard and sent to the countryside to dig in the fields. Although she first took part out of dedication to the revolution and to Chairman Mao, it was during the Cultural Revolution that she began to experience doubts about the revolutionary activity. A clash over her editorial decision while editing a Red Guard newspaper in 1967 was her first encounter with political infighting that had nothing to do with principles. During that time, Dai's mother was denounced as a traitor and revisionist. Not a single Party member would lift a finger on Feng's behalf; the only person who came to her assistance was an engineer in her organization who had been denounced himself.[2] It was during this period, when Dai first began to have contacts outside her privileged social stratum, that she began to learn what the Party had done to ordinary people and to discover how the Party destroyed lives. She found that her education had been filled with distortions and lies.

Meanwhile, Dai married, and when she returned to Beijing from the countryside in 1972 she and her husband found jobs in the Ministry of Public Security. In 1977, Dai entered the People's Liberation Army Institute in Nanking, where she studied in the English Department. By then she had begun to write short stories about the lives of the ordinary people who had so affected her. She published her first short story in 1979 and received a job in the People's Liberation Army intelligence section, where she worked undercover as a foreign affairs liaison officer in the Chinese Writers' Association, with the duty of making contact with East European writers and foreign writers' delegations. As part of her job in the Writers' Association she met Studs Terkel, author of oral history books, including *Working*. Dai accompanied him during his visit to Beijing, and her observations of his interviewing methods influenced her own future work as a reporter and historiographer.[3]

Her attendance, with the Chinese delegation, at a PEN (International Association of Poets, Playwrights, Editors, Essayists, and Novelists) conference in 1981 contributed to Dai's burgeoning disillusionment with the Communist Party. She received a leaflet that some young French students were distributing on behalf of imprisoned Chinese writers, an occurrence that filled her with shame. Her humiliation was compounded by the number of lies the delegation members told about the situation in China. She also recalls that when it was time for dinner and the participants could seat themselves with friends rather than with their delegations, the Chinese sat alone at a table. As a result of all these experiences, she dropped out of the writers' union. As someone who loves her country deeply, she was distressed by the behavior of the delegation and of the image that it projected abroad.

In 1982, Dai could no longer tolerate her position as a spy and relinquished her post. She received an offer from the *Guangming Daily*, a newspaper primarily serving intellectuals. That paper had already published some of her short stories, and she seemed a likely candidate to become a journalist, although she had no formal training for the position. She adopted the name Dai Qing as a pen name and served as a senior reporter until 1991.

Dai had laid down a number of conditions for accepting the job as reporter, including her refusal to report on government meetings, concentrating instead on the grass roots. Her work brought her into contact with a wide range of intellectuals, government figures, and many ordinary persons, thereby enabling her to gauge the changing mood of the country at the time, and also to discover the truth behind the masks of Party orthodoxy. It did not take her long to chafe under the Party strictures on what could be written. Because she was unable to write the stories she chose, she began interviewing all kinds of people and thus continued her painful education into the underside of reality in China. In the early 1980s she published a series of interviews called *Conversations with Scholars* and came into contact with noted historians such as Zhu Zheng and Li Shu, influential and controversial figures who had suffered for their rebellion against Party orthodoxy.[4]

In 1986, Dai launched a series of studies of major Party controversies involving leading intellectual figures. She produced two works of historical investigative journalism or historical reporting that struck at the basis of Party legitimacy in the realm of intellectual life. One of these writings covered the case of Wang Shiwei, who was executed by the Party in 1942 in Yan'an for his essays criticizing the elitism of party officials and whose works, including "Wild Lilies," were only made available during the 1980s. When Dai read Wang Shiwei's essays, she realized that the official version of his case was a distortion; and she began intensive research, which resulted in a publication entitled *Wang Shiwei and "Wild Lilies."* This was the beginning of a series of efforts to reconstruct party history and to examine the lives and works of major thinkers who had run afoul of the Party, who remained unrehabilitated, and whose writings were unavailable to scholars and the public.

As she interviewed scholars and read the original works of thinkers who had been victimized by the Party, Dai began to reexamine the nature of a political system she had never questioned as a member of the ruling elite. In this endeavor, she not only challenged journalism as practiced in China but also embarked upon a new historiography based upon a formerly proscribed examination of primary sources. She presented these investigations in her own unique style, with commentaries, asides, and extensive footnotes, a very bold move in a society that restricts the flow of information and controls the interpretation of policies and events.[5] "In my interviews I discovered that Chinese history has been completely distorted: it was written to delude the people. In individual terms, every life is in itself a living history, and it is of priceless worth both as history and literature. This is the realization I had."[6] Dai's historiographical dissent led her to the same conclusions as those reached by Vaclav Havel in his prison cell: the human spirit cannot be annihilated.

Dai was not only bold in her writing but was also outspoken in a society that demands active conformity and where individuals rarely have the courage to speak out. One of the many events that precipitated her downfall was her public questioning of the most powerful woman in China, Chen Muhua, at a meeting of the Chinese Women's Association. Dai confronted her on her record as head of the Bank of China, charging that she had presided over the worst inflation in thirty years.[7] Furthermore, she challenged her by asking what she had ever done on behalf of women. Her outspokenness, her history of criticizing Communist ideology as well as the foundations for its rule, and her activities against the construction of the Three Gorges Dam on the Yangtze River enraged the authorities. Dai's opposition to the dam project, which preceded her involvement in Tiananmen Square and the events leading up to it, brought her into direct conflict with the government and is, she believes, one of the most important factors that led to her imprisonment in June 1989. In fact, it continues to bear on her relationship with the Chinese government today.

Dai first became concerned with the environment as a human rights issue in 1988 when Li Peng, the prime minister, proposed the Three Gorges Dam Project for a two-hundred-kilometer stretch where the Yangtze, the world's third-largest river, surges through narrow canyons between limestone cliffs. It was the most ambitious hydroelectric power project ever proposed in the world and would affect a river that is the lifeblood of 400 million people and touches ten of China's thirty provinces, its fertile valley producing 40 percent of China's grain and 70 percent of its rice. Building the dam entails creating a reservoir that would stretch six hundred kilometers, flooding 44,000 hectares of farmland and displacing 1.2 million people during the proposed eighteen-year project. It would submerge parts of ten cities, including harbors, markets, temples, power plants, and industries, while destroying the habitats of endangered species and costing from $10 to $20 billion.[8] The government claims that the dam would generate eighteen thousand megawatts of electricity, improve navigation, control floods, and foster regional development. Critics warn that the dam could cause earthquakes, mudslides, deforestation, and other environmental problems.

Dai played a very prominent role in the opposition to the dam. Distressed over the lack of open debate on such a crucial project, she invited prominent scientists to write critical essays on the impact of the dam and published them, at her own expense, in a 1989 book called *Yangtze! Yangtze! Controversy over the Three Gorges Dam Project*. Fifty thousand copies were printed by a provincial publishing house that pushed the book through in fifteen days. Twenty thousand copies were sold before the enraged authorities confiscated the remaining thirty thousand. However, Prime

Minister Li Peng was forced to back down, and the project was postponed for five years, a retreat occurring just two months before the Tiananmen Square crackdown.

Since her release from prison in 1990, Dai has been very active in speaking out and publishing articles about the implications of the project. She arranged for the reprinting of the banned *Yangtze! Yangtze!* in Taiwan and for an English translation, which was published in 1994 by the Canadian environmental organization Probe International.[9] She is also planning to write on the problems associated with the Three Gorges Dam and eighty-six thousand other reservoirs built since 1949, information that has been unavailable to outsiders for the past fifty years and that will make an important contribution to the world's understanding of the difficulties surrounding large dams.[10] Dai has worked with organizations such as the Friends of the Earth, Green China, the International Rivers Network, and Probe International. These organizations formed a coalition in 1992 to campaign against the construction of the dam and to try to dissuade the World Bank, the Asian Development Bank, Canada, and Merrill Lynch from funding the project. As part of this campaign, Dai has given press conferences and has served on panel discussions.

She has since written that this project would be a continuation of others carried out in the 1950s that have resulted in environmental disasters in China, such as the development of large-scale water projects and large-scale steel smelting, an overreliance on grain production, and the encouragement of population growth. She notes that the results have been soil erosion, a reduction in forests, and increased flooding in the region of the Yellow River. In her articles, Dai has pointed out the environmental implications of the proposed Three Gorges Dam on farmland, climate, and wildlife, and she stresses that nobody has paid any attention to the pollution resulting from mines being engulfed by the reservoir; the damage to the drinking water of China's largest industrial city, Shanghai; or the social upheavals that could occur.[11] Because of these hazards, she has urged that, instead of constructing a dam on the Yangtze, the government should initiate an ecological program that includes forest and dike enhancement and the widening of the river channel for improved flow.[12]

Her own family experiences alerted her to the social impact of such endeavors, and she has expressed her concern that sociologists and anthropologists have not been consulted about the enormous social dislocation that would be caused by the project. In the

1950s, Dai's in-laws were displaced by plans to build a reservoir north of Beijing. They were ostracized in the village where they were relocated and suffered again when the government reneged on its promises that they would never have to pay taxes as a compensation for the move. Today, many of the peasants who would be affected by the construction of the Three Gorges Dam are being lured by promises of a higher standard of living and are unaware of the long-term consequences of such a move. Dai believes that those who will experience the effects of the project should be fully informed.

Dai's most scathing indictment of the dam has to do with the manner in which the decision is being carried out. She describes it as typical of Party rule, a handful of individuals controlling the natural resources of the entire country for purely political motives. In contrast, she suggests that people at the grass-roots level should be involved in the decision, and that the long-term good of the country should be considered as the plan would affect the environment not just in China but also in the entire world. Dai's efforts on behalf of the environment are concomitant with her work to ensure freedom of expression and historical investigation and to make certain that issues be publicly and freely examined and all shades of opinion be aired. In a recent article, Dai characterized the push for the Three Gorges Dam project as the death throes of an old state, and the resistance to the project as the emergence of a new society made up of independent individuals who require open decision making as well as international support.[13]

In April 1993, Dai received the Goldman Environmental Prize of $60,000 for her work alerting public opinion to the consequences of the Three Gorges Dam project.[14] Typically, Dai, upon her return to her home country in the spring of 1994, donated all of the prize money to start a journal concerned with the environment in China. The publication aims to make information on China's ecological problems available to countries around the world as well as to include articles and other material from abroad. As a result of this endeavor, the current government has characterized her work as having a sinister, anti-Party character.

Government disapproval, however, did not dissuade Dai from playing a very dangerous role in Tiananmen Square and the events leading up to it. In March 1989, shortly after her campaign to stop the Yangtze River-Three Gorges Dam project, she and some friends wrote an open letter to the National People's Congress that was signed by forty intellectuals and that appealed for the release of political prisoners. The letter provoked an outraged article from the *Guangming Daily*. The following April, when Qin Benli, editor of the *World Economic Herald*, was fired for publishing notes of a forum calling for the rehabilitation of the disgraced Hu Yaobang, former general secretary of the Communist Party, and expressing support for the student demonstrations in Tiananmen Square, it was Dai who persuaded other journalists to send messages of support for Qin Benli, urging his reinstatement.[15] In May, Dai and a number of Chinese intellectuals, supporting the demands of the students, called on the Party to continue with liberal reforms.

As a moderate and as someone with inside knowledge, Dai was concerned for the safety of the students and became a mediator between the authorities and student leaders. She was concerned that the student protests would be manipulated by Party leaders engaged in a power struggle. Fearing a bloody repression, she tried to persuade the students to end their hunger strike, leave Tiananmen Square, and return to their campus. As a result, she was criticized by both sides. The militant students received her suggestions with hostility, and some writers and journalists claimed that she was a government agent. The *Guangming Daily* insisted that her appeals to the students had an ulterior motive, criticizing her on the front page under the headline "Dai Qing Rebellion Reporter."[16]

Martial law was declared in Beijing on May 20, 1989, and the massacre that Dai had predicted occurred on June 4. Outraged, she helped circulate a protest petition. Few people had the courage to sign, and many retreated in fear. She then publicly resigned from the Communist Party, claiming that she wanted to distance herself from politics and preserve her individuality.[17]

Dai was arrested in July and taken to Qincheng Prison for investigation into her involvement in the Tiananmen rebellion, although she knew that her revisionist Party histories were the real reason for her arrest. There, she learned that she and several other inmates had been classified as an "antiparty clique," which could mean lengthy prison sentences or even the death penalty. She spent ten grueling months in solitary confinement, her hair turning white and falling out in clumps. Her guards repeatedly told her that she was on a list for execution. She wrote to friends that she would rather die than spend her life in prison and asked them to send her law books, hoping to learn whether a political prisoner would be allowed to seek a doctor's help to end her own life. While she was in prison, her daughter was asked to denounce her in order to gain entrance to the university, and, as her mother's daughter, she refused.

The following May, Dai was released from prison without formal charges or a trial and instead turned over to her newspaper for further discipline. The *Guangming Daily* kept her on its payroll but barred her from writing. She then took a job editing a Taiwan-based folkloric magazine.

Undeterred from her work toward a free press and freedom of expression, Dai Qing sued the author who had virulently attacked her in the article in the *Guangming Daily*. She regarded her suit as an assault against the Communist officials at the newspaper and the government's Propaganda Department, which would have approved the article. That action followed a similar effort by another writer, Wang Meng, a leading literary figure and former minister of culture, who had sued a newspaper for criticizing him.

Shortly afterward, on the suggestion of her sister-in-law, Dai applied to Harvard University and was accepted; however, the newspaper that controlled her passport refused to grant her permission to leave. After a number of unsuccessful appeals, she contacted Secretary of State James Baker, although she was detained in order to prevent him from meeting with her during his visit to China. It was the outrage of well-placed figures within the U.S. government that finally allowed her to come to Harvard, where she spent 1991 and 1992 as a Nieman Fellow and where she received the International Federation of Newspaper Publishers' Golden Pen of Freedom Award.

In 1993 she was appointed as a fellow of the Freedom Forum Media Studies Center at Columbia University, where she worked on a project to document the process by which the relatively free press that China had achieved before the Communists came to power was destroyed and turned into a tool of the Party. This historical study is written in Dai's unique style of a combination of personal stories, the work of journalists who played an important part in the transformation of the press (which she refers to as "intellectual rape"), and the primary sources documenting this evolution.

Dai returned to China in June 1994 with the full knowledge that she would be prevented from publishing her work. In fact, because she planned to arrive on the eve of the anniversary of Tiananmen Square, she was concerned that she would be forbidden to enter the country. To prevent this and to avoid being held up at the airport, she wrote directly to the security police informing them of her arrival.[18] She felt that returning to China was a risk worth taking, and she believes that members of the overseas democracy movement also should go back and face the potential harassment because her country needs real progress. In Dai's view, this can only occur on an issue-by-issue basis, with each individual combating the wrongs in his or her own arena and working toward the creation of democracy from the ground up, and with localities working together and preventing the usurpation of power by a privileged minority. Her courage and willingness to speak out on behalf of freedom, including her criticism of the lack of democracy within pro-democracy exile groups, have made her a lonely figure.[19] However, Dai Qing is not interested in power. She sees her role as that of a conscience, waking people up to the need for freedom and to their responsibility for achieving it in their own lives.

DAI SPEAKS

I think that freedom is more important than anything else, this is my fundamental belief. No excuses of any sort can be made to suppress individual freedom. Of course, people sometimes have to choose to restrict their own freedom of expression, to exercise self-restraint. I have often done this. I think, this is not the time to say this thing, so I'll just wait, and when the right time comes I will say it. This is because I choose to do it this way, not because someone prevents me from doing it. All restrictions on liberty are wrong.

[Interview with Sophia Woodman, *Human Rights Tribune* 3, no. 1 (Spring 1992): 23.]

"My father was a first-generation revolutionary who died in 1945 in a Japanese prison. My mother was a patriotic leftist student who went to Chongqing in southwest China, the capital during the war, in order to join the revolution. Theirs was a political marriage because the Party wanted to use my mother's family background to facilitate Party work. During that period, the Comintern needed some military intelligence badly, and they asked the Chinese Communist Party to send a person to Beijing, which was then occupied by the Japanese. They chose my father, but my father needed a background. He wanted a wife from a prominent family in Beijing so he could find his way among the upper class and also people who collaborated with the occupiers. At the end of 1940 my father was forty and my mother was twenty-two. Of course, later, my mother respected my father, but love was out of the question.

When I was just a baby, they brought me from Chongqing to Guilin, and then to Hong Kong, Shanghai, Tianjin. They made a roundabout journey on foot and in the heat through all of these cities to end up in Beijing so that nobody would know where they really came from. It was very, very hard and dangerous work. I didn't know much about it myself until 1988, when a person who wanted to write a biography of my father got together with my relatives. Then I learned about him and some of the details about the way they lived in Beijing.

They had to work undercover, so my father took a position as a professor. My parents lived in a nice house and were respectable on the surface, all on the Party budget. But when they were alone, behind closed doors, they ate only the most coarse food because they were so idealistic, and they wanted to save the Party's budget. That kind of idealism was instilled in me, and it contrasts with Party hacks who are now just leading a luxurious life. That generation gave up everything for the revolution.

The reason that my parents' cover was blown was that there was a young fellow who was sent to the Soviet Union to be trained when he was in his teens and then sent back to work in Beijing with my father. He just stood out with his terrible Chinese accent, but the Soviet Union insisted that he should be there because it was their kind of control. It didn't take long for the whole network to be exposed. Over a hundred people from my mother's side of the family were implicated and arrested, including my mother.

My mother was pregnant when she was arrested. When they were working undercover, life was so tense they never really had a sex life. The reason that my mother became pregnant again was that on one occasion she played with a key and just mislaid it; when my father came back he flew into a terrible temper because it was a life-and-death matter that he couldn't find his key to all his files. Later, he was apologetic and they had sex. My mother was unhappy because she didn't really know a married life. All she knew was revolution.

My mother's uncle had been educated in Japan, and her grandfather had seen the emperor of Japan during the time of the Qing dynasty. Because of their upper-class status, my mother's family was able to bail my mother out after a year. Just as she was giving birth, the Japanese surrendered, so she didn't have to go back to prison.

My maternal aunt took care of me while my mother was in prison. I was three years old, and my little brother was only one. At the time my aunt was only thirteen years old. One of my earliest memories from that time is when I was three and a half years old. My mother also remembers it; it's very strange. I was playing in the yard, and a woman came in who was very thin and emaciated but had a very big belly. Her face was very pale. My mother also remembers stepping into the yard and seeing a very dirty little girl picking dates from the ground, because there were date trees. She was eating them and wearing a cotton padded jacket with nothing underneath, no underwear. I was very dirty because there was nobody to take care of me.

I also remember when my sister was born. I went to the hospital to see her. Because my mother had been tortured when she was in prison, the baby was covered with bruises. My mother had been forced to drink cold water, and then they stepped on her stomach and water came out of all of her orifices; that is a typical kind of Japanese torture. So the baby bore the marks of the torture on its body. Later, during the Cultural Revolution, my mother was condemned as a traitor. They questioned her, 'How come your husband died in prison and you didn't?' They wouldn't believe how she had suffered during the war.

My teenage years were the best times for China, the middle fifties. At the time, the government and educational structure offered many opportunities for youth to join in all kinds of activities. I was still living with the family of General Ye, so during the summer the whole family could go up to the seashore to prestigious and restricted areas for swimming and other activities. I never went with them and always did something on my own. The first time I did was the summer of my first year in junior high; I became an assistant training youngsters in physical exercise. The next year I learned baseball, took part in speech competitions, paddling kayaks and parachuting, and learned to ride a motorbike. These were all youth activities which I joined and were not just for the children of the privileged. I did this instead of joining the Yes at their summer home. I feel that I am still privileged because I never had to do any housework.

My mother was in northeast China. It is a Chinese revolutionary way to give up her child. She also gave her youngest daughter to my aunt. I told my mother it was cruel to send her own child to another person. She had seven children and found them too much of a burden, believing all of her children must belong to the revolution. She could give them away to any organization, any family for the revolution, and then she herself could work hard for the revolution. I felt hurt, but this was in the past. Last December [1993] I went back to China, mainly to see my mother, because I don't think she has more time. I had to visit her and take care of her.

When I was growing up, one of the biggest influences on my life was Western literature. I used to be a solitary child, a little adult. I was always staying in General Ye's study and reading. The first three years of junior high school, the minute I was out of school and finished my homework, I would go to a local library and just sit there and read until it was very late. Recently, my daughter went to that library; it's the local library of the western district of Beijing, and she was shocked. It was in such a dilapidated state, and there was such a poor collection. My daughter exclaimed, 'Mother, you were reading there?' I have become what I am because of the library, so I am always moved when people want to set up a library in the poorest village anywhere. That's the most important thing. I first began by reading translations from Russian literature. I went through [Ivan] Turgenev. Then, in senior high school, I started reading translations from English literature, mostly nineteenth century: *Pride and Prejudice*, *A Tale of Two Cities*, *Jane Eyre*. I went through French literature after that. These books were all translated because they were protected by the commendation of [Karl] Marx and [Friedrich] Engels, so they were untouchable. All through the fifties and sixties, right up to the Cultural Revolution, these works existed in China on all the Chinese bookshelves and in many very good translations. Victor Hugo was a great favorite in China and was translated. I basically ended my reading of nineteenth century with romantic realism. I then read [William] Thackeray's *Vanity Fair*. In college I started reading American literature: [Charles] Dickens and Mark Twain. Mark Twain is still my favorite.[20] Bashevis Singer and Saul Bellow, the Jewish writers, became my favorites when I started writing myself.

I was in my late thirties in 1979. It was the beginning of the Deng Xiaoping era, when things were easing. I was writing short stories, which took up one or two pages in a national journal. I wrote a story called 'Anticipations.' The older readers were stunned. It inspired the greatest number of letters to the editor that the paper had ever received. I was writing about poor intellectuals (what we call mental workers) and how they were so isolated, and it was also a metaphor for other things. They were always longing to be together, and there were always promises dangled before them that never materialized. They were very poor and lived deprived lives. Readers were surprised because I was so privileged and wondered how I knew about the sufferings of such ordinary people because the subjects of my stories were not lofty intellectuals but just ordinary people—teachers, low-level engineers. They wondered how I could understand their feelings and empathize so much with them. I thought about it later and realized that what I hated most in life was officials using their power to deprive the smaller people in the name of the revolution.

It was during the Cultural Revolution that I began to reexamine the reality around me. Before the Cultural Revolution, I was sent to a very prestigious college, the highest educational institute. I was really educated to be a tool of the state, and I had never really realized how other people lived, that there were other ways of life. I lived in an enclosed world. The people that I interacted with were all people like me, coming from so-called good family backgrounds. They didn't know about suffering. I later considered them very naive.

The West has a very simplified notion of what a Red Guard is. The Western notion of the Red Guard is of teenagers on a rampage and beating up people. Of course, there was that side of it, but when the Cultural Revolution broke out, I was twenty-three years old and employed at the Ministry of Aerospace, working on missiles. When the revolution broke out, many people sincerely believed that Mao called on the younger population to be alerted because of the danger of revisionism among leaders implementing a revisionist line. Therefore, it was the younger people who were called on to rectify this line. It was more a matter of political correctness than patriotism. The young people were listening to Mao as he tried to correct revisionism. My group of Red Guards and the action we took was mainly to counter the revisionist line. It could be pretty extreme but was regarded as a rational thing. I drew the line at beating people, and I remember very clearly that in my research institute there had been an occasion when two people my own age put on a military Red Guard uniform with a big belt and decided to imitate the Red Guards in the city to learn how to beat up people. They decided to target one of the young men in the institute who was always chasing girls, and I interfered because I knew that this man was just mentally unstable, and I opposed the beating. It might have been because of my training as an engineer that I had a rational mind and wanted to think things through clearly. I would never just follow the herd. I had a strong will.

During the Cultural Revolution, I and many others started out with the idea of combating revisionism to make the Party and the revolutionary ideals purer. That was the starting point. Then, I saw the reality and realized that the revolution that my father and mother gave their whole lives for had degraded into a reality where so many people had been hurt and there was so much injustice. That first opened my eyes. Now I speak the truth. I thought back to the fifties when I was a happy teenager and of the movements when so many people had been implicated in one or another of these political campaigns. That's why I decided to dig back into Party history; I looked at the Party with new eyes.

Because of the turmoil during the Cultural Revolution, many writings and essays [primary sources] which were unavailable became accessible. It was complete anarchy, and so I read these essays by Qu Qiubai and Wang Shiwei which were critical of the behavior of Party leaders. There were so many things that had been censored and taboo that I now want to use my energy to unearth the hidden past and make it accessible. Only then can the Chinese people be normal and rational. So much is kept from us. Qu Qiubai was one of the Party leaders who was killed, and when I read his last testament, which was called 'Some Superfluous Words,' I suddenly realized that the revolution was not just romantic self-sacrifice with a sublime spirit, what the Party and my mother told me. In 'Some Superfluous Words,' you can see that sometimes there was a conflict within the personality that became very painful. That's when I developed a hunger for the truth. It seemed as if the demands of the revolution went against man's nature.

I originally wrote the critical essay 'A Pliant Rush' as a foreword to my second collection of short stories. I borrowed the metaphor of that essay from Dante's *Divine Comedy*, when Virgil led Dante into the gates of Purgatory and picked a reed to tie around his waist, saying, 'This is the emblem of pliancy because it bends with the wind.' I picked that image because I thought of myself as very modest in a literature regarded with cynicism by many writers at the time. I wrote this article to express my own attitude that I am very modest but very, very serious and that I didn't consider literature a game. Since then I stopped writing short stories. I don't think I really have the talent. I felt that there were more important demands on me.

In 1982, I was looking for a new job and the national paper, the *Guangming Daily*, suggested that I work for them. I didn't start out with the idea of being a writer or a journalist. In 1982, I had the advantage that the newspaper had published my short stories so they came to me. Nineteen eighty-two was the best time because it was the most liberal period in China. Now, no national paper will invite me to write anything or even publish me.

I had a great sense of responsibility when I accepted the invitation, so I worked very hard at my job. This was the early eighties. At the time, my husband was also very busy. I went on seven business trips all over China, leaving home and, as a result, we both neglected our home. We had ordered three bottles of milk delivered per day. Our daughter mainly survived on all that milk every day, and now she hates milk.

The first stage of my journalistic career coincided with the period when the whole of China and the leaders as well were very concerned with intellectuals. During the thaw the uppermost problems were how these poor trained professionals had been so deprived and maltreated. There was a dearth of talent as a result of the Cultural Revolution, so I had been sent on a mission to write stories on these intellectuals. There were many outstanding instances. In this first period what I wanted to do coincided with what my bosses wished me to do, mainly writing about many cases of intellectuals. The way these people had been shunted aside was an overriding national problem.

The *Guangming Daily* was always considered the paper for intellectuals because the big national papers had a division of labor. The *People's Daily* was the voice of the Party, while the *Guangming Daily* was the voice of intellectuals. It was at this period that the head of the propaganda department of the Party Central Committee pointed out that the *Guangming Daily* was not doing enough, that its level was too low, so I seized the chance to start a special column of interviews with scholars. It was a very famous column called 'Questions and Answers with Celebrated Scholars.' My column became very popular because it appeared just at the time when both scholars and readers were looking forward to a revival of the social sciences and humanities. Simultaneously, many old scholars who had been put down now had a voice and were allowed to work again. At the same time, there was a crop of younger scholars so it was a very good time for me. It was the beginning of openness, and people just wanted to know more. Since I was interviewing scholars in many different areas, I read a lot in economics and philosophy. I always studied everything before speaking with them. Later, when I entered into the current phase of my career, I realized that all this research had been very valuable for me. The column received national notoriety. Everyone wondered who I was going to interview next.

My historical investigations began in 1986 and ended with the massacre in Tiananmen Square on June 4, 1989. I interviewed the physicist Fang Lizhi. During those years, I met hundreds of people and discovered that they each had their own history and wealth of experience. They told me their hidden story, an alternative history. I thought, this is the truth, not the account the Party has written, and this was a way of getting at national history.

In 1987 and 1988, I had published some very important historical investigations, unveiling hidden events. One is 'Wild Lilies,' by Wang Shiwei, a great journalist, one of the earliest newspapermen in China, a very upright and brilliant man who graduated from the London School of Economics.[21] This man was labeled as a rightist in 1957 and actually disappeared. We don't even know where he died. Nobody dared mention his name. He was one of the main enemies in the 1957 Anti-Rightist Campaign. He was anathema. I wrote about him, and it was reprinted everywhere.

While I was writing and digging up these skeletons in the Party closet, I was a Party member myself, and I thought that what I was doing was for the good of the Party. I believed it should face its own dark past and exorcize all its evil spirits. That was my mood then. In 1987, before another minicampaign against bourgeois liberalization, there was still some free discussion. There was a writers workshop in Hanan Island down south, a very beautiful place near the sea, but we had a terrible argument because most of the writers (all very well known) were proposing a kind of art for art's sake and also linking up with the postmodernist school of writing abroad. I thought that in China writing was not only a moral responsibility but also that the mood, the atmosphere in China, would not allow a writer to dwell in an ivory tower. I thought that the real problem with these writers was that they didn't want to face up to reality. The danger was not the same as it was in the fifties when one could be shot and labeled as an enemy, be sent off to the wilds, and then disappear. You still run the risk of losing a good job, of not being allowed to go abroad, losing a promotion, falling out of favor. It is still taking a chance but not as dangerous.

Now I feel very differently from what I did when I first took up reporting. The Party that would achieve its own victory at the expense of so much suffering and loss of dignity for so many people gained a very questionable victory. In Yan'an in the forties, the Party had this power base, and many scholars since the 1960s and

1970s had written very positively about the Yan'an base because they saw only one side of it, as a very idealistic, hardworking, and committed group of people. I saw the dark side of this period, and I wrote about it.

My aim is to restore to Chinese society the consensus of what journalism should be in a normal society. This is what I am doing here in the Media Center. In the nineteenth century, China had a free journalism, and then in the 1940s the Communist Party transformed journalism from a pluralistic to a monolithic enterprise.

In China before Tiananmen, Deng Xiaoping was not limiting his efforts to just economic reform; he also had in mind eventual political reform. This was the 1980s. If the situation had been allowed to develop, it might have taken a positive turn. My stand in Tiananmen Square was that the students should be restrained and reasonable, just to push for reform. That was the role I was going to play. In the beginning, I didn't agree with the concept, which is still a Communist concept, that a mass movement would develop into a revolution and then push history forward. I felt that the students were starting out with this Communist concept, and that if the whole society is not changed, the people in power would be just like the old ones. I think that for a society to be normal, everyone should play their own role and do their own job. At the beginning of the movement on May 13, I did something which was just part of my job as a journalist. I called a meeting of celebrated scholars and wanted them to speak out about the problems of society. I considered it as a kind of safety valve, offering alternative ideas. I don't agree with the notion that everybody should take part in a revolution. The scholars could offer a pluralism, different ideas. What I did in Tiananmen Square was to go to the students because there was a moderate party in the government which asked people like myself, celebrated scholars, to go and talk to them. I talked to the students, trying to instill some moderation and rationality. Qia Ling's husband snatched the microphone away from my hand. She and her husband were directing the operations of the students, and they just wouldn't listen. I felt that as a journalist and writer that was all I could do. I couldn't go and start another revolution on the square. For this I was later arrested and spent ten months in prison.

The government was punishing me for something else which they couldn't really say, all my digging up of skeletons in the Party closet. Also, I had allowed myself to be interviewed by thirty different members of the foreign media while in Tiananmen Square. At the time, it was a very dangerous thing to do. People are usually afraid to be interviewed by the foreign press, but I felt that at the time the voices were too extreme, both the government and the students, and thought there should be a different kind of voice. That enraged the government. Apart from my writing, this made the government angry. After students were shot in Tiananmen Square, I publicly resigned my membership from the Party. That was like slapping the Party in the face and was why they arrested me.

You must understand that, although we have a one-party system, sometimes underneath there are differences. After Tiananmen there was such a big problem; the legal system didn't want the extra burden on their hands. But it was the propaganda people, those in charge of ideology, who wanted me punished. In prison, when I was questioned, I was only questioned about my role in Tiananmen and, of course, I only played a very innocent role there. They couldn't find anything wrong. There were only twelve people who went to the square to preach moderation to the students and didn't succeed. Only nine were on the list to be mentioned by the mayor of Beijing as these 'evil bourgeois liberalization elements,' fanning the flames of this chaos. My name was at the top of the list of twelve people. Later, when the order came for arrest, three names were dropped from the list. Of these nine, my name was moved down to the fourth. There is a special department under the Propaganda Department of the Central Committee, which is called the First Department, and they pondered the so-called bourgeois liberalization elements, prominent people who write. Their job is just to study their cases, follow their writing and their movements. They were just looking for an excuse to arrest me. Being in the square was just what they were looking for. As far as the legal system was concerned, they didn't want to be burdened, and that is why they shut one eye and allowed so many people to come abroad. Many people were able to escape because they turned a blind eye.

I was arrested on July 14. On the day before, the West German ambassador had come back from his holiday in Italy and came to visit me in my home (I had agreed to make a program about the Cultural Revolution as part of a normal cultural exchange). He rushed back from Germany and said, 'Come with me.' I was very moved because I understood what it meant. I cried a little, but decided I just couldn't go. After the ambassador left, the local police came and asked, 'Where will you be tomorrow?' It was like a broad hint that something would happen tomorrow, giving me time to get away. But I still decided to stay. This decision reflects something deep in the Chinese mentality. I thought, this was the eighties, not the fifties, and that perhaps I might not be arrested, and, if I would be, it wouldn't be so serious. However, I still didn't exclude serious consequences. In the Chinese mentality is a spirit of loyalty and honor, that when you are called upon to do something, you shouldn't run away.

I absolutely disagree with Fang Lizhi going to the American embassy, and I had many arguments with him and with other foreign journalists who defended him. I felt that if it was my role under the circumstances to be arrested, I should just take the consequences as a point of honor. By that time, we were considered symbols, and we should have acted honorably. I disagree with Liu Binyan and all those who left. I stayed because I was innocent. Even if I suffered extreme punishment, I wouldn't have been the first. I feel that people who are directly responsible for what happened on Tiańanmen Square, the student leaders, had no right to leave. Scholars like myself, who could be considered indirectly responsible because we had preached all these theories of individualism and liberalism, shouldn't leave. One should stay and prove one's innocence, thus revealing the nature of the Communist Party. In this case, it's my Chinese mentality and culture which runs very deep in me. There's also a precedent in Chinese history. In 1889, before the republic, during the last gasp of the Manchu dynasty, there was a great reform movement. The reformers are all now big names in Chinese history. One of them was publicly beheaded in the square. He repeated these famous words: 'If the reform needs blood to be spilled, let it be my blood.'

I had never been a very good wife and mother. I was interested in my career, but when I was in jail and I was in solitary confinement, the highest jail for political prisoners, I suddenly found I had a soft spot for my family. I missed my husband and daughter and worried about them in a way I had never done before. In November, when I had been in prison for six months, the situation was extremely tense, and words floated about that some would be executed, some would be exiled, and some would get long prison sentences. I got a hint from a friendly jailer that I was among the six who were to be executed. In this prison, there was no physical violence, but they watched us incessantly through a peephole.

I was crying once, and the female jailer came in and asked me what was wrong because they were trying to change my mind. My family had sent me things, and one of the things they sent was a towel with a big and little monkey printed on it. It was just like my husband and daughter, and that was why I was crying. I told the jailer, 'I'm so sorry I only nursed my daughter for fifty-six days' (that was the legal time limit for a break after a delivery). When the jailer asked my daughter's age and I said she was twenty and in college, the jailer told me I was a fool and said, 'Why worry about her now?' She couldn't understand how my mind went back.

I read this poem around Christmas, already looking forward to an open trial when I could defend myself, but also afraid that they would not just execute me but sentence me to life imprisonment. I would rather have died and thought about mercy killing. I knew of a scholar at the Chinese Academy of Social Sciences who was a philosopher studying the issue of mercy killing. I was trying to find the wife of a prominent scholar who knew this philosopher because I couldn't write a letter to him. I smuggled out a little note written on the back of a chewing gum wrapper. I copied a poem from memory by one of our most outstanding modern poets, who had spent much time in England. I wrote that poem so that the person receiving the note would know that it was from me. It was by word of mouth that I wanted to get in touch with this scholar and try through my lawyer to reach a doctor. 'I leave now so softly/as softly as when I came/With a flutter of my sleeve/Not taking even a cloud.'[22] ”

Notes

1. The Comintern was the Third International of Socialist Parties, founded by V. I. Lenin in 1917 and used by him to tightly control Communist parties around the world.

2. Geremie Barmé, "The Trouble with Dai Qing," *Index on Censorship* 8 (August 1992).

3. Ibid., 17.

4. Geremie Barmé, "Using the Past to Save the Present: Dai Qing's Historiographical Dissent," *East Asian Studies* 1 (1991): 147–50.

5. Ibid.

6. Quoted in Barmé, "Using the Past to Save the Present," 149.

7. Tom Regan, "Chinese Nieman Fellow Wins Golden Pen Award," *Nieman Reports* (Spring 1992).

8. Probe International press release, Monday, April 19, 1993, Toronto, Canada, 1–3.

9. Dai Qing, *Yangtze! Yangtze! Controversy over the Three Gorges Dam Project*, ed. Patricia Adams and John Thibodeau (Toronto: Earthscan Publications), 1994.

10. Probe International press release, April 19, 1993.

11. Dai Qing, "The Three Gorges Dam Project and Free Speech in China," *Chicago Review*, no. 39 (December 1993): 275–78.

12. Ibid.

13. Ibid.

14. The Prize was established in the late 1980s and is awarded to environmental activists from each of the six continents for their grass-roots efforts.

15. Lek Hor Tan, "Caught in the Memory Hole," *Weekend Guardian* (November 11–12, 1989).

16. Ibid.

17. Barmé, "The Trouble with Dai Qing," 17.

18. Before leaving the country, Dai would telephone the security police telling them that because they followed her so frequently, she might as well ride with them to her destination and thus avoid having to take a taxi.

19. The author is grateful to Carmelita Hinton (daughter of William Hinton) of Dorchester, Massachusetts, for her insights into Dai Qing's character.

20. Over dinner one night Dai and the author discussed the works of Milan Kundera and Vaclav Havel.

21. "Wild Lilies" reveals the Party leaders and cadres at the time as self-indulgent, clinging to privilege, and unfeeling toward the masses. The essay criticizes the hierarchy already instituted by Party officials and points out the disparities between Party rhetoric and the everyday reality of common people. See Dai Qing, *Wang Shiwei and "Wild Lilies": Rectification and Purges in the Chinese Communist Party, 1942–1944*, ed. David E. Apter and Timothy Cheek (Amonk, NY: M. E. Sharp, 1993), 1–93.

22. Dai Qing, "My Imprisonment," *Index on Censorship* 8 (August 1992).

Part II

Struggling with Race and Ethnicity

5 / *Daisy L. Bates*

ALMOST FORTY YEARS HAVE PASSED since the crisis in Little Rock, Arkansas, over school desegregation, but the name Daisy L. Bates continues to evoke the power of the human spirit against hatred, violence, and intolerance and the ongoing struggle of her people for justice and human dignity. Daisy Bates served as mentor to the nine children who entered the first desegregated school in Little Rock in 1957 and has devoted her life to working for the civil rights of African Americans. She occupies an important place in the galaxy of leaders on behalf of equal rights. However, as a woman, she has borne the double burden of racism and sexism, obstacles that she and so many others have overcome through sheer tenacity and moral courage.

Born and raised in Huttig, a company-owned sawmill town in southern Arkansas, Daisy Lee Gatson first confronted the bitter consequences of racism and segregation as a seven-year-old child. While running an errand for her parents in a white-owned store, she experienced the humiliation of being made to wait until everyone else was served and to pay for an inferior grade of meat. When she came home in tears from that first encounter, she learned that the father she looked up to was unable to protect her because of fear for his own life and for the safety of his family. It was a lesson that filled her with anger and grief, and one that haunted her for years.

Not long after this incident, Daisy discovered that her mother had been kidnapped and murdered by a group of white men and that, overcome with despair, her father had left town shortly afterward, leaving his daughter in the care of friends. Her adoptive parents had tried to shelter her from this brutal reality, but a friend unwittingly mentioned something to the child, believing that she already knew. That same year, Daisy met her mother's murderer. As she paused outside on the steps of the general store, waiting for her friends, she felt someone staring at her. Daisy had been told that she was the image of her mother, and, as she watched the white man's expression change from puzzlement to fear, she understood that she was confronting her mother's killer. She stared him down and continued to do so relentlessly over the years in the same manner as she pursued the rights of her people, unafraid and fueled by righteous anger.

When Daisy was in her teens, her adoptive father died of cancer, leaving her a legacy that was to sustain her throughout her battle for her people's rights. While dying in his hospital bed, he admonished Daisy against the hatred of whites that was causing her grief and advised her instead to direct that anger against the humiliation, insults, and discrimination black people endured and to work toward eliminating them.[1]

The year after her father died, Daisy married L. C. Bates, a friend of his and a journalist. The couple settled in Little Rock and in 1941 decided against all odds to establish their own newspaper, the *Arkansas State Press*. Daisy soon turned the paper into a vehicle to unmask the racism endemic in aspects of daily life and in social and economic structures. In so doing, she was building upon a vigorous tradition of black women journalists who had used their careers to advance civil rights throughout the nineteenth century.

With the outbreak of World War II and the presence of black soldiers in Camp Robinson near Little Rock, Daisy began a crusade in the *State Press* against the all-too-frequent killing and beating of these soldiers by the local police. The stories that she published proved so unsettling to the white community that the paper faced an advertising boycott. Undaunted, Daisy and her husband worked long hours to keep the newspaper afloat and watched its circulation rise and attract a new group of advertisers who catered to their readers. The *State Press* became a noted advocate on behalf of a wide spectrum of civil rights for the African-American community, from better housing and working conditions to their entitlement to exercise rights guaranteed by the U.S. Constitution.

From their first days in Little Rock, Daisy and her husband were active members of the local branch of the NAACP (National Association for the Advancement of Colored People). Daisy served as cochairwoman of the State Conference's Committee for Fair Employment Practices, and in 1952 she was elected president of the Arkansas State Conference of NAACP branches. Meanwhile, NAACP lawyers, such as Thurgood Marshall, had been filing suits against segregation in public education, which ultimately led to the historic 1954 Supreme Court decision that declared all segregation unconstitutional.

In *Brown v. Board of Education of Topeka*, the Supreme Court ruled that schooling for black and white children cannot be equal under segregation, overturning the separate-but-equal doctrine established by an 1896 case, *Plessy v. Ferguson*. In the latter case the Court ruled that separation of the races is constitutional as long as equal accommodations are made for blacks.[2] The most severe test of the 1954 decision occurred in Little Rock as state politics became embroiled in efforts to prevent desegregation. At the time, Governor Francis A. Cherry was seeking reelection and his challenger, Orval Faubus, made political capital out of the recent court ruling by declaring that the state was not ready for complete and immediate desegregation, especially under outside pressure. Faubus won the election and took office in 1955. In 1957 he would call out the National Guard to prevent the entrance of nine black students into Central High.

The Little Rock school board issued a statement of compliance after the Supreme Court's decision, and in the summer of 1954, Virgil T. Blossom, Little Rock's superintendent of schools, drafted a plan for a gradual implementation of desegregation, with the school board adopting a much weaker version. It limited integration to just one school, Central High, and postponed implementation until 1957. Even though the Phase Program was vague and applied to only a limited number of black children, it roused the ire of segregationist groups, prompting the governor to announce a poll indicating that 85 percent of white people in the state opposed integration and to claim that he would not force a change that was so overwhelmingly opposed.[3]

As a result of the governor's announcement, the state chairman of the NAACP Legal Defense Committee and a regional attorney for that organization filed suit in federal court for immediate integration to start in grades one through twelve. The federal judge ruled in favor of the school board, deciding it had acted in good faith in scheduling its integration plan. NAACP attorneys then appealed this decision to the Eighth Circuit Court of Appeals, which upheld the lower court but also ordered the school board to put its plan into effect by September 1957, ruling that the district federal court retained jurisdiction over the case to issue any further order that might be necessary.[4]

In retaliation for this litigation, Arkansas legislators introduced and passed four prosegregation bills in the state legislature, establishing procedures to jail and intimidate citizens who spoke out against injustices such as segregation. One bill allowed school boards to hire lawyers to contest suits for integration; another made attendance at integrated schools voluntary; the third required organizations and individuals "challenging the authority of local or state officials" to register with the state; and a fourth created a state sovereignty commission with a broad mandate to protect the sovereignty of Arkansas from "encroachments by the federal government."[5] Daisy Bates would be harassed and arrested in 1958 as a result of this legislation.

As the date for the integration of Central High approached, the hate campaigns waged by segregationist groups, including the Ku Klux Klan, mounted. A month before Central High was scheduled to open, a rock with a message was thrown through Daisy's front window. She was warned not to go ahead with the integration of the nine black students. Governor Faubus fanned the flames of hatred by championing the cause of the segregationists under the guise of states' rights. Believing in the justice of her cause and the principles of the U.S. Constitution, Daisy Bates braved these formidable opponents to ensure that the children would open the way for equal education.

The admission of the nine children into Central High in September 1957, with the aid of federal troops, was not the end of the battle. Daisy spent that year seeking help in order to protect the youngsters from the continual acts of physical and psychological harassment that they were subjected to by other students and to keep the schools open. The school board and local authorities were unwilling to protect the students, and the governor threatened to shut down the schools, although he was circumvented by the Supreme Court. Throughout that period the hate campaigns continued against Daisy, and she was hanged in effigy.

The cruelest blow for Daisy and her husband came in 1959 when they were forced to shut down their newspaper by white segregationists. A woman representing a group of "Southern Christian women" visited Daisy and made it clear that unless she withdrew the nine children from Central High, her life would be ruined. When Daisy refused, the advertising agencies that had supported the *State Press* canceled their contracts, and the paper lost its largest clients.[6] The smaller advertisers succumbed to threats. Daisy and her husband not only lost sixteen years of dedicated work but also struggled for their economic survival and their lives.

Daisy Bates then went to New York City, where she wrote her memoirs of this period. She later joined the Democratic National Committee and worked out of National Headquarters in Washington, DC, during the Kennedy-Johnson administration.

In 1984 she decided to revitalize the *Arkansas State Press* as a tribute to her husband and as a vehicle for the African-American community in Arkansas. That same year, she was awarded an honorary doctorate from Washington University and the University of Arkansas and was recognized by the *Arkansas Gazette* as one of the hundred most influential persons in the state.

Daisy L. Bates is the recipient of over two hundred citations and awards, including the Harriet Tubman Award, the NAACP Spingarn Medal, the Diamond Cross of Malta, the Sojourner Truth Award, the Robert S. Abbott Award, and many others. However, she has written that despite her efforts in achieving integration, and regardless of the gains of the civil rights movement and the presidential candidacy of the Reverend Jesse Jackson, racial hatred still seethes below the surface of daily life. She has observed that the changes enacted in Little Rock in response to these events were mostly cosmetic and represent attempts to appease African Americans without providing them with substantive improvements in their lives. As a result, she has concluded that much remains to be done to break down the barriers of prejudice and assure equal rights for African Americans in the United States.[7]

DAISY SPEAKS*

In the great struggle of the colored peoples of the world for equality and independence—the struggle that is one of the truly crucial events of the twentieth century—the episode of the children in Little Rock is a landmark of historical significance.

"My husband, L. C. Bates, and I had moved to Little Rock in 1941 and started a newspaper, the *State Press*. In spite of its crusading spirit, the paper prospered; and L. C., as my husband was always known, looked forward to a life of, if not serenity, at least quiet, progressive, journalistic endeavor. We had, of course, hailed the 1954 Supreme Court decision on school integration as a great forward step in achieving true equality for our race. We felt that the school board of Little Rock, while moving all too slowly, was determined to obey the law, at least in token form, and make a start on integration according to plans it had formulated and announced well in advance.

The plans called for the entrance into Central High School of nine Negro pupils when school opened on September 4, 1957. The city had apparently accepted the board's plans, and there seemed little reason to expect serious opposition, much less what followed. The summer passed quickly for those of us active in the National Association for the Advancement of Colored People in preparing the children selected for this initial move toward integration to hold their own academically. And, almost before I knew it, we were deep into August and the opening of school but a few weeks away.

On the evening of August 22, I was sitting in my living room listening to the eleven o'clock news broadcast on television. I heard the announcer say: 'Governor Marvin Griffin of Georgia and Roy V. Harris, two of the South's most ardent segregationists, tonight addressed a statewide meeting.' The report continued that approximately three hundred fifty persons attended the dinner and heard Governor Griffin attack the Supreme Court decision and praise the courage of the Arkansas groups who were fighting to preserve the rights of states. He referred to them as 'patriots.' He urged the support of a national propaganda campaign to support their stand. The announcer went on to state that the Capital Citizens Council, a

*From *The Long Shadow of Little Rock* (Fayetteville: University of Arkansas Press, 1987), 47–56 and 61–67, 99–101, 110–11 passim. © 1986 Daisy L. Bates. Reprinted by permission of Daisy L. Bates.

local segregationist group, was host, and that while the governor of Arkansas, Orval Eugene Faubus, had not attended the meeting, he would entertain Governor Griffin at breakfast the following morning.

After the broadcast I took Skippy, our dog, for his nightly walk. Little did I realize that this would be the last quiet walk that Skippy and I would enjoy for many years. After we reentered the house, I sat down on the divan in the living room, directly in front of our large picture window, and started glancing through the newspaper. Suddenly a large object came crashing through the glass. Instinctively, I threw myself on the floor. I was covered with shattered glass. L. C. rushed into the room. He bent over me as I lay on the floor. 'Are you hurt? Are you hurt?' he cried.

'I don't think so,' I said uncertainly. I reached for the rock lying in the middle of the floor. A note was tied to it. I broke the string and unfolded a soiled piece of paper. Scrawled in bold print were the words: STONE THIS TIME. DYNAMITE NEXT. I handed the note to L. C. 'A message from the Arkansas *patriots*,' I remarked. As he left the room to telephone the police, I heard L. C. say, 'Thank God their aim was poor.'

Suddenly, I realized that the calm I had so taken for granted was only the calm before the storm, that this was war, and that as state president of the National Association for the Advancement of Colored People, I was in the front-line trenches. Was I ready for war? Was I ready to risk everything that L. C. and I had built? Who was I really, and what did I stand for? Long after I had gone to bed my mind ranged over these questions and over the whole course of my life. Toward dawn I knew that I had found the answer. I was ready. I drifted off into the sleep of a mind no longer torn by doubt or indecision.

~

It was Labor Day, September 2, 1957. The nine pupils who had been selected by the school authorities to enter Central High School—Carlotta Walls, Jefferson Thomas, Elizabeth Eckford, Thelma Mothershed, Melba Pattillo, Ernest Green, Terrance Roberts, Gloria Ray, and Minnijean Brown—were enjoying the last day of their summer vacation. About midafternoon young Jefferson Thomas was on his way home from the pool and stopped at my house for a brief visit. While Jeff was raiding the refrigerator, a news flash came over the radio that the governor would address the citizens of Arkansas that night.

'I wonder what he's going to talk about,' said Jeff. The youngster then turned to me and asked, 'Is there anything they can do—now that they lost in court? Is there any way they can stop us from entering Central tomorrow morning?' 'I don't think so,' I said.

About seven o'clock that night a local newspaper reporter rang my doorbell. 'Mrs. Bates, do you know that National Guardsmen are surrounding Central High?' L. C. and I stared at him incredulously for a moment. A friend who was visiting us volunteered to guard the house while we drove out to Central. L. C. gave him the shotgun. We jumped into our car and drove to Central High. Under the streetlights stretched a long line of brown Army trucks with canvas tops. Men in full battle dress—helmets, boots, and bayonets—were piling out of the trucks and lining up in front of the school.

As we watched, L. C. switched on the car radio. A newscaster was saying, 'National Guardsmen are surrounding Central High School. No one is certain what this means. Governor Faubus will speak later this evening.' I don't recall all the details of what Governor Faubus said that night. But his words electrified Little Rock. By morning they shocked the United States. By noon the next day his message horrified the world.

Faubus's alleged reason for calling out the troops was that he had received information that caravans of automobiles filled with white supremacists were heading toward Little Rock from all over the state. He therefore declared Central High School off limits to Negroes. For some inexplicable reason he added that Horace Mann, a Negro high school, would be off limits to whites.

Then, from the chair of the highest office of the state of Arkansas, Governor Orval Eugene Faubus delivered the infamous words, 'Blood will run in the streets' if Negro pupils should attempt to enter Central High School. In a half dozen ill-chosen words, Faubus made his contribution to the mass hysteria that was to grip the city of Little Rock for several months.

~

The citizens of Little Rock gathered on September 3 to gaze upon the incredible spectacle of an empty school building surrounded by National Guard troops. At about 8:15 in the morning, Central students started passing through the line of National Guardsmen—all but the nine Negro students.

I had been in touch with their parents throughout the day. They were confused, and they were frightened. As the parents voiced their fears, they kept repeating Governor Faubus's words that 'blood will run in the streets' of Little Rock should their teenage children try to attend Central, the school to which they had been assigned by the school board.

The NAACP attorneys, Wiley Branton and Thurgood Marshall, appealed to Federal Judge Ronald N. Davies for instruction. Their question was, in effect: What do we do now? The judge stated that he was accepting the governor's statement at face value, that 'his purpose in calling out the Guard was to protect "life and property" against possible mob violence.' Therefore, Judge Davies directed the school board again to put its plan for integration into operation immediately.

On the afternoon of the same day, September 3, when the school was scheduled to open, Superintendent [Virgil] Blossom called a meeting of leading Negro citizens and the parents of the nine children. I was not notified of the meeting, but the parents called me and asked me to be present. At the meeting Superintendent Blossom instructed the parents not to accompany their children the next morning when they were scheduled to enter Central. 'If violence breaks out,' the superintendent told them, 'it will be easier to protect the children if the adults aren't there.'

During the conference, Superintendent Blossom had given us little assurance that the children would be adequately protected. As we left the building, I was aware of how deeply worried the parents were. That night the Reverend J. C. Cranshaw, president of the Little Rock branch of the NAACP, was at my home. His presence immediately gave me an idea: 'Maybe,' I said, 'maybe we could round up a few ministers to go with the children tomorrow. Maybe then the mob wouldn't attack them.'

I called a white minister, the Reverend Dunbar Ogden, Jr., president of the Interracial Ministerial Alliance. I did not know Mr. Ogden. I explained the situation, then asked if he thought he could get some ministers to go with the children to school the next morning. 'Well, Mrs. Bates, I don't know,' he said. 'I'll call some of the ministers and see what they think about it.'

Next, I called the city police. I explained to the officer in charge that we were concerned about the safety of the children and that we were trying to get ministers to accompany them to school the next morning. I said that the children would assemble at 8:30 at Twelfth

Street and Park Avenue. I asked whether a police car could be stationed there to protect the children until the ministers arrived.

The police officer promised to have a squad car there at eight o'clock. 'But you realize,' he warned, 'that our men cannot go any closer than that to the school. The school is off limits to the city police while it's "occupied" by the Arkansas National Guard.'

By now it was 2:30 in the morning. Still, the parents had to be called about the change in plan. At three o'clock I completed my last call, explaining to the parents where the children were to assemble and the plan about the ministers. Suddenly, I remembered Elizabeth Eckford. Her family had no telephone. Should I go to Union Station and search for her father? Someone had once told me that he had a night job there. Tired in mind and body, I decided to handle the matter early in the morning. I stumbled into bed.

A few hours later, at about 8:15 in the morning L. C. and I started driving to Twelfth Street and Park Avenue. The bulletin over the car radio interrupted. The voice announced: 'A Negro girl is being mobbed at Central High.' 'Oh, my God!' I cried. 'It must be Elizabeth! I forgot to notify her where to meet us!'

L. C. jumped out of the car and rushed to find her. I drove on to Twelfth Street. There were the ministers—two white and two colored. The children were already there. And, yes, the police had come as promised. All of the children were there, all except Elizabeth. Soon, L. C. rushed up with the news that Elizabeth finally was free of the mob. He had seen her on a bus as it pulled away.

The children set out, two ministers in front of them, two behind. They proceeded in that formation until they approached the beginning of the long line of Guardsmen. At this point they had their first brush with the mob. They were jostled and shoved. As they made their way toward the school grounds, the ministers and their charges attempted to pass the Guardsmen surrounding Central High. A National Guard captain stopped them. He told Mr. Ogden that he would not allow them to pass through the Guard line. When Mr. Ogden asked why, the captain said that it was by order of Governor Faubus.

The ministers returned to the car with the students, and Mr. Ogden reported what the captain of the Guardsmen had said. I told him that in view of the school board's statement the previous evening that Central High School would be open to Negro students in the morning, it was my feeling that the students should go immediately to the office of the superintendent for further instructions.

When we arrived at the office, the superintendent was out. When he failed to return within an hour, I suggested that we appeal to the U.S. attorney, Osro Cobb, since Federal Judge Davies had ordered the Federal Bureau of Investigation [FBI], under the direction of the U.S. attorney, to conduct a thorough investigation into who was responsible for the interference with the court's integration order.

Mr. Cobb looked surprised when we entered his office. I told him that we were there because the students had been denied admittance to Central High School by the National Guardsmen, and we wanted to know what action, if any, his office planned to take. After questioning the pupils, he directed them to the office of the FBI, where they gave a detailed report of what had happened to them that morning.

I might add here that during the school year the FBI interviewed hundreds of persons. Many of those who had participated in the mob could easily have been identified from photographs taken in front of the school. Yet, no action was taken against anyone by the office of the U.S. attorney, Osro Cobb, or the Department of Justice.

Thurgood Marshall and Wiley Branton appeared in U.S. district federal court to ask for an injunction against interference with the integration of Central High School by the governor and the adjutant general of Arkansas and the unit commander of the National Guard. The hearing was set for Friday, September 20.

That evening Governor Faubus went on television and announced that he had withdrawn the National Guardsmen in compliance with the federal court order. Having created the mob, he tried to shift the responsibility onto the Negro community. He said he hoped the Negro pupils, of their own volition, would refrain from exercising their rights under the court order by staying away from Central High until such time as school integration could be accomplished without violence. Shortly after his broadcast, the governor departed for the Southern Governors' Conference at Sea Island, Georgia.

~

As president of the Arkansas State Conference of NAACP branches and as the publicized leader of the integration movement in Arkansas, I was singled out for 'special treatment.' Two flaming crosses were burned on our property. The first, a six-foot gasoline-soaked structure, was stuck into our front lawn just after dusk. At the base of the cross was scrawled: 'GO BACK TO AFRICA! KKK.' The second cross was placed against the front of our house, lit, and the flames began to catch. Fortunately, the fire was discovered by a neighbor, and we extinguished it before any serious damage had been done. A rock was thrown through our living room window, and it barely missed me. A few nights later, a volley of shots was fired at our house from a passing car. One bullet pierced the window, entered the living room, and lodged in the wall. Other bullets ricocheted off the brick front of the house. We experienced the horrifying feeling that in our own hometown there lived people who wanted us dead.

The violence intensified after Governor Faubus ordered out the National Guardsmen. Often we were forced to call the police two and three times a day. We appealed to the chief of police for protection, but he said that there was not enough manpower to station a policeman in our neighborhood. Our friends, concerned for our safety, organized a volunteer guard committee. We also installed floodlights along the wide eaves on the front of the house. The floodlights went on automatically when darkness came. Each evening our friends joined L. C. in the darkened carport and watched as cars cruised by filled with teenagers shouting insults and exploding firecrackers in the street. Other cars filled with rough-looking, silent men filed by.

It took many weeks for me to become accustomed to seeing revolvers lying on tables in my own home. And shotguns loaded with buckshot, standing ready near the doors. As Ted Poston, covering the Little Rock story for the *New York Post*, remarked, the house, by necessity, had become a fortress.

~

On Monday morning, September 23, all nine children, accompanied by their parents, arrived at my home before eight o'clock. All but two parents had to leave for work immediately. The two who remained were Oscar Eckford, a night worker, and Mrs. Imogene Brown, an unemployed practical nurse.

Reporters came and went. They wanted to know whether the children were going to school. A few of the newspapermen called me aside, lowered their voices, and asked, 'Mrs. Bates, are you really sending the children to Central? The mob there is really vicious now.'

There were several radio outlets in our home, and the children stationed themselves all over the house to listen. Radio commentators were broadcasting sidewalk interviews with men and women in the mob gathered in front of Central. A man was saying, 'Just let those niggers show up! Just let 'em try!' Someone else said, 'We won't stand for our schools being integrated. If we let 'em in, next thing they'll be marrying our daughters.'

None of us said anything, but all of us were watching the hands of the clock move closer to 8:30. The radios blared, but the children were strangely silent. Elizabeth sat alone, almost motionless. Carlotta and Ernest walked restlessly from room to room. The faces of all were solemn but determined.

Once, when I entered the living room, I saw Mrs. Brown seated on the sofa, her hands clasped tightly on her lap, her eyes closed, her lips moving in prayer. Across the room Mr. Eckford sat with bowed head. For the first time I found that I was praying, too. At last the call came from the police. They told us it would be safer to take a roundabout route to the school. They would meet us near Central and escort the children through the side entrance.

The white newsmen left my home for Central High. The Negro reporters remained, seating themselves around the table drinking coffee. They were L. Alex Wilson, general manager and editor of the *Tri-State Defender* of Memphis, Tennessee; James Hicks, managing editor of the *New York Amsterdam News*; Moses J. Newsome of the *Afro-American* of Baltimore, Maryland; and Earl Davy, *State Press* photographer. I told them they must take a different route from the one the children would take, but that if they were at the Sixteenth Street and Park Avenue entrance to Central, they would be able to see the nine enter the school.

We had two cars. I went in the first car with some of the children, and C. C. Mercer and Frank Smith, field secretary of the NAACP, followed with the rest of the nine. To this day, I cannot remember which of the nine were in our car. Nor can they. As we approached the side entrance to the school, the main body of the mob was moving away from us. I got out of the car and told the children to go quickly. From the sidewalk I watched the police escort them through the door of the school. Someone in the mob saw them enter and yelled, 'They're in! The niggers are in!'

The people on the fringes of the mob started moving towards us. A policeman rushed up to me. 'Get back in the car, Mrs. Bates. Drive back the way you came, and fast!' I tumbled into the car. Mr. Mercer was waiting at the wheel. The car radio was on and a hoarse-voiced announcer was saying: 'The Negro children are being mobbed in front of the school.' I knew the children were in the school and, for the moment at least, safe. But who was being mobbed? We sped back to the house to reassure Mrs. Brown and Mr. Eckford. Then I called the other parents at work to quiet their fears.

A series of false radio reports followed. Newscasters, broadcasting from the school grounds, reported that the children were being beaten and were running down the halls of the school, bloodstained; that the police were trying to get them out, but the nine children, hysterical with fright, had locked themselves in an empty classroom.

A young white lawyer, who was very close to Assistant Chief of Police Gene Smith, devised a plan by which he would keep me informed of the goings-on inside the school. When I called him, he assured me that the reports were false. After each report I would check with him, then call the parents. Once Mr. Eckford screamed at me in exasperation, 'Well, if it's not true, why would they say such things on the air?'

Later that day we learned that a white teenage girl had been slipping in and out of the school, issuing false reports to the radio broadcasters. They had put her statements on the air without checking them. Gene Smith had finally caught up with her and ordered her arrested. One could say it was the answer to Mrs. Brown's prayer that the Negro reporters arrived at Central about five minutes ahead of us. Jimmy Hicks of the *Amsterdam News* later told me just what did happen that morning.

'We parked our car near the school and made a dash for the Sixteenth Street entrance. When the mob saw us, they yelled, "Here they come!" and came rushing at us. The women screamed, "Get the niggers! Get 'em!" About a thousand folk blocked the streets. One big, burly guy swung at my head. I ducked. The blow landed on my shoulder, spinning me around. I ran between two parked cars which concealed me from the mob. Two men jumped on top of Earl Davy, dragging him into a bank of high grass. Others were kicking and beating him while the two held him. They took his press camera and threw it to the sidewalk and smashed it flat with their feet. Several men jumped on Alex Wilson, knocking him to the ground and kicking him in the stomach. As he was getting up, one of the mobsters hollered, "Run, nigger!" Alex wouldn't run. The brute, with a brick in his hand, jumped on Alex's back and raised the brick to crush Alex's skull.

' "The niggers are in the school! The niggers are in the school!" The man jumped off Alex's back, calling to the others, "Come on! The niggers are in!" The mobsters beating Davy, Newsome, and Wilson all charged toward the school like a pack of wild animals.

'We probably saved you and the children, but I know you saved us. Some of the mob had spotted me between the cars and were advancing on me with sticks and clubs. And when they charged toward the school, we got the hell out of there. But you know, during all that beating, Alex never let go of his hat.'

The frenzied mob rushed the police barricades. One man was heard to say, 'So they sneaked them in behind our back. That's all we need. Let's go get our shotguns!' Hysterical women helped to break the barricades and then urged the men to go in and 'get the niggers out!' Some of the women screamed for their children to 'Come out! Don't stay in there with those niggers!' About fifty students rushed out, crying, 'They're in! They're in!'

Around 11:30, Gene Smith realized his police force was inadequate to hold the mob. He ordered the nine removed from the school. They were taken out through a delivery entrance in the rear of the school, placed in police cars, and driven to their homes. When it was announced that the children had been removed, the reporters rushed to my home and asked me what was our next step. Would the nine return to Horace Mann, the all-Negro school? I said, 'No, they were going to remain out of the school until the president of the United States guaranteed them protection within Central High School.' This was interpreted by the reporters as my having requested troops.

The mob, thwarted in its attempt to put its hands on the Negro children, switched momentarily to another field of battle. They went after the 'Yankee' reporters. The entire *Life* magazine staff on the scene was beaten. Most of the citizens of Little Rock were stunned as they witnessed a savage rebirth of passion and racial hatred that had laid dormant since Reconstruction days. As dusk was falling, tension and fear grew. The mob spread throughout the city, venting its fury on any Negro in sight.

Two Negro women driving through the city were pulled from their car and beaten. Two Negro men in a truck were surrounded by the mob near the school and beaten, and their truck windows were smashed with rocks. Mayor Woodrow Mann wired President [Dwight D.] Eisenhower for protection. The Justice Department called Harry Ashmore, editor of the *Arkansas Gazette*, and asked him to describe the situation. He said, 'I'll give it to you in one sentence. The police have been routed, the mob is in the streets and we're close to a reign of terror.'

That evening I sat in the semidarkened living room with L. C. and the reporters, watching the empty, quiet street through our broken living room window. The police car that had been assigned to guard our house was barely visible across the street. A cab stopped in front of the house. All of us stood up. I heard a soft click. L. C. had released the safety on his .45 automatic. Dr. G. P. Freeman, our next-door neighbor and dentist, was aimlessly running his hand along the barrel of a shotgun he held in his left hand. When Alex Wilson of the Memphis *Tri-State Defender* stepped from the cab, I breathed a sigh of relief. As he entered the house, Alex said, 'I had planned to return earlier, but the story of the mob was a little difficult to write.' He took L. C.'s gun, saying, 'I'll watch for a while.' I thought, 'What a guy! He took the brunt of the mob today, yet here he is, holding a gun to help protect *us*.'

The radio commentator reported that teenage mobs had taken to cars and were driving wildly through the streets throwing bottles and bricks into Negroes' homes and places of business. One of the white reporters jumped out of his seat. 'Ye Gods!' he demanded. 'Aren't they *ever* going to stop? Such hate! I heard a woman say today, "I hope they drag out nine dead niggers from that school." '

I left the room to call the parents of the pupils to see whether they had adequate protection. They reported that the city police were on the job. About 10:30 P.M., I returned to the living room. Brice Miller, a reporter for United Press International, was talking to L. C. I saw his photographer in the shadows across the street.

'What's up, Brice?' I asked.

'Oh, nothing. Just checking.'

'Oh, come now,' I said. 'We've all heard the rumor that the mob would ride tonight, and this will probably be their first stop. Isn't that the reason your photographer is across the street?'

'Well, yes,' he admitted.

'Where did you hear that rumor?'

'One of the segregationist students told me. She was so pleased to have a reporter hanging on her words. I, of course, notified the police and the FBI.'

L. C. broke into the conversation. 'Something's up—things are too quiet.' He asked Brice Miller about the radio reports.

'Oh, they're just a bunch of wild kids getting in on the act. They're not the real dangerous ones,' he guessed.

'Say, Freeman,' said L. C., 'maybe we should stand guard outside for a while.'

L. C. got his shotgun from the closet and, with Dr. Freeman, went outside. I went into the kitchen to make coffee. Just then L. C. rushed back into the house. 'Something's up! A car just passed driving slow with its lights off and a bunch of tough-looking characters in it. And the police car outside is following it.'

Miller plunged past L. C., calling his photographer. 'Come on! This might be it.' Not only his photographer but all the reporters except Alex Wilson followed him.

'Do you have plenty of ammunition for these guns?' Alex asked.

'Yes,' L. C. said.

'Well, we'll be ready for them if they show up.'

Dr. Freeman stood guard at the bedroom window, Alex Wilson at the living room window, and L. C. at the kitchen window. L. C. told me to turn out the lights and go downstairs. I turned out the lights and sat on the top step of the stairway. We heard the wail of sirens approaching us. The minutes seemed like hours as I sat in the darkened stairway waiting for something to happen.

'The police are back,' said L. C. He opened the door and turned on the lights. 'Turn that light off!' commanded the policeman as he entered. 'And stay away from the window.' The policeman, a big, red-haired man, was tense with excitement. 'We just stopped a motorcade of about one hundred cars, two blocks from here. When we followed that car that passed, we ran into the mob head on. We radioed for help and a whole group of city and Federal agents showed up. We found dynamite, guns, pistols, clubs, everything, in the cars. Some of the mob got away on foot, leaving their cars. We don't know what will happen tonight, so no one is to leave the house.'

No one slept that night.

At about 2:30 A.M. the phone rang. I answered. A man's voice said, 'We didn't get you last night, but we will. And you better not try to put those coons in our school.' The next day, the children remained at home. A tense and weary city waited to hear from the White House.

In midafternoon the city was electrified by the news that President Eisenhower had federalized all ten thousand men of the Arkansas National Guard unit. He had also authorized Charles E. Wilson, secretary of defense, to send in such regular U.S. troops as he deemed necessary 'to enforce any order of the U.S. District Court for the Eastern District of Arkansas for the removal of obstruction of justice in the state of Arkansas with respect to matters relating to enrollment and attendance at public schools in the Little Rock District.' Under the authorization of this order, the secretary of defense ordered one thousand paratroopers to Little Rock from Fort Campbell, Kentucky. The soldiers were part of the 101st Airborne 'Screaming Eagle' Division of the 327th Infantry regiment.

Around 6 P.M., the long line of trucks, jeeps, and staff cars entered the heart of the city to the wailing sound of sirens and the dramatic flashing of lights from the police cars escorting the caravan to Central High School. The 'Battle of Little Rock' was on. Some of the citizens watching the arrival of the troops cried with relief. Others cursed the federal government for 'invading our city.' One got the impression that the 'Solid South' was no longer solid.

A young white reporter rushed to my house and grabbed me by the hands, swinging me around. 'Daisy, they're here! The soldiers are here! Aren't you excited? Aren't you happy?' 'Excited, yes, but not happy,' I said after getting myself unwhirled. 'Any time it takes 11,500 soldiers to assure nine Negro children their constitutional rights in a democratic society, I can't be happy.'

At 9:22 A.M. [the following morning] the nine Negro pupils marched solemnly through the doors of Central High School, surrounded by twenty-two soldiers [Airborne troops]. An Army helicopter circled overhead. Around the massive brick schoolhouse, 350 paratroopers stood grimly at attention. Scores of reporters, photographers, and TV cameramen made a mad dash for telephones, typewriters, and TV studios, and within minutes a world that had been holding its breath learned that the nine pupils, protected by the might of the U.S. military, had finally entered the 'never-never land.' ”

Notes

1. Daisy L. Bates, *The Long Shadow of Little Rock* (Fayetteville: University of Arkansas Press, 1987), 29.
2. Juan Williams, *Eyes on the Prize: America's Civil Rights Years, 1954–1965* (New York: Viking, 1987), 8–11.
3. Ibid., 94.
4. Ibid., 95–99.
5. Ibid., 96.
6. Bates, *The Long Shadow of Little Rock*, 174–76.
7. Letter to author from Daisy Bates, May 9, 1987.

6 / Hanan Mikhail Ashrawi

SINCE HER FIRST TELEVISION APPEARANCE in April 1988, when she spoke on ABC's "Nightline Town Meeting," Hanan Mikhail Ashrawi has been demanding justice for the Palestinian people and insisting upon their right to be heard. In public, she is passionate and articulate. In private, she is a poet who loves literature and music, and a loving wife and mother whose eyes glow when discussing her family. She is firm in her humanistic beliefs and in her dreams of a just future for her people, one that ensures pluralism, dignity, and freedom.

When I met Hanan Ashrawi in September 1993, she was spokesperson of the Palestinian delegation to the peace talks with Israel in Washington, DC, and in the throes of a delicate and complex diplomatic situation. Without consulting the group in Washington, Yasir Arafat had just concluded an agreement with the Israeli government over the autonomy of Jericho and the Gaza Strip, two tiny areas within the occupied West Bank. Hanan, along with other PLO (Palestine Liberation Organization) officials, had always envisioned a two-state solution to the problem of the area, a far cry from that agreement. In fact, it was Hanan Ashrawi who suggested in 1992 to Yair Hirschfeld of the Economic Cooperation Foundation (a nonprofit, nonpartisan organization devoted to the prospects of peace) that he contact Abu Allaa, the PLO finance minister, to discuss possible spheres of economic cooperation. An initial encounter in London was followed by fifteen other secret meetings with the PLO in Oslo, Norway. However, the September 1993 agreement concluded between Arafat and the Israeli government was filled with loopholes and left many crucial issues unresolved, such as the boundaries of the territories in question. As chief spokesperson of the fourteen-member delegation negotiating with Israel, Hanan was asked to appear on CNN and comment on these events. With her usual aplomb, she claimed that the Palestinians had not given up their goal of statehood.

Hanan Ashrawi was born in Nablus in 1946, the youngest of five daughters, each of whom was born in different parts of Palestine because the family was continually forced to move. The Ashrawi children grew up in areas that are now part of Israel and, as a result, are heirs to the anger and mistrust dividing Arabs and Jews. Despite the upheavals of her family life, Hanan received her B.A. at the University of Beirut and a doctorate in medieval studies from the University of Virginia. She married Emile Ashrawi in 1975 and is the mother of two teenage daughters.

Although she did not experience the misery of desert prison camps, Hanan nonetheless suffered from the Israeli occupation of her homeland. Her brief stints behind bars, the torture and death of a beloved uncle who had served as her political mentor, and frequent interrogation by Israeli authorities are what shaped her beliefs. Her father, Dr. Daoud Mikhail, also served as her political mentor, and he exerted an equally profound influence on her development. He was socially progressive, believing that women should have an equal role in all spheres of life. He devoted his life not only to his patients but also to the Palestinian people's struggle for freedom, serving time in prison for his efforts.

In 1964, the year Hanan enrolled in the American University of Beirut, Daoud Mikhail helped form a new group in Cairo—the PLO—to speak for the Palestinians and also to launch a guerrilla struggle against Israel. While her father was in the throes of his new activities, Hanan received her formative political education through her exposure to the squalor and misery in the Palestinian refugee camps in Lebanon. As a result, she immediately joined the General Union of Palestinian Students (GUPS). In the late 1960s the Palestinians in the refugee camps revolted against their strict control by the Lebanese secret police, and a new leadership of PLO members took responsibility for running them. Student members of the GUPS were expected to volunteer among the refugees, and Hanan worked at Bourj al-Barajneh and Tel Zatar, the largest camps, where she taught classes in political awareness. She was also assigned to accompany reporters through the camps and began to act as a liaison with journalists, helping them to meet eminent Palestinians. In that capacity, she met some of the most important members of the Western media, such as Peter Jennings.[1]

When Hanan received her degree in literature, she decided to remain in Beirut to continue her work among the Palestinians. In the fall of 1969, she attended the first GUPS convention in Amman, Jordan, as spokesperson of the Lebanese chapter, the only woman among three hundred men. There, she met Yasir Arafat, beginning a long political association.

Hanan left Beirut the following year to begin postgraduate studies in the United States, where she entered a doctoral program at the University of Virginia. She maintained her political activism by working with the Black Student Alliance and by establishing a group in support of Palestinian rights. However, once her studies were completed, she was unable to return to her home in Ramallah because Israel prohibited from returning to the West Bank any Palestinians who were outside of the country in 1967, when the West Bank was lost to Israel. Hanan has referred to this exile as the "invisible deportation, the silent transfer."[2]

The Israeli government passed a law in 1973 permitting family reunification, and Hanan returned to Ramallah for the first time in six years. There, she became head of the English Department at Bir Zeit University and, eventually, dean of the Faculty of Arts. However, she was not allowed to live a normal life and, while pursuing her professional activities, suffered continual harassment by the Israeli authorities. She was often followed to her house, where the powerful spotlights from the Israeli prison across the street shone through her bedroom window. She also was detained on numerous occasions and interrogated in that prison. She learned to carry books, cigarettes, and chocolates in her purse in case she was arrested. She has described this way of life as "any day, in everything, you cannot make plans, you cannot take anything for granted, you wake up not knowing if you are under curfew or not, if you are going to be detained or arrested or not, or who is going to be killed today."[3]

Under Israeli military law governing the Occupied Territories, any Palestinian can be arrested and placed under administrative detention for up to a year without being charged or tried. The allegations typically brought against Hanan included "disturbing the peace, breaking the terms of her family reunion, inciting others to demonstrate, and threatening the security of the state."[4] Nor was she allowed the luxury of a private life; the morning after her wedding to Emile Ashrawi, in the midst of a Christmas Day celebration, she received a summons from the Israeli authorities for an interrogation.

Despite the problems of living under occupation, Hanan began thinking about peace and talking to the Israelis as early as 1970, after the Egyptian attack against Israel on the eve of Yom Kippur. She realized that any future for Palestine meant accepting the existence of the Israeli state and that any peace would have to involve a two-state solution. Following the example of her father, who had Israeli friends, Hanan tried to engage the Israeli peace movement, which is mostly composed of women. One of her closest friends is an Israeli lawyer who has defended her and her students on numerous occasions and whose children have grown up with her own. Hanan's view of a free Palestine includes a democracy guaranteeing the rights of all groups.

The Intifada uprising against the Israeli occupation, which exploded in 1987 and which Hanan supported, was interpreted by the media around the world as fomenting unchecked violence and represented by images of children throwing stones at Israeli soldiers. However, it represented a grass-roots effort to create local leadership and community organizations and to replace institutions, such as schools, that had been closed by the Israelis. The fact that these institution-building efforts were illegal did not stop people such as Hanan from participating in establishing schools and women's consciousness-raising groups.

Another of Hanan's political mentors, Faisal Husseini, regarded by many as the potential head of an eventual independent Palestinian state, asked Hanan to join a group of Palestinians preparing position papers in 1988 for conferences abroad and talks with Western envoys. In 1991 these people became the core group representing the West Bank and Gaza during eight months of negotiations with U.S. Secretary of State James Baker, and the main channel for

Baker's unofficial dialogue with the PLO. Although she was not a member of the Arab delegation to the Arab-Israeli Peace Conference in Madrid in the fall of 1991, Hanan's presence on the advisory committee proved to be extremely important. She took a prominent place among the press corps and played a role in drafting the speeches that transformed the image of the Palestinians.[5]

In the speech she helped write for Haidar Abdul Shafi, head of the delegation, she equated Palestinian suffering with that of the Israelis and stressed both their mutual dependence and the fact that their experiences mirrored each other. Thus, she transformed the Palestinian image from that of terrorists to victims. American pressure on Prime Minister Yitzhak Shamir to allow his rivals to give a speech and to begin talks with them represented an important turning point for the Palestinians.

The sixth round of Arab-Israeli talks began in Washington, DC, in August 1992 and resulted in the September 1993 agreement granting autonomy to enclaves within the West Bank. The accord concluded between Arafat and the Israeli government did not make a reference to Jerusalem, one of the Palestinians' major claims. However, it was the first crack in the frozen sea that had kept the two sides apart through four wars since the creation of the state of Israel in 1948, and the successive displacement of a people that had caused a diaspora of four million Palestinians. Unfortunately, it also opened gulfs between the various groups representing Palestinians such as the PLO, Hamas (the Islamic Resistance Movement), and the Islamic Holy War (one of the more radical groups that opposed the peace treaty). These fissures were mirrored in the Israeli population, with a radical group of settlers in the West Bank turning to violence.

In December 1993, Hanan resigned as spokesperson for the PLO and declined Yasir Arafat's offer to serve as foreign minister or in any official capacity in his proposed government. Instead, she created and headed the Palestinian Independent Commission for Citizens' Rights to monitor and protect human rights in the Occupied Territories once the PLO would take charge, viewing this effort as an important part of institution building. Ever the diplomat, she denied that this decision was a protest against Arafat and other PLO leaders, although there was great concern expressed over his autocratic ways, both within the Occupied Territories and among prominent Palestinians.

When Gaza and Jericho attained self-rule in May 1994, Arafat formed a governing council of fourteen members and once again invited Hanan to join, this time as minister of information. As head of the Palestinian Independent Commission for Citizens' Rights, she refused, stressing that her human rights efforts were her paramount moral commitment. Since then, she has become a full-time activist, spending twelve to fourteen hours a day working for her citizens' rights group and organizing Jerusalem Link, a feminist alliance she cofounded with Naomi Chazan, a member of the Knesset, the Israeli parliament. She continually speaks out on issues such as freedom of the press and on the need for broader participation in the new government. Hanan Ashrawi's goal always has been to assure justice for the Palestinian people, a vision that includes the reconstruction of society to reflect genuine democracy and due process at all governmental levels.

On January 20, 1996, the Palestinian people voted in the first general elections held in the Occupied Territories, selecting the president of an executive branch, Yasir Arafat, as well as an eighty-eight-member legislature, the Palestinian Council. Both the Legislative Council and the Interim Self-Government will serve until Israel and the PLO reach an agreement on the final status of the West Bank, East Jerusalem, and the Gaza Strip in a peace accord currently targeted for May 1999. Hanan Ashrawi was elected to the Council and was one of the candidates who had run as independents against the official slate dominated by Yasir Arafat. Thus, she begins a new stage in her struggle to achieve nationhood and democracy for her people.

HANAN SPEAKS

Women's role is to humanize things all the time.

"Like almost all Palestinians, I was involved in politics from the moment of my birth. It was impossible to think of being born in a situation of either occupation or exile, where your whole Palestinian identity is being denied, and then to say, 'I'm not involved.' Although I was always aware of what was happening because of my father's activism, my deliberate participation began when the 1967 war erupted, and the Israelis occupied our land. I was an undergraduate at the University of Beirut when the occupation occurred, preventing Palestinians abroad from returning. It wasn't an abstract place, it was my home. The fact that I or my parents or members of my family couldn't go home made me feel that it was my responsibility to take action. So I started working with the General Union of Palestine Students and with the General Union of Palestine Women in the area of information. I also worked in the refugee camps. What I did was 'political consciousness raising,' education, information, and writing analyses.

From then on it's been a continuum, in different ways, different incarnations. While I was in the United States in the early 1970s, I worked with various American organizations such as the Black Students Alliance. I even talked to the Appalachian mine workers and with women's groups, and formed the American Friends of Free Palestine. I worked with the Charlottesville Resistance and with the Virginia Weekly Collective.

When I returned home, I immediately began to work on women's issues, human rights issues, and alternative education programs. In 1974 I formed a legal aid committee at Bir Zeit University that acted with community groups and a number of volunteer faculty to defend our students. Many of these volunteers were foreigners, even Americans, who went with students to interrogation centers, waiting for them outside in the dark, in the rain, sometimes all night. We got them lawyers and attended their trials. When they were detained we tried to get them food and supplies such as underwear and toiletrics. Not only did we have to worry about their legal and human rights, but we also had to attend to their daily needs. We wanted to make prison less dehumanizing and to let them know that we were there for them. That effort gradually evolved into the human rights project, which I have headed since 1974.

I became very active with the Intifada, not just in women's groups but in community work and neighborhood committees. When the Israelis closed down our schools and universities, we set up our own neighborhood school in a single weekend. We discovered that we had eighty children, from preschool to high school graduates, and we had to establish an alternative school program in people's homes. It was illegal. You could go to jail for ten years for setting up a popular committee, but we did it anyway. All the people in our neighborhood helped. When you close down schools, you're not just robbing children of their right to education but also of their right to their childhood. Holding children hostage to political ends seemed incredibly cruel and malicious. This was the price for the Intifada. It was a very difficult price, but we managed. One thing about the Intifada is that we were always creative; whenever the Israelis built a wall, we found a way around it. That movement was a collective effort of children, men and women; as such, it began to change the stereotyping of roles and people.

In Palestinian society we have always had a long tradition of emphasizing education. Even though we are a traditional society, we have been open to international influences. We have never been a fundamentalist, introverted, or self-enclosed society but have upheld pluralism, religious tolerance, and diversity. The first women's organizations, of course, were charitable groups formed in the nineteen twenties. In my mother's, and even in earlier, generations, we had instances of women going abroad to study when this wasn't done anywhere else. Ingrained within Palestinian society is a need for women to express themselves and a desire for an open and diverse social life. The Israeli occupation presented a challenge and a form of oppression. I think it destroyed the fabric of our society, its infrastructure and institutions.

The Intifada was a corrective force, an effort to assume control over our lives. We called it a period of acceleration and intensification, creating back-up institutions and an alternative, authentic community. We felt the occupation was a distorting force, and we wanted to take matters into our own hands, to present ourselves directly. That's why I agreed to be spokesperson. I was involved in political work at the beginning of the Intifada. I was in demonstrations, in the political committee, also in coordination, human rights, and neighborhood committees. We were trying to present the essence of the Intifada as the voice of a people who refuse subjugation and oppression, who have rights, and who have said, 'Our will cannot be broken regardless,' and 'We will be heard directly without distortions and intermediaries.' I think in that sense we have succeeded, but we paid a very heavy price for it.

At the time, I was already meeting with politicians and diplomats. I was part of the group that negotiated with different people who came to the region. I had traveled to the United States several times on behalf of the PLO to work out issues and to explore ways of making peace. When Secretary of State James Baker's visit led to the Madrid talks, three of us were chosen to carry out a dialogue with the United States. There was a sort of political agreement about my involvement, but ultimately the choice of my position was a PLO choice.

When we were discussing our political work and the peace process, I said that 'we deserve honesty, we deserve to present ourselves for ourselves, we deserve a hearing.' I remember that in the maiden speech we wrote that we will not have our voice confiscated. We insisted, 'In order to do justice to a people who have suffered so much and quite often in silence and in the dark, we have to present this case in a direct and forthright manner.' We had to address people's hearts as well as people's minds, to convince them that this was not just a political statement but the fate of a nation. Palestinians have to be presented in all their humanity. That was the one thing that was always denied us. We were stereotyped and called terrorists, still a favorite word here. These stereotypes have to be shown for what they are. People gave themselves the right to call us all sorts of names and to see us as subhuman. It was as if we had to prove ourselves all the time. So we had to take the initiative and tell people who we really are.

Nelson Mandela came to visit us in 1990 after his release from prison. He is a good friend, a man we respect very highly. He never lost his essential humanity, and this is very important. When we were meeting with James Baker, I told him, 'If you lose sight of the focus of our work, which is the human dimension, all this work is useless. We're not interested in political virtuosity and in one-upmanship, we are interested in alleviating human suffering and working for the well-being of the human being, not for political careers.' In James Baker's speech, he included the human dimension, and everyone said, 'That's Hanan's.'

I don't say I am an artist, I say I am an aspiring poet. I try to write poetry. It may not be the best poetry, but at least it's honest. Poetry is more than just a literary exercise or endeavor. I have always felt that you need poetry in public speeches and in political discourse. The Madrid speech has lots of literary and poetic quotations. At the heart of that speech is a quotation from our national poet, Muhammad Tarsis, in which he says 'my homeland is not a suitcase and I am no traveler.' That, in essence, captures our situation.

When I gave a talk at the Schlesinger Library* at Radcliffe, I started with a poem. My friend Yael† was quite upset. She's someone I know politically; we have carried out a women's dialogue for a long time. She got up and exclaimed, 'We're not here to read poetry.' I replied, 'Listen, Yael, I think the main problem is that you don't have poetry in your soul and if you don't have poetry, then you cannot make peace.' Everybody can make a political argument, but to give it human substance, to give it creativity or imagination, you need to have poetry. I continued, 'Maybe that's the

*The Arthur and Elizabeth Schlesinger Library on the History of Women in America.

†Yael Dayan, daughter of the late war hero Moshe Dayan and a member of the Knesset from the Labor Party, is a supporter of Palestinian rights.

problem with all the political endeavors that have continued for so long; they lack this deep, authentic human voice and an awareness that is beyond the here and now, a vision for the future.'

What I would like to see goes beyond what is happening now. We are undergoing a very difficult phase. I am realistic enough to recognize it, to be awed by it, and, sometimes, to be scared by it. I have a tremendous sense of apprehension. I also have a tremendous sense of faith, not just in the justice of the cause, but in this striving for peace and reconciliation, and this drive for ascertaining, not only our own humanity, but the humanity of the other. So I feel that in order for us to really begin to engage in the shaping of our destiny, this step (agreement between Israel and PLO of September 1993) is a necessary first step that will put us on the proper path toward freedom, dignity, and recognition.

Beyond that is the challenge of shaping very concrete things like institutions, and of healing a society that has been traumatized. We are a wounded people who have suffered under occupation for twenty-six years. For three quarters of a century we have been deprived of either our own homeland or our freedom, so we need a period of rehabilitation and of learning how to work together as one people. Beyond that we need to come together as a nation among other nations and to reach out to others. While we have reached out to the Israelis to make peace, I still feel that it is necessary to ascertain the identity and the dignity of the Palestinians. From there we can work on a regional perspective. I have told the Israelis that if they wanted to dehumanize us, they have succeeded in dehumanizing themselves first.

I keep going through sheer determination and tenacity. I am obsessive about peace. I don't have a constructed belief system, but I have inherited a very humanistic approach from my father. You focus on the human being, and on the difference that a person can make, and you don't evade responsibility. I've seen so much suffering, but I've also observed a will, not just to endure, but to overcome and to begin again. I feel that if we are always looking backward, we will never look ahead. What we have to do is to transcend our pain and reach toward a future that can incorporate the past but not be a captive of it. By believing that you can make a difference, you can be an instrument; you can be an active part of things.

Personally, I have lots of advantages. My parents, and my father in particular, firmly believed in women's rights and in our ability as his daughters to be daring, to pursue the truth and not be intimidated or accept injustice. He was an intellectual, a humanist, and a man of the arts as well as a doctor, who said, 'I'm a farmer; I'm a peasant at heart.' He was as close to his roses, his trees, and his shrubs as he was to his patients. They said that when Dr. Mikhail came to your bedside, you healed just by his attitude and the way he talked to you. He was unusual for his time and his society. I am also fortunate that I have a husband who is like that, a warm, supportive, and intelligent man who doesn't need to prove his masculinity by suppressing women. He is very confident about his own abilities, so he doesn't regard marriage as a relationship of competition but as one of real partnership and mutual reinforcement. I also have two wonderful daughters.

Motherhood and politics are inseparable. A real mother goes beyond just the here and now of her children. She's not a captive of the daily routine but has a vision of what she wants for her children, and therefore she has to create that future and be part of it. She can't be passive. I'm extremely possessive about the future of my children: I have to be part of shaping it for them, not by molding them as human beings, but by giving them their rights, doing whatever I can to ensure them a life of peace, dignity, and freedom.

My children and I have a very close relationship, immediate and direct. I am very proud of them. They also have difficulties because they are children. Both of them are almost teenagers; one has just turned sixteen, and the other has just turned twelve. They need their mother, and though they may intellectually understand my need to do this work, emotionally they say, 'We need you with us.' It's not easy for them. I have conflict with that, too, but we do talk about it. On the one hand, I want to give them security at home to compensate for the insecurity of the occupation, the fear, the death, and the violence. However, I inadvertently contribute to their insecurity because I am often in danger. I don't want them to experience a paralyzing fear and to believe that life is dangerous, and we are taking risks. We compensate for that by talking about things, by having a secure life at home. I know they are afraid for me most of the time, so I tell them I am safe, that I can take care of myself, that I'm all right. I've been in situations where I saw death staring me in the eye, but I don't go around being afraid. There is a certain amount of healthy fear which leads you to caution. You don't take unnecessary risks. But sometimes you don't have the time to stop and worry. You just do what you have to do.

I've never given up hope. You get discouraged at times. You have your ups and downs: sometimes you're angry, sometimes you're outraged, sometimes you're sad, but if you get to the point of despair, that is self-destructive. I've had my moods; I'm a human being. Most of the time it's the need to continue and to work that keeps me going because the status quo will not stop or wait for you. If you don't do anything, things will degenerate. But I also have a very strong support system in my family, in my husband, in my daughters, my friends, people who have learned to understand my moods. I also have several outlets. I read a lot of poetry and literature. I talk to people. Before undertaking this work, I was always a very private person. Now, I have to be in the middle of events, but I try to retain my internal self intact. I love music as well as poetry. My husband is a musician, and my daughter is a good pianist. We have long talks at home, and we sit in the garden. That is important to maintain perspective. What keeps one sane is to be deeply rooted in your own human and natural context.

I used to take bad press personally. Then I realized that there is this whole public discourse; journalists look for the dramatic, and I've noticed that they create a version of the truth, and they believe it. They become very possessive about it, and it gains a life of its own. I don't see myself in most of the articles I've read about myself. It's like reading about somebody I don't know. My husband and my daughters get hurt when they read things like that. But I learned that it's one of the prices you pay for being public, for taking on this work. There are many people who are willing to destroy, there are many people who are looking for sensation, and there are many people who can be very, very cruel. I just wish I could shield my daughters and the people who love me from it. But I just say they want to sell copy, after all. They want to be sensational and dramatic and different. They look for an angle. I don't resent it personally; otherwise, I would never get anywhere. I would never talk to anyone. I would become a suspicious person. But I keep trying to explain myself and my work.

Part of the disempowerment of people is when they feel helpless, when the individual feels that he or she cannot make a difference. I firmly believe in collective, community work, but I also believe that you as an individual must work, regardless of how visible, how low-key your work or your life is. What keeps me and many people going is the belief that every person has something to contribute, no matter how modest. All of us have positive and negative sides, but you minimize the negative and look for the positive and work with that. Then, you go beyond the fact that you can make a difference as a human being and create or work within a support system which could be very fluid. You join a collective approach to reality that can transform the individual input into a real current for change."

Notes

1. John and Janet Wallach, *The New Palestinians: The Emerging Generation of Leaders* (Rocklin, CA: Prima Publishing, 1992), 17.
2. Ibid., 24.
3. Ibid., 28.
4. Ibid., 25.
5. Ibid., 32.

7 / *Awiakta*

BORN IN KNOXVILLE, TENNESSEE, IN 1936 to a Cherokee-Celtic family that has lived in the Southern Appalachian mountains since the 1790s, Awiakta has become one of the voices of a people the U.S. government continues to oppress by betraying its agreements with the Nation and encroaching upon its lands and sacred burial grounds. She grew up in Oak Ridge, at the time a closed city for atomic research, and in 1957 graduated from the University of Tennessee with a degree in French and English. The same year she married and moved to Memphis, where she taught high school English and French while her husband, Paul, completed his university studies. A mother of two daughters and a son and a grandmother of three children, Awiakta is a widely published author of poetry, essays, and books whose work has also appeared in many anthologies. Among her many honors and awards are the Distinguished Tennessee Writer Award, the National Organization of Women's "Person of Quality Award," the National Conference of Christians and Jews Leadership Award, and the Women of Achievement's "Woman of Vision Award" from the municipality of Memphis. Awiakta is a cofounder of the Far Away Cherokee Association of Memphis and was part of a fifteen-year struggle to protest the construction of the Tellico Dam by the Tennessee Valley Authority. The dam flooded the Cherokee burial mounds in 1979 and was a futile project that ultimately decimated the environment as well as robbed a people of part of their cultural and spiritual heritage.

Although the Cherokees and the early settlers had periods of living in peaceful coexistence, ultimately the Cherokee Nation was practically decimated by forced removal from Cherokee lands and the breakup of the Nation. In her book *Selu: Seeking the Corn Mother's Wisdom*, Awiakta writes that when the Europeans arrived in 1540, the Cherokee Nation covered parts of what are now eight southern states, following the Appalachian Mountains from southeast Virginia to north Georgia and covering the territory from eastern North Carolina to middle Tennessee. Through a series of broken treaties, the Nation experienced a steady attrition. In 1838 the federal government forced seventeen thousand Cherokee on a fifteen-hundred-mile march to Oklahoma, during which about a fourth of the people died. The Cherokee called it "the place where they cried," or the Trail of Tears. In North Carolina a small group eluded the federal troops and fled to the mountains, where they managed to survive. Later, they became the nucleus of what is now the Eastern Band of Cherokees.[1] All southeastern Indians were forced to go to the West, and Awiakta has written about the experience of removal in *Rising Fawn and the Fire Mystery*, the story of a Choctaw child in Mississippi.

Today, there exist two major groups of Cherokee, the Eastern and the Western. Awiakta describes them as separated by twelve hundred miles, federal bureaucracy, and lack of formal contact for nearly a century and a half.[2] The Eastern Band is located in North Carolina, while the Cherokee Nation of Oklahoma occupies tribal lands in that state. Although it includes a population of 53,097, as compared to the 8,882 of the Eastern Band, most of its members participate in the dominant culture and also maintain their own.[3] The councils and peoples of the two groups met at Red Clay, near Cleveland, Tennessee, in April 1984 at the very same site of the last meeting in 1837, in order to discuss matters of mutual concern. It was an event signifying the renewal and the continuation of the culture, and also attracted thousands of well-wishers from around the country. Today, the Cherokee is the second-largest Indian Nation in North America, with forty thousand members living in states other than North Carolina and Oklahoma.

As a poet, writer, and storyteller, Awiakta has kept the history of her people alive within a culture that has consistently sought to eliminate its traditions and render its members invisible. This task did not come easily, because she has had to confront the negative and false portrayal of her people in history books, the media, and public perceptions. Although she was nourished by her mother's Cherokee wisdom, the Indian within her was silenced so that she felt divided against herself, suffering untold anguish. When she found her voice in her poetry and rediscovered the attainments of her Nation, she began using this knowledge, not just on behalf of her own people but for all of us. Rather than reacting with vengefulness, Awiakta looks toward a society in which nations and their peoples will coexist peacefully and draw strength from each other. Her goal now is not only to help return her people to their rightful place but also to share the insights of the Cherokee in order to combat the contemporary assaults on human dignity, which she has described as racism, sexism, and disdain for Mother Earth.

Awiakta uses her artistic gifts on behalf of social and cultural justice, which she views as encompassing individual dignity, and relations between the genders and within the family, the community, the nation, and the world, connections many traditional human rights workers have not perceived. Coming from a culture that upholds the precepts of community and equality, and a balance between the genders in which women take an important role both in the economy and in the decisions of the Nation, she has promoted values that women working for human rights have sought to realize. She regards the well-being of her people as connected to world peace and the preservation of our species and planet.

She invites each one of us to join her as a traveler on the road to mutual understanding, a message of inclusiveness our world sorely needs. For example, Awiakta describes herself as the product of three cultures—the Native American, the "high tech," and the Appalachian. The silver pendant that shines on her dress is engraved with a deer leaping within an atom. The deer represents Awi Usdi, Little Deer, a spirit whose story embodies the Sacred Circle of Life and the Cherokee law of taking and giving back with respect. Awiakta, whose name means Eye of the Deer in Cherokee, recalls standing in front of a giant model of an atom in the Museum of Science and Energy at Oak Ridge. She gazed at the whirling lights representing electrons until she reached an altered state of consciousness and saw Little Deer leaping within the heart of the atom, signifying a synthesis of her three cultures. It became the vision of her life: to build bridges between cultures and to restore harmony to a troubled world.

In her publications and her many appearances, Awiakta brings the perceptions of the Cherokee to bear on contemporary problems. However, the sophistication of these perspectives requires a significant reorientation on our part. For example, the Cherokee society is egalitarian in all spheres of life; Awiakta identifies herself as only one of the people who speak and not as the spokesperson of her Nation. Furthermore, the Cherokee mode of thought differs from that of the dominant culture in the United States and the West, which separates the mind from the heart, the practical from the spiritual, and the public from the private. Drawing upon the oral tradition of her people, Awiakta often recounts their myths, lending them an immediacy and a relevance, for Native Americans view time as a continuum in which the past, present, and future are fused.

In telling the Cherokee creation story in *Selu*, Awiakta addresses the needs of the present. "In the beginning, the Creator made our Mother Earth. Then came Selu, Grandmother Corn,"[4] who produced the corn, nourishing her family from her own body. One day, as she was preparing the corn, her grandsons spied on her to learn her secret. Once it was revealed, Selu knew that she would soon die, but she left her grandsons specific instructions on growing and caring for corn, assuring them that, if they showed respect, there would be plenty for everyone. The message is clear; the individual cob contains seeds of different colors and sizes, representing our heterogeneity, and "as a single stalk will bear nothing, so the people must draw strength from their clan."[5] For the Cherokee, corn is not only food but a way of life that incorporates a love of liberty and a balance between the good of one and the good of all. Awiakta thus challenges traditional liberal philosophy, with its focus on the individual as the ultimate reality, and brings the message of community, members of which are held together spiritually, historically, and practically in a union that respects diversity.

In contrast, she recalls how the settlers that came to the New World took the grain for themselves, misunderstanding the true message of the corn, which is taking and giving back with esteem. She points out that, besides the oppression of Native peoples, the more basic issue today is how we treat Mother Earth in the name of material progress. Referring to the Tellico Dam controversy, Awiakta warns us that "the waters are rising for us all."[6]

One of the messages of Selu that Awiakta brings us through her book and her presentations is that we can begin to heal our culture and the earth when we restore the balance between genders, giving women their rightful place beside men as leaders and mothers of the nation. For Native Americans, reverence for women, the earth, life, and the spirit are interconnected. They interpret disdain for any one of these as a bent for destruction. In the nineteenth century, when the famous Cherokee chief Attakullakulla came to negotiate a treaty with the whites, he asked the all-male delegation, "Where are your women?"[7] That question was fraught with meaning, for he perceived a culture out of balance, and he was filled with foreboding for the future.

The path to the future for women is embodied in the past. Awiakta invokes the memories of the Beloved Woman Nanyehi, adviser to the Cherokee Nation, who served both as warrior and peacemaker. She describes the Clan Mothers of the matrilineal Cherokee Nation and how the practice of according women a predominant place has continued underground despite generations of white repression, suggesting that the time has come for the broader culture to learn this history and put it into practice. The values of balance and harmony so important to Native Americans reflect the laws of nature. "One of the unchanging elements (in the story of Selu) is that a basic imbalance, lack of regard, between genders disturbs the balance in the environment, just as imbalance in an individual invades the web of his or her life and affects all relationships."[8] We are all too familiar with the results of treating women and the earth as objects: rape, economic inequality, and ecological disaster. Awiakta continually tries to remind us to place the person back in the center, for a healed individual is the source of national well-being, just as a true balance between the genders is the source of a harmonious culture.

Awiakta invites us to examine our own thought patterns in the context of the Native American world view, which stresses connection, attachment, and ceremony as opposed to detachment and alienation. She characterizes our world as one of little boxes, the squared world, of time slots that separate us according to sex, occupation, race, ethnicity, and economics. The way back toward healing is to return to the circle, "the silken strands attaching us to the web."[9]

The final lesson of the corn, as retold by Awiakta, is that, just as the seeds were spread throughout Europe by Native Americans who were brought there and by returning explorers, elements of Native American thought penetrated European thinkers, including the work of John Locke. However, Awiakta believes that these philosophers did not fully understand the democratic life of the Native peoples they encountered; otherwise, they would not have excluded women and the lower classes from the polity. Throughout her career, Awiakta has sought to bring the untold stories to the world. She stresses that those in power are the ones who write history, overlooking a treasure of experience and wisdom. One of these stories is that of John Rutledge, who participated in the writing of the first draft of the U.S. Constitution at the Constitutional Convention in 1787. Familiar with the Great Law of Peace of the Iroquois Nation, he included aspects of that law in the final document. Another part of the untold story is that emerging aspects of our society, such as changing attitudes toward women, also stem in part from Native American teachings, proving that centuries of white domination have not been able to eliminate the indigenous civilization and that it continues to offer us the insights and tools with which to survive as a species.

In her work on behalf of human dignity, Awiakta advises us to relinquish the cultural, scientific, and material pride that causes us to overlook Native American contributions, and to practice mutual respect toward each other and all of creation. She urges us to become involved in the world at whatever level and to whatever extent we are able, to engage in "unified thinking"—a synthesis of mind, heart, and spirit—and to join the sacred web of our common humanity. Like the Cherokee and the Iroquois, indigenous peoples are the voice of the earth. In offering us a path to the future, they reveal a grasp of cause and effect that we seem to barely understand in our relentless pursuit of technological and material gain—that as we are connected in our humanity, we are also linked to all living creatures. Acknowledging that link signifies a reverence for nature and the Creator. It is that difficult and that simple. In sharing her Nation's heritage, such as the myth of Selu, Awiakta offers us the message of "strength, balance, harmony, adaptability, cooperation and unity in diversity."[10] This is the gift of wisdom that the

Cherokees have kept burning throughout the years, along with their sacred fire, and which Awiakta gives us with much grace.

AWIAKTA SPEAKS

All of my work follows the Native American tradition of art. The true artist must help create a disease-free environment—that is, create harmony and healing.

"The minute I opened my eyes when I was born I wanted to be a poet. That's the way I saw the world; my mother told me I spoke of things in images. When I was three and a half and we were walking together, she remembered that a monarch butterfly died in the air and grazed my shoulder as it fell to the sidewalk and that I picked it up and said, 'Oh, little butterfly, how I wish you weren't dead, so you could fly with other butterflies.' Then I put the butterfly on the window ledge out of harm's way. Looking back on myself at that age, I realize that I sounded what would be my song, which is regret and sorrow for pain, but to move as much as possible out of harm's way. My work now—with my poetry, stories, and speaking to people, working in the schools or in prisons or wherever—is still the same theme: I wish pain weren't here, but I want to move people out of harm's way toward harmony for the future.

When I was young and I said I wanted to be a poet, my mother would reply, 'That's good, but what will you do for the people?' Poetry in America, at that time and now, is not a high-market item, and people don't think of it as something to use for the good of the people, but the traditional way of thought is to turn the young person toward using what one has for the good of the whole. It was that instruction from my mother, the tradition of my people, that directed the path of my work.

My mother's question, 'What will you do for the people?', indicates an idea of success that is different from what is usually thought of. For example, in the dominant culture's concept, if one is a college student and is gifted in writing, there is a career path. You try to get published in certain magazines and that leads you to the next rung and the next rung and the next rung, on to the top rung. But my mother's question, which was a traditional question, indicates a communal path, where the value of what you do is whether you really help your people and the community with it or whether you just use it for yourself. That's a diametrically opposed value system to going for the top. Also, in Western thought, the utility of art is very often viewed as diminishing its value. If an art form is useful, it becomes a craft. A basket is a craft, a Fabergé egg is an art form. But one does nothing with a Fabergé egg but look at it. A basket is useful. There's class bias inherent in the West's attitude toward art, if you think about it. A very fine piece of Native pottery that's used to cook in is not art. King Tut's chair is art because it belonged to a king. The degree of skill in making the object is not measured. I have chosen to use my work according to the values I respect the most: Art for life's sake instead of art for art's sake.

I began to write poems about how we're using nuclear power—the abuse of that great force, the lack of respect—and also about women and the place of women in our society, what's happening to the planet, the trees. I began to sing these songs. Then people would ask me to say these poems or stories in order to help with an issue they were working on in their communities. For example, in the Great Smoky Mountains, acid rain was destroying the forests from the top down, so the Conservation Department came and asked me, 'Can we use some of your poems, to help people see? We'd like to use them with a statistical article, and they will move people's hearts and then we'll hit them with the statistics.' Then the National Colloquium on Nuclear Waste Disposal, the most statistical conference you could imagine, asked me to give a talk and read poems. They said they'd never had anybody from the arts come to do something like this. 'We want you to use your poetry and songs to help move people off the mental gridlock and help them to more creative ways of seeing.'

I worked to help preserve the Indian mounds in Memphis that the municipal authorities were preparing to bulldoze. Native leaders put together a community response that involved African Americans, Native Americans, European-descent Americans. The people of Memphis that cared united to help save the mounds. My contribution was to write a poem for it, 'Old Students of the New Physics,' and help educate the community by speaking to different groups about how Native people felt about the mounds. Other people were leading the confrontational part who were gifted at doing that.

That's one thing I like to make clear to young people: In a movement it's important to find which strand of the web you're suited to help with. The fact may be that your place is not on the front line or the barricades. That is the place for people who are warriors. Once the public is shocked, people are also needed to go behind the scenes and help educate the public about what's really at stake. The people that occupy the mounds and shut down archaeological digs are important; those of us who were in the movement and had other tasks were important, too. It was the combination of everyone working together that saved the mounds in Memphis.

Sometimes, what I see happen in the dominant culture is that a certain act or attitude gets defined as politically correct. I think that's because Western culture is set up in little boxes and has categories. Perhaps it stems from that kind of thought. 'Here's what you do if you are this,' they say, and then you are labeled in a box. The Native way is the web. So one strand of the web is not more important than another strand and it takes many strands to get something done. With a movement it takes the people who are confrontational, who educate the public; it takes the people who sing, the people who dance, the people who just go about their daily rounds and talk to others. Put it all together and you have a very strong web. Mutual respect and cooperation is my way.

I think it's very important to define terms, especially because the dominant culture now has the right-brain/left-brain paradigm in mind—that the right brain is intuitive and the left brain is analytical. Even though this concept is an advance, it still is in the Western dichotomy, which separates thinking and feeling. If you are speaking from the heart, for example, you are not speaking from the mind. The Cherokee way has a lot in common with other Native ways of thought. In the Cherokee language you don't separate thought and feeling. There's no way to separate it like in the West. There is a verb for 'thinking purposefully,' and from the root of this verb come the nouns for the heart, the mind, and the soul. When you think purposefully, you are thinking with the mind, the heart, and the soul. In English, there's not an analogous verb; you either think or feel. Even when the Cherokee says 'thinking purposefully,' in English it doesn't really translate. This kind of thinking is very difficult to defeat—to conquer—because the intellect works in a linear A, B, C, D way. When a person speaks from a unity of thought and heart, the listener can't tell where the thought is coming from, because it analyzes from every point of view like a web, thinks about something from every direction, and comes to a conclusion. It's very hard to fool somebody or shake somebody who is thinking like that. This is not speaking from an emotional base, as the West would call it.

I grew up in a highly scientific world, with the traditional teachings of Cherokee and Appalachia. The first thing I had to do was to make a synthesis of those three cultures. The high-tech world has its own view and its own language and value system, so it is a culture. Today, all of us have to deal with that culture with whatever ethnic background we have. I grew up in Oak Ridge, where the atom was split in the 1940s. It was the beginning of tomorrow. When I made a synthesis of those three cultures, the high tech, the Cherokee, and the Appalachian or Celtic, I could move out and begin to go among the people, the mountain people or whoever asked me to come. I would bring poems and stories about making new harmonies for the future based on mutual respect for all.

I was recently invited to come to Alaska for a statewide self-esteem conference to train teachers. The conference title was 'Full Esteem Ahead.' Two of the keynote speakers spoke on building self-regard. I titled my section 'Full Esteem Around.' I made the point that it's good to have a sense of self-worth, but it has to be shared to allow other people a sense of self, a place in the circle. That means not only saying, 'I'm okay, you're okay' but also 'there's a place for your value system here,' which requires other people moving over a bit, which they don't often want to do. It won't work to say, 'I'm okay, you're okay, do it my way.'

The women's prison in Memphis asked me to give poetry workshops. When you're put in prison, everything is taken away from you, and you are depersonalized. Many of these women were mothers separated from their children. Also, in Memphis, the women who had committed misdemeanors were put in prison with men who were felons. The men who committed misdemeanors were sent to the penal farm that has television, swimming pools, means of working on the GED (high school equivalency). So, here were these women, some of whom had only written bad checks, with felons and on the same schedule in prison, having breakfast at 3:00 A.M., lunch at 7:00 A.M., dinner at 3:00, and bedtime at 6:00. Women in the Memphis community were leading a political movement to have that changed, approaching the judges and so forth. I was helping the prison women develop self-esteem and taking their poems back out to the community and saying, 'Here are some voices coming from prison, please listen. They're not saying what you probably thought they'd be saying.' That's a very quiet, gentle way of working. That's what I mean about going where the need is.

I've been part of the Arts in the Schools Program in Memphis for seven years. I go into the classrooms with my work. *Rising Fawn and the Fire Mystery* was chosen to be the art project in the city. The whole point of that book was mutual respect between Native people and white people. You can take that story and apply the principle to all races and people who are different from the mainstream, like the physically handicapped. They asked me to train the teachers and then work with the children. That is very quiet, grass-roots work. With our children is where we begin.

By blood and life experience I am a bridge myself because I have Cherokee/Celtic heritage and I grew up on the frontier of science, the high-tech world. Then I moved to France, where I worked as a translator for the U.S. Air Force. There I was in a completely different culture from my own. My whole life experience has been seeing the importance of mutual respect among people who are different. Emphasizing the differences all the time can lead to no progress whatsoever. I also see my work as a bridge. I mean a swinging bridge, not a concrete or steel bridge. A swinging bridge is native to my region, to Appalachia. It's made of rope and is very pliant, very flexible, and very much alive. You have to be very respectful to walk over it, or it will flip you off. I see myself weaving connections that are alive, between the dominant culture and the Native culture, between science and people whose wisdom is experiential. I do it through my Native heritage and my mountain heritage—poems and stories about life there taken to universals.

It's not to devalue the dominant culture, but I've started with a different premise. This made a big difference on how I've organized my life and work, because the main thing for me was to keep my life in balance. Balance is the great teaching of Native peoples. Balance in family and work, balance with the children, and balance with the community. To do that, I have to be in control of how many times I travel to speak and to choose where I go. When you're with an agent, to a large extent, you go where they want you to go and when. I think it's very important in speaking with young people and with college students, to stress thinking through in a very pragmatic way, how you want your life to go, and what you will have to do in order for it to go in that direction. I only go where I feel there's a need, where people express a need and where the circle is going—where the giving and taking is mutual. Arranging things myself, I can negotiate everything one to one with the person who is asking me.

The Native tradition for women in the arts—all the way back to the guide stories of women like Selu—is of healing and teaching. In many Indian cultures, the tradition for women has always been an egalitarian one; our entitlement to move into the public sphere comes through the mothers' line. As a woman, if I stand in the Memphis city council, I don't feel I've intruded into the male sphere. It's my right to stand in the council because I'm a Mother of the Nation, and I should be heard. That doesn't go over big in some dominant culture places, but the point is that one way women are controlled in the dominant culture is to be told that if they run for political office, for example, they are trying to be men. But in the old Cherokee Nation the women always served powerfully on the council, it's traditional. Today, when you want to be on the council you are fulfilling your woman's role to move in the public sphere. You are supposed to be the center of the home and the center of the nation. In the West, it's the male who traditionally has had the public sphere and the female the private sphere. There are even some women who take on male characteristics and look at other women and say, 'Oh, well, they're just mothers.' In the Native way, the fact that you are a woman entitles you to a public place and a say in the policy of the people.

For me to talk about nuclear reactors might seem to a Western view that it's a woman butting into the male world. To the Cherokee mind, it's like one of the clan mothers walking in and having something to say about how the government is run. It's her duty and obligation and right, not to tell the men what to do but to add her wisdom, her half. If you have a balance in the home and then in the country and nation, things go better when you have the two points of view, the male and the female.

Someone asked the chief of the Cherokee, Wilma Mankiller, if she would like to dance the men's dances, and she replied, 'Oh, no. We women have our own dances.' There's a balance of power there. It's not like the men do the important dances and the women do the frilly stuff. The women's dances are very important and, ceremonially, when the Cherokee women danced for the poor, no one could leave the dance ground until the Mothers of the Nation judged that there was enough donated to care for the people who hadn't had as good fortune that year. It's a totally different way of reasoning gender roles and that's why it's sometime very difficult to talk with radical Western feminists who see an automatic devaluation if women are concerned about children and family. That's a Western concept. The Native concept is that because she is the life-bearing force, whether physical, intellectual, or spiritual, a woman has the right to speak and to be heard. From the Native point of view, it's very interesting what's happening in Washington now that the president's wife (Hillary Rodham Clinton) and other women are in government. This could be seen as a return to the way the Mothers of the Nation were before white contact.

I see my work as contributing a strand of hope. If we give up hope, we certainly will lose it all. I think there is a calculated risk that we might make it a little longer. In one poem I say, 'Our courage is our memory/Out of ashes peace will rise/if the people are resolute./If we are not resolute/we will vanish/and out of ashes peace will rise.' That's hope, but it's very pragmatic. If we are resolute and try hard to restore our planet and restore harmony to our people, peace may come. If we are not resolute, peace will also come but we may well not be here. Mother Nature is a businessperson, and she may look at Homo sapiens as a failed species. Mother Earth will return. She is eternal. We'll just be phased out. I have a poem which is called 'Mother Nature Sends a Pink Slip.' It says, 'To Homo sapiens, re: termination/I'm in the life-producing business/ The bottom line is you're not a cost-effective species,' and she goes on to say why Homo sapiens is a disloyal species. It's humorous, but it's also true. My work brings the message that we should face the sunrise, face tomorrow. We must honor the past, look to the future, and do what we can, trusting the Creator will take care of the rest.

Native people have been through a horrible destruction and a constant undermining of our culture and a killing of the spirit, yet we have survived. I think one of the reasons is this teaching that we're all connected in one web of life and that we must maintain a positive mind. That's what the Cherokee spiritual leaders teach. The whole Nation was almost wiped out in the removal and the Trail of Tears but the leaders always say, 'Don't deny what happens to you and honor the past, but don't dwell on bitterness and let it drag you down.' The focus is to the future. The Cherokee have just developed a whole computer program for the language so that, now, all of our archives written since 1821 can be translated. The language was forbidden for a hundred years, and there were so few people that still spoke it. For a long time it looked as if these archives would be forever lost to the people.

It's very difficult to talk directly about pain, but to take painful experience and transform it into something positive is the teaching. Consider the Trail of Tears, where the whole Nation was virtually destroyed, and the hundred years when the U.S. government forbade teaching the history and language—if the Cherokee had dwelled on what had happened in the past, the Nation would not be rising like a phoenix as it is today. They would have headed West toward death. The direction of life, hope, and power is East, toward the rising sun. I follow the traditional teaching that everything is related in a web of life and try to maintain a positive mind. Great leaders like Wilma Mankiller exemplify that you face problems squarely. If there is a big problem, like that of the self-esteem of our young people, or economic problems, you face them, but eastward. We will network among all different groups to do something about a problem, through what is the same among us as opposed to what is different. It's a consensual form of government, democracy. I'm a strand of a whole web of that type of thought. My work takes on that focus because of my culture. I give myself credit that I try to maintain it and discipline myself spiritually. If you read my work, it certainly doesn't shirk from the difficulties of what's out there.

It's very important for young women of all races today to think through for themselves where their center is and what they are about and then look at the culture they live in and see how affirming it is of a woman following her chosen path. If that culture is not affirming, action needs to be taken. For instance, we have so many young women today with anorexia or bulimia. That is a direct result of the attack on women's power and her soul through the media, advertising a culture which projects an unrealistic image for a woman. Our young women are being fooled, are being trapped. I really have a lot of faith in our young women and our young men that we are going to move toward a new harmony.

I'd like to finish with the last four lines of my poem, 'An Indian Walks in Me.' 'My Cherokee left no sign/except in hair and cheek/and this firm step of mind/that seeks the whole/in strength and peace.' Seeking the whole in strength and peace is my work."

Notes

1. Marilou Awiakta, *Selu: Seeking the Corn Mother's Wisdom* (Golden, CO: Fulcrum Publishing, 1994), 44.
2. Ibid., 107.
3. Ibid.
4. Ibid., 9.
5. Ibid.
6. Ibid., 51.
7. Ibid.
8. Ibid., 26.
9. Ibid., 175.
10. Ibid., 229.

8 / *Navanethem Pillay*

IN JANUARY 1995, NAVANETHEM PILLAY'S long career as an opponent of apartheid was vindicated when she was appointed by Nelson Mandela's government as the first black woman to serve as acting judge for the Supreme Court of South Africa. In the spring of 1995 she was also nominated by her government for and elected to serve as judge on the United Nations' International Criminal Tribunal to review abuses in Rwanda. Throughout her life, Dr. Pillay has been at the forefront in seeking change for the oppressed through her work as a human rights lawyer, her membership in the black consciousness-aligned New Unity Movement, and her efforts to transform the subservient role of women in South African society.[1]

Born of Indian parents in 1941 in Durban, South Africa, and of grandparents brought from India as indentured servants by British sugar planters, her family suffered discrimination in all of its forms.

Given the structure of apartheid, neither of Navanethem's parents had access to education, but her mother helped ensure that she enter school at an early age. Because of her hunger for learning, Navanethem, or Navi as she prefers to be called, began pushing at the limits imposed by apartheid when she was in high school. With the financial help of the Indian community she managed to obtain a university education and graduated with a B.A. in 1963 and an LL.B. in 1965 from Natal University.

Despite all the obstacles that Navi encountered, she became the first black woman* to start a law practice in Natal in 1967, defending some of the most notable opponents of apartheid and developing highly creative legal strategies to move forward in the struggle for justice. She was awarded a Harvard University scholarship for graduate study in 1981 and became the first South African to receive a doctorate in law from Harvard Law School in 1988. Navi is married to an attorney, Gaby Pillay, and is the mother of two daughters, aged twenty-one and eighteen years.

As a human rights lawyer, Navi spent more than twenty years involved in political trials, including numerous visits to the notorious Robben Island Prison, where Mandela was held for twenty-seven years, as well as to other security prisons. Her most impressive achievements include the successful denunciation in court of evidence extracted under detention through the use of torture and solitary confinement, and the victorious court application for the right of prisoners on Robben Island to have access to lawyers. She always has regarded court battles as opportunities for challenging the laws and gaining public exposure for political grievances and police brutality.

I interviewed Navi Pillay a few months before President Frederik Willem de Klerk stepped down and the new regime was established with Mandela as president (May 1994). Activists like her were still the target of harassment by the security police, living within the omnipresent web of apartheid. From the vantage point of an open society, it is hard to imagine what it is like to live in a goldfish bowl, to have one's telephone tapped, one's every move monitored, and, most of all, to have one's family life disrupted by the state. Working for political change in a society that denies the most basic right to privacy and freedom of thought and that pun-

*Under apartheid South Africans were classified into three major groups: blacks, whites, and coloreds, who were of mixed race. Indians were considered a subcategory of the blacks.

ishes opponents with torture and death requires an inner strength and fearlessness that few Americans can fathom.

Navi considers herself fortunate because she was never in prison or even banned, a fact that she attributes to her great care. However, while she was working on the cases of important dissidents, her offices were bugged, she was under continual surveillance, she was often the target of threatening phone calls, and, at one point, the security police planted a spy in her office. In addition, Navi was denied a passport for many years; she received permission to travel abroad for the first time in 1972 and then for only four days. None of these pressures ever deterred her from pursuing her human rights work.

One of the most difficult periods in her life was in 1971, when her husband was in detention. While Navi was trying to help him, a member of the security police made a special effort to wear her down by threatening her and using obscene language. At the time, she was juggling work, important trials, and family with efforts to free her husband. However, she feels that these were minor sufferings compared to what was happening to others.

In "The Role of a Conscientious Lawyer in the South African Legal System," Navi Pillay has written about the difficulties of working within a political system in which the reins of political, legal, social, and economic power are in the hands of a small minority. Apartheid was officially established in 1948 when the Nationalist Party won its first full election victory and was able to form a government and systematically reshape South African society. Traditional forms of segregation were replaced by formal apartheid ("separateness") in every conceivable sphere of private and public life. Any political liberties that nonwhites had enjoyed previously were eradicated, the entire population was classified into racial groups, and the civil rights of white critics were curtailed. Gradually, the military, police, and civil service bureaucracies were filled with Afrikaner nationalists. The institutions supporting apartheid—government, economic, and the Dutch Reformed Church—were held together by a secret organization, the Broederbond (brotherhood), that in turn controlled the government. The facade of democratic institutions reserved for the Afrikaans and English minority masked a shadowy control by a network of political elites from the major institutional supports of the regime.

Apartheid meant not only the separation of the different racial groups but also a systematic oppression of black, colored, and Indians by disenfranchising them economically as well as excluding them from the political process. The white population appropriated the agricultural and mineral resources of the country by forcing Africans off the arable and mineral-rich lands. This was accomplished by the creation of so-called black homelands, which were little more than reservations, where, typically, hundreds of thousands of people were crammed into small areas of agriculturally unviable land. The homelands also instituted the separation of diverse ethnic groups, setting the stage for future ethnic conflicts and creating a vast pool of urban laborers living in crowded hostels with the status of a permanent underclass.

Pass laws that required every African over the age of sixteen to carry a pass at all times indicating his or her status in the "white areas" meant that Africans were restricted in their movements and in their choice of residence. They became aliens in their own country. Because African laborers who worked in the mines and in the cities were not allowed to bring their families with them, the African family was disrupted and women found themselves as the heads of households struggling for survival.

The South African government exercised its tyranny over nonwhites by means of a vast network of laws and regulations. Rather than viewing the law as a guarantor of basic rights and liberties, of habeas corpus, and of the presumption of innocence and equality, the government has viewed it as a bastion of order against the threat of anarchy and as the foundation of its racial dominance. There were literally thousands of statutes, regulations, and official circulars not in the public domain but treated as law by officials governing the daily life of the nonwhite population.[2] There were also the laws, regulations, and circulars relating to the administration of the Group Areas Act, the basic statute guaranteeing absolute residential segregation. It divided the land into racially designated areas and homelands and the population into racial castes and subcastes. Blacks, coloreds, and Indians were able to move around the country but were barred from owning land in more than 85 percent of it. Black South Africans were subdivided by law into six distinct categories: urban and rural blacks, insiders and commuters among urban blacks, migrants who live in urban townships, and blacks who live in white rural areas as farm laborers. Those who defied these apartheid laws ended up in prison as common criminals. There were also many members of the white population who wound up in prison for their anti-apartheid views and activities.

The problem for a human rights lawyer, as Navi saw it, was how to work within a judiciary that is part of such a tyrannical system, how to work toward human rights without compromising one's own integrity and without supporting the political system. Navi describes the reality in which she functioned as a lawyer: "White Person's courts and Black Person's prisons: the distinction correlates with the polarized extremes of the real world outside the courtroom: enfranchised vs. disfranchised, exploiter vs. exploited, rich vs. poor, . . . power vs. powerless, . . . it is all part of the grand scheme of apartheid and in the vision of the black population, the judiciary system is an integral part of the oppressive system."[3]

As a black woman lawyer in South Africa, Navi Pillay grappled with the injustice of racist courts: that they were not representative of blacks, coloreds, and Indians who were in the main not legally represented in the courts and that they acted as a support for governmental policy, with justice serving the interest of those members of the white minority who supported the government. Because of this, Navi believed that no person of color should act as either magistrate or judge within the legal system because that would entail upholding unjust laws rather than assuring individual liberties. By implication, they would also uphold a political system based upon neither the representation nor the consensus of the people and therefore lacking in legitimacy. Navi believed that even so-called liberal judges were acting to preserve the status quo in South Africa and that a lawyer working to achieve human rights by necessity challenges the system and raises the political and moral issue of injustice even though the courts refuse to deal with political questions. Throughout her years of work, Navi has seen her role as that of seeking relief within the courts for those unable to protect their basic rights within the political process, thus challenging the political system while seeking redress for her clients.

Now that the political system has changed, Navi is able to serve as judge without compromising her views. She notes that her appointment represents the first time in South Africa that an attorney was selected as acting judge, rather than such posts being reserved for longtime advocates and senior counsel, thus guaranteeing judgeships for white males. She believes that her years of experience have qualified her for such an important position.

Like many women activists, Navi Pillay has a vision of human dignity that is all encompassing, including the rights of men and women to work, fair wages and working conditions, a clean environment, education, and health. She regards a truly democratic system as the best protection of rights provided that it also assures economic and social equality among ethnic groups and between genders.

NAVI SPEAKS

The role of conscientious lawyers is to confront the reality and not turn a blind eye to the injustices that prevail. The reality is that justice is inaccessible to the vast number of the black population.

["The Role of a Conscientious Lawyer in the South African Legal System," *African Law Review* (October 1990): 27.]

"Apartheid was fully in place. We were Indian children educated in Indian schools and living in slums. We grew up with our parents constantly in utter fear, advising us not to get involved in politics, not to oppose the white man, and not to have any grand illusions about being the same as whites. They instilled in us that the whites were superior and what our place was.

All the jobs were restricted. When I was a child there was no sewerage system, so the household refuse was removed by the bucket system, and African males used to carry these horrible buckets. But the driver of the van was white because that job was supposed to be a skilled job and therefore for white people.

In school the teachers didn't speak about politics because they would have lost their jobs, and teachers did lose their jobs. The teachers were all Indian. I remember, when I was in grade six, I won an essay competition on why we should buy South African-made goods and was awarded a medal instead of the money prize that had been offered. Some of the teachers were saying, 'If she was white, she would have won a money award instead of just receiving a medal.'

Constantly one would hear these comments and realize that we were underprivileged. We knew we were not getting the same opportunities. We would go to shops and we would stand on line while they served white people first. I went to the public hospital once when I was eleven to have some teeth extracted, and I remember I had to wait for about ten hours. When I started to lean against a vehicle in the hospital yard, a white doctor stuck his head out of the window and yelled at me for leaning against his car. As a child of apartheid I couldn't go to the beaches or parks. They were for white people.

When I was in high school and among my peer group, I became more conscious of discrimination. In 1957 I wrote an essay for a competition which was organized by the Union of Jewish Women. I don't know who these wonderful women were who reached out to different racial groups and organized a national essay-writing competition on the role of women in South Africa. I won the competition, and my picture, together with extracts from my essay, were published in the newspaper. What I had written was that the role of women in South Africa was to inculcate values in children so that we would all struggle for our rights.

In high school I also took part in debates. We would debate capitalism and socialism and the different value systems. But we couldn't talk about our own oppression. I couldn't write an essay about the discrimination I was experiencing and about all the discriminatory laws in South Africa. The security police would come into our schools very often to question the prefects. They would want to know, for example, why the students had supported Human Rights Day.

The only reason that I was able to attend high school was because I received a scholarship. I was only able to attend the university because I received a scholarship. The high school went out to the community on my behalf and raised the money for me to go to the university for the first year. Thereafter, the university gave me a grant on merit. I received the award for the best first-year student. It was a minimal sum of ten dollars, but it meant that, given the opportunity, a black woman from a disadvantaged background could do well at the university. I also received a grant from the city council. If it wasn't for the system of scholarships and fee remission, I wouldn't have had the opportunity of a university education. I felt very deeply for the rest of my classmates. There were thirty of us and no one else had the opportunity of going to the university, even though they were all so keen.

At the university, I became more politicized. I joined student organizations, including the Durban Students Group of the New Unity Movement. That's the liberation movement that I belonged to and still do. I came directly into confrontation with apartheid because the university was segregated. We were in a nonwhite section. The white students were in the university proper, while we were in a potato warehouse. We studied bills of exchange and negotiable instruments from one textbook. About thirteen of us shared that textbook. Each of us had an hour to read it in the library. There we were studying bills of exchange and negotiable instruments without ever having seen a check. We often joke about it now.

When I finished my B.A., I was not allowed to do the LL.B., the law degree. Because I received credit for four law courses for my B.A., I could enter the second year of the LL.B. But the university could not admit me to the second-year course. The Separate Universities Act decreed that all nonwhite students had to go to their different ethnic colleges. There was a college opened for Indians in that year, 1963, but I couldn't go there because they were just starting the first-year law courses and had no provision for me to do a second-year LL.B. I appealed to the minister of education, and my appeal was rejected. Instead, the minister gave me permission for the teachers' diploma. It wasn't something that I wanted to do. I lost six months of the year.

In July of that year, they opened up a Ministry of Indian Affairs. The Indians didn't want to have anything to do with that ministry because we were citizens of South Africa. We wanted a nonracial, democratic South Africa and believed that these were all ploys by the government to create separate homelands, to divide and rule. On principle we didn't want to have anything to do with this ministry, but I knew I wanted to play a role as a lawyer and so I had to apply to the Ministry of Indian Affairs. We had no access to typewriters, so I wrote my application by hand. Every time I telephoned, the secretary of the honorable minister of Indian affairs, she would say, 'Oh, you are the girl that sent in the handwritten application.' They finally issued me a special study permit, and I entered the University of Natal. I was one of two nonwhite students.

I completed the LL.B. in one and a half years. Then, I went to see the registrar about an internship. Lawyers in South Africa are required to serve two years of internship with a law firm before being admitted to practice. The registrar told me there was no way he would help me to find an internship because one could not have a situation where white typists had to take instructions from black persons. I inquired about postgraduate study and the registrar replied, 'Why do you want to study? Get out there and work.'

I walked the city, looking for placement as an intern. All the lawyers were men, almost all white. There were less than ten Indian lawyers. Of course, white firms wouldn't take on a black person. Every year the white firms would accept one or two students who were at the top of the class. The year I finished, they didn't pick the top student because it was a black woman who had the highest score. Finally, I found a two-year position with a lawyer who insisted on the condition that I not become pregnant for that period. My husband and I had known each other for five years at the university and had waited until final examinations to get married. So I went on the pill for two years.

The person I was articled to was a politician, a member of the African National Congress [ANC]. At the time almost everyone was active, and everything was regarded as political. You could get into trouble just for having written a poem. Many people were coming out with opposition literature. Anyone who left the country or tried to leave the country for training could be sentenced to life imprisonment. The authorities prohibited literature, and they prohibited certain people from leaving their homes after 6 P.M. They prevented people from leaving the city. These restrictions were carefully spelled out in what were called banning orders or house arrest orders. The principal lawyer I worked for was under house arrest. He couldn't leave the city of Durban, so he sent me to all the cases outside Durban, even though I was totally inexperienced. I was thrown into the deep end.

I would go out on cases, in the rural areas, and find that a whole village of men was being charged because their cattle had strayed onto certain land which had been fenced off and was owned by white people. The land contained all the green pastures, and the villagers were charged under environmental laws. White landowners used environmental and health regulations to confiscate the cattle owned by black people. The real intention was political, to deprive these people of their cattle, drive them off the farms, and force them to become laborers in the city, where they would depend on cash for income and have to pay taxes. I defended these villagers. Naturally, their cattle would stray onto the grassy areas from the barren rocky areas to which black people were forcibly removed. Not only were their cattle confiscated but they were also charged for trespassing. I would defend these people on technical grounds. I would question the police or the white farmer's wife with queries such as, 'What color was the cow?' and 'How do you know it belonged to him?' I would get them acquitted, and then I would address the villagers through an interpreter (I was speaking English) to point out that this was not a political victory, that all I did was to get them off on technical grounds, and that they could be caught again. I felt it was my duty to inform them. But I soon realized that they were making a political stand, while I was seeing it from the perspective of a lawyer. This was a real turning point for me.

I also became perturbed with my principal, the lawyer for whom I was working. I felt that we shouldn't be misleading these people. While it was true that they needed a lawyer, we were charging them money to defend them. I felt we should have identified more with our clients' causes, although that would be a political stand and a community issue. These were political offenses, and this work was my grounding for the big political trials I handled later. I was learning from my clients that the issues were not just about losing ten head of cattle because they had strayed. That's when I understood all the forces functioning in the rural area, what forcible dislocation of entire peoples meant, and how great was the courage of ordinary people.

One morning, when I drove up to court outside Durban, in the rural area, my client didn't come on time, which put me in a panic. When he came I was very agitated, and I asked him what was wrong with him and told him that a warrant of arrest would be issued for him. It turned out that he had left his home at three in the morning and had walked all the way to arrive at court at 10:00 A.M. In this way, I learned about how people suffered and what they were struggling against.

In those early years I also acted for many people who were under restriction orders and who had to report to the police every Monday morning. One couldn't just forget, that was not an acceptable excuse in court. But there was one man who simply forgot. By then I was a little more experienced, but still just an interned clerk, a trainee. Other trainees were running errands, while I got landed with all this responsibility because my principal attorney was himself restricted. But I jumped into it eagerly because I had identified with these injustices from an early age. So, in defending this man charged for failing to report to the police, I went to elaborate lengths to get a medical certificate that he had piles, and we presented all the graphic details of his condition. The reply was, 'Yes, you had piles, but why couldn't you walk to the police station to report?' We could never get an acquittal. Invariably, our clients were convicted.

The day I was admitted to the bar, I started my law practice on my own; that was in 1967. I was the first woman to start a law practice in Natal Province, and one of the few black women lawyers in the entire country. When I started I heard the men saying,

'She's very presumptuous, a woman and starting a law practice.' But you know, I had no choice. Nobody would employ me as a black woman. Anyway, I didn't want to work for anyone else. I thought I would try it for six months and see if I could make it. If not, I would close up and start looking for a job. It was a question of having very few choices.

One of the first cases I handled on my own was on behalf of a woman who was still a law student, but she was older than me and deeply involved in politics. Her name was Phyllis Naidoo, a very well-known ANC person. She had been charged for failing to report to the police station. She was studying for law exams, and she also had very young children. They were sick at the time, and she was tending to them. She was tired and, when she got up in the morning, she just went off to write her exams, forgetting to report to the police as a banned person. She wanted me to defend her but she couldn't afford a lawyer. I told her I would do it but that I had just started to practice and had no experience.

We went to court and explained all the circumstances, but both the magistrate and the prosecutor said, 'Well, why didn't she report the next day, or why didn't she get a car and go and report?' The sentence was one year in prison, but, thankfully, they suspended most of it. Generally, people would spend four days in prison. My unfortunate friend Phyllis had to serve seven days. I was conscience stricken and thought that probably I had done such a bad job that she had gotten three more days than most people. I had been in and out of prison consulting with clients, and what was going on inside was terrible. The women weren't issued sanitary pads, and they had to use newspapers. All the warders were white women. They were big and strong, and they used to kick the women prisoners.

I continued my practice, and some of my colleagues started to refer work to me. They were African male lawyers who specialized in criminal work. They would take on too many cases for the day and would call me at a quarter to two and say, 'Can you take on this case at two o'clock?'

I did everything. I did criminal work. I did civil work. I did estates and trusts. I did ordinary common-law crimes, but everything was political. I acted for students and trade unionists. I acted for members of all the political groups in South Africa. I still do all of it, except for criminal work.

Without even me choosing, my work immediately became focused on human rights. People started to phone me for advice. One school principal telephoned me when, during school holidays, four of his students who had gone for a picnic in the Transkei, about five hours outside Durban, were detained. They were held in prison for no reason and spent the entire weekend in the crowded cell. I made numerous phone calls and managed to get them released at the end of the weekend. When they were released, the live chicken they had been carrying for the picnic was returned to them, and they were asked to pay fifteen cents to cover the cost of feeding the chicken. Yet the students hadn't been fed the whole time.

In the '70s there were huge strikes in Durban. I acted for workers and for students who were charged as instigators of the strikes. Some of the people I represented have become very well-known for the major contributions they made to the struggle. They include Saths Cooper, a member of the black consciousness movement, who served six years on Robben Island. Strini Moodley was head of AZAPO [Azanian People's Organization], a student organization. Chris Albertyne is now a well-known trade unionist lawyer. I acted for quite a few of the people who were in opposition politics.

Most of the political activists couldn't pay because they had no money. I usually just charged the minimum. Black lawyers functioned differently from white lawyers. We were not the big corporate law firm working for money. We were working for a different purpose. I was making a reasonable income from registering bonds and transferring properties, which paid the rent and enabled me to act for indigent people. Now, I'm doing mainly women's rights work, and the majority of the women can't pay. They are the most disadvantaged group.

I laid the grounds for my human rights work in an early case. That was the case in which my husband was detained in 1971. In that year hundreds of people were detained. They were members of the New Unity Movement. The New Unity Movement started in 1941 in Cape Province. It's regarded as some kind of intellectual organization, but it's not. It's a people's movement. It doesn't have a large membership but actively prints and distributes leaflets and critical literature. The New Unity Movement is a nonracial democracy movement. There is a ten-point-minimum program, which is adhered to uncompromisingly. The movement is critical of the compromise solution that has been recently worked out by the ANC with the apartheid government, which has been the oppressor for so long. They compromised many issues, agreeing to a balkanized state and recognizing cultural law and traditional chiefs, all very oppressive to women.

The New Unity Movement case also involved another group, the African People's Democratic Union of South Africa. The charge was that, in conspiracy with members of the movement who were outside of the country, mainly in Zambia, the accused had plotted to overthrow the government by armed and military warfare. The authorities picked up hundreds of people and held them totally incommunicado. My husband was among them. He was detained for five months under the terrorism laws. I kept going to the Durban police and asking about him. They were very scornful and said, 'He is being held under Section 6 of the Terrorism Act. You are supposed to be a lawyer, and you don't even know that.' It was utterly humiliating. I was terrified of those fellows. I looked up that statute for the very first time. It's very much like the English statute that is used against the Irish, allowing the authorities to pick up anybody and hold them indefinitely.

My husband was asked to be a state witness. He refused and, therefore, was kept in detention. After about six or eight months, ten of the detained were charged. Three of them were lawyers. Some of them wanted me as their lawyer, and some of them were reluctant because I was a woman and inexperienced. All of them had been brutally tortured. My husband wasn't tortured, but they kept threatening him. He was thoroughly intimidated. I was at the police station every day, making noise, and I used to pick up his laundry and bring him fresh clothes. The first time I saw that his handkerchief was in a tight ball, I realized that he had been crying, and I had never seen him cry. It was a terrifying experience. I found it very hard to function as a lawyer because I was emotionally involved.

During the trial we discovered that all the accused had been tortured, and we took statements from all ten of them. Then, my husband was detained again in the course of the trial after having been released earlier. The chief security policeman wanted to use him as a state witness against his comrades. He wouldn't do that on principle, and he also said that they wanted him to lie. He insisted that all the New Unity Movement did was to send people out for education and training, but the security police and the interrogators wanted him to say that it was for military training, not just training.

I rushed around, consulting various people with more experience than I had, including one very well-known Jewish lawyer called Rowley Arenstein, a real doyen in the struggle. Rowley gave me the idea to bring application in court to stop the police from using unlawful methods of interrogation. We could never do that before because we did not get affidavits to support our allegations that the police had been using torture and other unlawful methods. This was an ideal situation for such an application. My husband had left the power of attorney in my favor, which enabled me to file the application for him. I had the affidavits of these ten brave men, who had described their ordeal in detention. So we filed the application, and a very sympathetic judge granted it, issuing an order that the security police were not to use unlawful methods of interrogation. He also ordered the sheriff to serve this order to my husband, who was being held incommunicado. That was a real first. Many people asked how we had managed to get the order, or even think of applying for it, since it had never been done before. The Terrorism Act specifically provided that no court could inquire into the validity of the detention or order the release of a detained. Well, I think you have to look for first-time solutions when there's no other way. Maybe it was because my husband was involved, and I felt I had to do something from the outside. Previously, the courts had had affidavits from people who had come out and were living in exile, mainly ANC people. In 1972 the UN's Subcommittee of the General Assembly on Apartheid adopted that application as a document in their collection on torture.

As defense attorney in another political case I was sent to London to obtain similar sworn statements from political activists in exile who had experienced detention in South Africa. This was my very first trip outside the country, but I didn't see anything in London, like Hyde Park. We rushed around, trying to get lawyers and notaries to expedite everything. Everything was very slow there, and we were pressed for time. We used these affidavits, together with those of the men inside the prison standing trial, to show that the police were using a system of torture. The case was covered by all the major white newspapers. The *Rand Daily Mail* had it on the front page. There were many committed journalists who were helpful in exposing the conditions of detainees. This was not a black-white struggle in South Africa. White people were always deeply involved in serving the cause of justice and human rights. Whites who were Jewish especially identified with the struggle. Many served time in prisons, were banned, and were placed under house arrest restrictions.

At the trial, the judge refused to allow us to call the expert testimony of an American, Dr. Louis West from UCLA [University of California at Los Angeles], who did research on the effects of solitary confinement. He had conducted research on what had happened to American prisoners of war in Korea to make them say to their captors that America had used germ warfare when it wasn't true. The American government was very interested in the cases of these people. Dr. West had done research and published material on the 'DDD syndrome': the dread, debility, and dependence that result from being held incommunicado and tortured. We were making the argument in court that you could not rely on the testimony of witnesses who were being held incommunicado, brought into court in chains, and then dragged back again into detention. They have no access to lawyers, and we don't know whether they are speaking the truth or whether they are saying whatever will please their interrogators. Therefore, this evidence should not be used to convict. We didn't succeed in that case, which was *State v. Kader Hassim and Twelve Others*. It was a precedential case involving the Terrorism Act, but the prisoners were all convicted and sent to prison for periods of six to eight years on Robben Island, where Nelson Mandela was being held.

We appealed the Hassim case, which gave us cause to request permission to visit Robben Island Prison. I was probably the first woman to enter that prison as a lawyer. We found that no lawyers had been allowed in the Robben Island Prison for at least seven years before that. Prisoners would tell you that they had been very badly treated. It has all been documented in the book by Albie Sachs on prison conditions there. Prisoners weren't allowed lawyers. Supposedly, if they broke prison regulations, the authorities held an internal inquiry and subjected them to further punishment, six months of solitary confinement with a spare diet. But when we went into the prison, we were only supposed to speak about the appeal and nothing else.

The prison visits were out of hearing but within sight. The warder watched through the window, but we knew that the whole conversation was being taped. We would communicate in writing, and then erase what we had written. In this way, we learned about prison conditions. The authorities would do things like increase the number of prisoners in a cell from twenty to eighty without increasing the food supply. The prisoners weren't allowed to study and couldn't get law books, although there were three lawyers among them. One of the prisoners, who was a lawyer, drew up a petition setting out their grievances. Kader Hassim handed this petition to a prison official and was promptly thrown into six months of solitary confinement.

After I left the prison we waited for the wives to have an official visit. The wives were able to visit about three times a year. It was a very difficult trip because of the rough seas. The boat would lift right up into the air and bang down on the waves again. Everybody was sick, so we used to take Dramamine before we got there and fast the whole day. The boat left at 8:00 in the morning and returned at 4:30. So it wasn't the usual lawyering, where you could control your own hours. But the idea was for the wives to bring an application to court, asking what the rights of prisoners were. Inside the prison there was a discussion about it, and Nelson Mandela was of the view that an application might be lost, which would close doors, and that it would be much better to negotiate for privileges and rights. Kader Hassim disagreed, arguing that conditions had not improved over the past seven years, and there wasn't even access to lawyers. So the application was filed.

Of course, the prison denied that Kader Hassim had been sentenced to six months in solitary. They said that he had been segregated, that it was a prison practice to segregate prisoners so that they knew how to classify them. While the case was going on, I was visiting Robben Island for consultations on the appeal and was to learn from Kader Hassim that this was not true. He drew a description of the card outside his cell door, which read in Afrikaans, 'SIX MONTHS' SENTENCE IN SOLITARY.' The court's verdict was that a prisoner has a right to a trial and a right to a lawyer. Thereafter, prisoners on Robben Island had access to lawyers. The case was widely publicized in the newspapers because, for the first time, it spelled out the rights and privileges of prisoners.

The next major political trial in which I acted as defense attorney was an ANC trial in 1978. That was the case of Harry Gwala, the leader of the ANC for Natal Province, and nine other members of the ANC charged under the Terrorism Act. Harry Gwala had spent ten years in prison for a previous conviction. He was released and had several months of freedom before being charged again with nine others. Two of these men were exiles who had been living in Swaziland for five years. They were kidnapped from Swaziland and brought to trial in South Africa. Of course, this was disputed by the state. The state contended that the men voluntarily jumped over the fence on the border and fell into a police trap on the South African side of the fence. They couldn't explain why the police blackened their faces, why they were standing at midnight near the border fence, and why there were cuts and bruises on the wrists of the prisoners. The prisoners maintained that they had been handcuffed and dragged over the barbed-wire fence. They were also charged in common purpose under the Terrorism Act for plotting an armed overthrow of the government. We were able to produce evidence that each and every one of these men, although they were members of the ANC, were also deeply involved in the trade union movement and that they had been attending a meeting of trade unionists.

The state based its case on the evidence of another ANC member, Harold Nxasana, who stated that, at a meeting, the accused had discussed a document issued by the ANC in exile, supposedly dealing with the use of dead letter boxes to receive literature from the outside outlining how to disseminate pamphlets throughout the country and how to send people out for military training. My clients were deeply shocked by the testimony of Harold Nxasana, which they found to be untrue. Then, we heard from the witness's wife that she had managed to visit him in detention and that he told her that he had been brutally treated and forced to make a statement that pleased the police. He wept and begged to be returned to the witness stand, promising he would tell the truth to the court. He was recalled and recounted his ordeal of torture, which had permanently damaged his ear drum. They had put a wet sack over his head and subjected him to electric shock.

Each one of the prisoners suffered some kind of permanent damage. The security police used to boast to them that they had been trained by the CIA [Central Intelligence Agency] and were using the most advanced equipment from them, and that Scotland Yard was also helping them. Women were also detained. The wife of one of the men was detained, and she was released months later with a skull fracture which totally disoriented her. Harold Nxasana recanted his testimony and said he had been brutally tortured and that various suggestions for his testimony had been made to him. The judge ruled that he was simulating tears, that when he gave evidence for the first time he was speaking the truth and when he testified the second time he was lying, and that therefore the judge would rely on the first half of Nxasana's evidence to convict Gwala and the nine others of the crime of terrorism.

At this time we were able to call the American expert, Dr. West. We secured all the affidavits to show that the police used a system of unlawful methods of interrogation, including torture, as well as long hours of sleep and food deprivation and withholding of medicine. Harry Gwala was asthmatic and needed medicine. They detained his wife and children. His daughter was breast-feeding one child at the time, so they detained the baby with her. She was held for quite some time, although I was pleading with the security police to let the daughter and her baby go. I asked why they were being detained, as they were not going to be called as witnesses. He asked how old the child was, and I told him two years old. He said, 'Well, a black child of two is old enough to go and graze cattle.'

Dr. West came from California and gave his services to the case free of charge. His airfare was paid for by the Lawyers Committee for Civil Rights in Washington, DC. Our Supreme Court and our appellate division, which is the highest court in the land, recognized Dr. West as an expert and accepted his testimony on the effects of DDD syndrome on detainees, but the judge said, 'That's the way Communists behaved towards the American soldiers, that's not the way our security police treated these people.' The court chose to disbelieve the witnesses' evidence on torture and ill-treatment. It had no comment to make on the fact that people can be held indefinitely because the law provided for that. That was the whole purpose of the Terrorism Act. That was in 1979, and we lost the case. Five of them were sentenced to life imprisonment, and the others were sentenced to fifteen and eighteen years. They all went to Robben Island.

We appealed the Gwala case and simply lost. I visited Harry Gwala and the others who had been sentenced to life imprisonment, and I was so despondent. We had really done a good job in the defense, but our senior advocate was given literally no chance to even address the issues properly. I was feeling really conscience stricken that I had failed as a lawyer. But the prisoners said to me, 'You don't understand. This is a political struggle. We needed to defend ourselves in court. You played your role.' They added, 'Take our court record and go overseas. Get some judge to look at it and see whether the American judges would have convicted us on that.' They were encouraging me and pointing out that this was a political matter and that they were going to get out of Robben Island. That's the positive thing I came out of the prison with—the hopes of these men who were in for life. Nelson Mandela had already spent twenty-five years there, yet they were talking about coming out anytime. They did eventually release Harry Gwala from Robben Island, shortly before they released Nelson Mandela. He has some neurological disease which affected both his arms. They thought he was terminally ill and released him on compassionate grounds.

By 1980–81, after these experiences, I realized that I was deluding people into thinking that there was such a thing as achieving justice in our court system. I had reached the bottom line. In the meantime, all along I had been carrying on a normal law practice as well—doing the political cases, registering bonds and trusts, and defending somebody who had stolen five cents. Officials in the state government were misappropriating millions with impunity, and ordinary people were being charged with stealing five cents to buy food. One fellow was charged for staying overnight in a park even though he said he had nowhere else to go. He was sentenced to thirty days in prison. People who stole bread or fruit from a food store because they were hungry were being charged.

One day I saw an advertisement for a scholarship in the newspaper, and I wrote for an application. When the form arrived, I looked at the bottom and realized that I knew one of the persons listed, a John Samuels. I called him up and asked him whether the scholarships were open to all black people, including Indians and coloreds. He said yes and asked me who the application was for. I told him it was for me and explained that I wanted an opportunity to expose these cases and to study the reliability of evidence taken from detainees. It's because of what Harry Gwala and the others had said that I applied for the Harvard South Africa Scholarship.

So I had the good fortune of spending the year at Harvard in 1981–82. I worked on the LL.M. degree, the master's in law. I owe much of my subsequent development to Harvard. It helped me focus on human rights, women's rights, and labor issues, and gave me a broader perspective. I returned to Harvard in 1984, having been accepted for the doctoral degree in law, the S.J.D.—doctorate in juridical science. That was a first for the country when Harvard gave a doctorate to a South African. The papers insisted on saying a black woman was the first, instead of saying a person, a South African.

I left the cases for a while to acquire more skills. I realized that the way I had been conducting the cases, strictly focusing on legal issues, hadn't helped the clients. We needed more community involvement and more international focus on the injustices. We needed to get American judges involved to discuss this kind of evidence. I spoke to a number of American judges about this. While I was at Harvard, I took a class taught by Alan Dershowitz on human rights. Professor [Alan] Stone, a well-known psychiatrist at Harvard, also dealt with how incarceration affects people. The South

African courts were a no-win situation because the judges would say that their hands were tied because parliament was sovereign and they were obliged to enforce the law. We needed outside help. This is what I worked on from 1981 onwards, to create links with international human rights organizations and to get more media involvement.

I had already established clandestine links with Amnesty International as early as 1966. In 1970 there were no Amnesty groups in the United States, but there were groups in London and Europe. The purpose of those contacts with Amnesty was to get political prisoners and their families accepted. The prisoners I was representing were ANC, and Amnesty International had taken the position that they couldn't adopt prisoners who had chosen violent means as their method of struggle. For the first time I was able to explain to Amnesty groups that they should look at the defense put up by the people charged and not at what the state alleged. In most cases the accused said that they had not resorted to violence. We sent out information to Amnesty about prisoners and children in detention. We managed that by traveling to Swaziland or Lesotho to post things or asking people who were going abroad to take them. Students would ask how lawyers could function under apartheid. We had to be very careful. A conviction results in being struck off the roll because you owe allegiance to the state if you are a lawyer. That's why students kept asking how we functioned. I answered that we helped in defending people, in keeping them out of prison. When you are charged you want somebody to defend you. But often I played a different role from what is normally seen as a lawyer's role.

As lawyers, we distinguished between our role and the role of judges and prosecutors. We didn't think that black people should be prosecutors and judges because that meant implementing unjust laws. My youngest sister chose to become a prosecutor and that caused grave problems in our family. My husband still doesn't speak to her. He felt she joined the other side. She said she was doing a job as a professional, doing cases like theft and murder and all the common-law cases, and that in all her career she has never had a political case. She's now a magistrate. We maintained that many persons charged with crimes such as theft were also victims of the laws of apartheid.

In 1988 I was invited to join the Amnesty International Human Rights Now! concert tour to popularize the Universal Declaration of Human Rights. The tour was organized by Jack Healey and Jessica Neuwirth, whom I knew from Harvard Law School. Jessica had come to South Africa on a human rights fellowship to work with me and subsequently had gone to work for Amnesty International. I traveled on this world tour with Jack and Jessica, and with the musicians Bruce Springsteen, Tracy Chapman, Peter Gabriel, and Youssou N'Dour. By that time I had a passport, but there were sanctions and boycotts in place. Many countries wouldn't give a South African passport holder a visa. Japan, for instance, wouldn't even give a visa to people who were coming to trade with them. I was able to get most of the visas; the United States, Canada, England were no problem, and neither was India. African countries were a real problem, and Japan was a problem. I kept phoning the local embassy in Johannesburg. They said they would consult Tokyo and kept asking me so many questions. They also asked my husband whether he would grant me permission to go, and that's when I finally got the Japanese visa.

Despite the new government in South Africa, there is still a role for organizations such as the New Unity Movement. We do not take funds from anybody because we feel that imperialists have had a lot to do with perpetuating apartheid in South Africa. The battle for justice does not end with the Afrikaner government, but continues with all those people who have been taking profits and exploiting the resources and workers of the country, taking the money out of the country without giving anything back. We also object to the policies of such bodies as the IMF [International Monetary Fund] and so-called aid agencies which impose conditions and effectively lock countries up. We've seen it done in South America and in other parts of Africa. Puppet regimes have been established in Africa and supported by outsiders to further their economic purpose. Most people in South Africa do not view the struggle in this way. They feel that once you knock out the white government and put in a black government, everything will be different. It won't be. The ANC is still working on economic policy that will best serve the development of the people.

People who are all for free enterprise have the idea that with economic growth, everything will be all right. Economic growth functions in a particular way, and women have felt that not all initiatives and aspects affecting humanity are covered in the so-called economic growth theory. We see ourselves as heading for disaster and feel conscience bound to stick to our principles even though it has made the New Unity Movement very unpopular. One of our leaflets reveals the background of those in governmental positions who have records for misappropriation of funds, people who have committed murder and have criminal records. The New Unity Movement is a small voice, but it is not alone. PAC [Pan-African Congress] and the black consciousness movement, the Azanian People's Movement, are with them. The students at the campuses are with them. We might well have a black government in place, but all the structure of apartheid is still in place. We aim to carry on and popularize our ideas and we do it by education and critical study."

Notes

1. The New Unity Movement is a multiracial movement started in the early 1940s in Cape Province, with branches all over the country. Its program is for an end to apartheid, redistribution of land, equality between genders, and the right to work. The black consciousness movement was founded in the late 1960s by Stephen Biko.

2. Joseph Lelyveld, *Move Your Shadow: South Africa, Black and White* (New York: Random House, 1985), 82–84.

3. Navanethem Pillay, "The Role of a Conscientious Lawyer in the South African Legal System," *African Law Review* (October 1990): 24–27.

Part III

Seeking Environmental Justice

9 / Dollie B. Burwell

THROUGHOUT HER YEARS OF POLITICAL activism, Dollie Burwell has proved the power of the so-called powerless. Her organizing skills and ability to think creatively during times of crisis have enabled her to mobilize her own community and rural black neighborhoods within her state and across the country to rise up against injustice. She is a tireless worker, often staying up into the early hours of the morning to prepare for her next political forays. While disarmingly soft-spoken and quiet, she is fiercely committed to her battle for human rights.

Before assuming the leadership of the Warren County Environmental Justice Movement, Dollie had participated in civil rights activities with the Southern Christian Leadership Conference and the United Church of Christ's Commission for Racial Justice for more than twenty-five years. As a result of her many achievements in human rights she has been awarded the Southern Christian Leadership Conference's Woman Award for Outstanding Activism in Civil Rights, the Rosa Parks Award for Outstanding Leadership and Activism for Racial Justice and Human Rights, the Vance County Ministerial Award for Outstanding Community Service, the Ernest A. Turner Citizen of the Year Award for Outstanding Civic Leadership, and the Vance County African-American Leadership Caucus Award for Outstanding Leadership for Justice, Equality, and Human Rights. Her successes in leading the Warren County citizens against environmental racism led to her election as the first African American and the first woman to be selected as register of deeds for the county. She also served as a peace monitor and election observer during the first multiracial elections in South Africa in 1994.

Dollie was born in 1948 and grew up in rural Warren County, North Carolina, one of ten children. She became politically active when she was only twelve years old, working toward voter registration during the height of integration and the civil rights movement. She was involved in sit-ins to integrate lunch counters in Durham, Henderson, and Warrenton, North Carolina. In fact, she was suspended from school for her activities because her principal was afraid of the repercussions on his career and the school. Often working in dangerous situations, she helped the elderly overcome their fear of reprisal for voting and spent long hours bringing people from isolated rural areas to the polls. While still an adolescent, she revealed a passionate dedication to justice and civil rights.

Although raised in poverty, Dollie experienced a rich and loving family life, unaware of what lack of money meant until she wanted to attend college and discovered the cost of higher education. Undaunted, she took out student loans and worked while attending Durham College and Shaw University. Dollie married William J. Burwell in 1971, and they subsequently had two children: Kimberly, now twenty-one years old and herself an activist, and Wiletra, age fourteen. As a young army wife at West Point, Dollie immediately began organizing black enlisted couples who had experienced discrimination in finding housing and managed to get the offending parties dropped from the army's housing list. She also obtained a job in a predominantly white college near the base by visiting the president and threatening to file a lawsuit when she was turned down because of her race.

As soon as the couple returned to Warren County, Dollie resumed her civil rights work while raising her young family. She was also active in seeking to improve the schools and the conditions of women prisoners in her state, often ferrying family members for visits who would otherwise be unable to make the long trip. However, her true abilities would reveal themselves when the state of North Carolina selected Warren County as a burial site for thirty thousand cubic yards of soil contaminated with highly toxic polychlorinated biphenyls (PCBs). She then became the lead organizer of one of the largest civil rights demonstrations since the 1960s, a highly publicized protest campaign that would earn her the title of "Mother of the Environmental Justice Movement," by environmental justice activists.

In 1978 the Raleigh-based Ward Transformer Company illegally sprayed thirty-one thousand gallons of PCB fluid along 240 miles of North Carolina roadways in fourteen counties, the largest PCB dispersion in U.S. history.[1] In some areas, the concentrations were two hundred times above the level the Environmental Protection Agency (EPA) designates as the criterion for contamination. The state had a number of options for disposing of the waste and in 1982 decided to bury it within the state with monies provided by the EPA's superfund, which finances the disposal and storage of hazardous wastes. EPA guidelines required that in selecting a site, the bottom of the landfill be at least fifty feet above the groundwater and that it be located where there are "thick relatively impermeable formations such as large-area clay pans."[2] Although Warren County was selected as the site for the landfill, it hardly fulfilled these criteria, given the presence of a high water table only five to ten feet below the surface, the fact that residents derived all their drinking water from local wells, and the predominance of sandy, permeable soil. Yet, the EPA waived the guidelines in this instance. Given that Warren County's population was predominantly black and one of the poorest in the state, there appeared to be a clear link between human rights and environmental policies.

Urged by Dollie and Ken Ferruccio, another Warren County resident, community members began discussing the problems of the siting of the landfill and educating themselves on environmental issues. By inviting speakers such as Lois Gibbs, organizer of New York's Love Canal residents, and William Sanjour, branch chief of the Environmental Protection Agency's Hazardous Wastes Management Division, the citizens learned that landfills inevitably leak and that safe landfill technology was not yet a reality.[3] They linked their growing environmental knowledge to the political and economic factors behind the choice of location when they discovered that the site would be three miles from a new regional industrial wastewater treatment plant, connected by pipeline to one of the potential industrial parks. Residents of Warren County also discovered that the state's selection of the site was based on the need for a legal chemical waste dump and that the landfill would have to store waste not only from the state but imported from various parts of the region as well.

During August 1982 the residents filed a suit in district court for an injunction to halt the construction of the landfill. The injunction was denied on the grounds that there was no evidence to support the claim that the decision was motivated by race. The community then turned to direct action and engaged in protests throughout the six weeks that the state trucked the waste to the landfill. During that period, the state transported 7,223 truckloads of waste to the twenty-acre landfill through a gauntlet of persistent and determined citizen demonstrations.[4]

Although the protest failed to prevent the landfill from being completed and the Concerned Citizens' Group led by Dollie and Ken Ferruccio is currently pressuring the state to detoxify the landfill as soon as possible, the community won some concessions from the governor. These were that no more landfills would be built in Warren County and that well water would be monitored. However, the protest had an unexpected effect. It was the first time in U.S. history that over five hundred people had been arrested for direct action against environmental injustice, and it demonstrated that grass-roots activism was a viable route to securing human rights as well as an example to communities around the country, providing them with expertise as well as leadership. That activism ultimately provided the impetus for the 1992 federal law on environmental justice. The Warren County protest also succeeded in getting more African Americans elected to political office locally, statewide, and nationally. In 1993 a newly elected black member of the state legislature successfully introduced legislation prohibiting hazardous and toxic waste facilities within a one-hundred-mile radius of the county.[5]

Because of Dollie Burwell's efforts, a connection was established between human rights and environmental justice. A General Accounting Office study sponsored by Congressman Walter Fauntroy, who had marched with Dollie, revealed that all of the hazardous and toxic waste facilities in the South were in predominantly black and poor communities. That study inspired the Commission for Racial Justice of the United Church of Christ to compile a report in 1987 on toxic wastes and race. The findings revealed environmental injustice on a national scale and received widespread attention, leading to the first People of Color Environmental Summit in October 1991, in Washington, DC. Based upon these and other reports, Benjamin Chavis, former executive director of the NAACP, defined environmental racism as "racial discrimination in environmental policy-making and enforcement of regulations and laws, the deliberate targeting of communities of color for toxic waste facilities, the official sanctioning of the presence of life-threatening poisons and pollutants in communities of color, and the history of excluding people of color from the environmental movement."[6]

From the beginning, Dollie has insisted that the siting of hazardous wastes is not an isolated problem: it has ramifications not just throughout the United States, but for the world, especially for Third World countries that are too often the recipients of waste from the industrialized West. When Dollie traveled to South Africa to help monitor the elections, she brought her expertise in environmental affairs to that country and helped to widen the network of global concern. Her years of experience within her own community have helped her to redefine the community as worldwide and to take the lead in urging us to transcend race and class in confronting the problems of environmental justice.

DOLLIE SPEAKS

I think some environmentalists see the environment as being this place in space, or this place out on the ocean. It doesn't make any difference what you do for the whales if little children are dying of lead poisoning or dirty water and pesticides. You've got to save the people first.

"I was around 12 or 13 years old at the height of the civil rights movement when my older sister and I were involved in sit-ins and in efforts to integrate the lunch counters in Durham, Henderson, and Warrenton, North Carolina. In fact, I was suspended from school because my principal didn't want me to be involved in after-school activities he feared might jeopardize the school. He was a black principal. In rural communities, even now, the older educators are really intimidated by the system. To this day I'll have teachers call me and say 'I can't get equipment, I can't get books for my classroom, and I think something needs to be done about it but I don't want my name used.' They still have that sense of intimidation.

Right after that I began massive voter registration drives with the Negro Voters League in Vance and Warren Counties. (This was between 1959 and 1960.) I would go with my neighbor, who worked as a secretary for the only black attorney, Charles Williamson. She was always involved, and my older sister and I would accompany her. My parents were not that active, but they encouraged both me and my sister to be.

Dr. James Green was another person who influenced me because he was leading a Negro League. For the most part these were people who didn't depend on the system. Unlike teachers, they had their own businesses and were therefore independent enough to lead that kind of movement.

From there I began participating in trying to integrate the schools with marches. This took me up to about the middle 1960s. I've always been a member of the United Church of Christ, which has a field office in Raleigh, North Carolina. My pastor, Reverend Leon White, was the director of that field office. So, naturally, I was encouraged to take part in the demonstrations and marches it sponsored.

I must have been about fifteen or sixteen when the schools in Henderson were being integrated. I remember marching from the black junior college, Kittrell College, downtown. We were trying to march to the courthouse. All I could remember was a huge fire with Klan members and the police everywhere. I remember Reverend Ben Chavis, the former director of the NAACP, was working with the Commission for Racial Justice, and we were marching with him. He was very young then, probably no more than eighteen or nineteen.

Then I got involved with the Southern Christian Leadership Conference when they would hold meetings at some of the historically black colleges in North Carolina, like St. Augustine's College. I also became active with SNCC (Student Nonviolent Coordinating Committee). I worked with the Southern Christian Leadership Conference [SCLC] and the Commission for Racial Justice in sit-ins and demonstrations all over the state and even throughout the country when there would be communities who needed help organizing. In the small communities there would only be a minister and one or two other leaders doing all the work. They would call SCLC, and SCLC would call us.

Sometimes I've driven all night, or I've taken a group of young people on a bus. As soon as we arrived, we participated in a daylong march or demonstration. Since we didn't have money to stay in a hotel, we would get back on the bus. This was in the 1970s, after integration, when we could find a rest stop to use the sink for washing up and changing clothes.

I've always gone to where there has been a need. I realized how people coming into a community from the outside really motivates those who are struggling. I try to do it because I know how one can feel isolated and lose hope, but when others come in and relate some of their success stories, it gives people enough energy to keep on fighting the system.

I married in 1971. After my husband got out of the service and we moved back home, I started working in my own community again, doing voter registration, voter education, and becoming active with the Commission for Racial Justice, the North Carolina Black Caucus, and other organizations that were doing social justice work.

My daughter Kim was four when she started marching with me. On election day my children have worked at the polls. They've called people on the telephone to remind them to go vote. When I was pregnant with Mia, I would still participate in demonstrations and rallies.

My husband is very supportive, but he doesn't get involved. He works on election day and in voter education and voter registration. The only time he said Kim couldn't go with me was when she was old enough to want to go. It was when this young white guy in Forsythe County, Georgia, wanted to coordinate a Martin Luther King birthday march. As people began marching, the Klan started throwing rocks. They had run all the black folk out from that town years ago. It was on TV because I remember Oprah doing a show from Forsythe County. SCLC decided to try to pull together a march to support the black people and the white guy who organized the march and sent out a national alert to ask people to come to Georgia the next Saturday. The Klan appeared on television saying they were going to be ready for the marchers. Kim wanted to go with me, but her father said she couldn't, and she was really disappointed. I think that's about the only time that he has just said, 'No, your mother can go, but she's going to have enough to do to protect herself and so I don't want you to go.'

When I first heard that PCBs had been spilled along the roadside, the thing that puzzled me was that they knew about it before they actually caught the guy who did the dumping. They knew exactly where the spills were because they had posted signs along the roadsides in fourteen counties. Apparently this person opened a valve, drove some, cut it off, drove some more, going through another county, opened it back up, poured out some more, and just kept on until he got rid of all the PCBs.

When the state of North Carolina decided that the only thing they could do was to pick it up off the roadside and bury it in a county, I thought they were going to put it somewhere where the soil and the water table were suitable and that the operation was going to meet all the established criteria. From 1978 to 1982 they tested about ninety different sites in Warren County. When they first began testing, Warren County was last in terms of scientific suitability for a landfill site. Then, they conducted another study and Warren County suddenly became number one. We never figured out what happened to bring Warren County from last to first. They claimed that the roads in Warren County were not suitable for transporting PCBs, but they did nothing to improve them. The Department of Transportation changed the grading on some of the roads, but not enough to make any difference.

A lot of things that the state and the EPA did infuriated me. I knew that those of us who understood the danger of PCBs would have to educate the people. I felt that if the people came out in massive numbers and voiced their opposition that it would somehow make a difference. From 1978 until 1982 we worked to organize people and get them out to hearings. I lived within a three-mile radius of the proposed site, and I didn't want my children or any of the other children in that community to have to risk their health and life.

Even before the PCBs were placed in that landfill, Warren County had one of the highest cancer rates in the country. There's no hospital there, and people can't afford health care. Those folk who work in factories might have a minimal amount of health insurance, but they don't have insurance that would cover specialized testing for illness. So people have a tendency to go to doctors when they're just about dead. Warren County's lack of adequate health facilities was something that ought to have been taken into consideration because you know that landfill is going to leak. In a county like Warren County where you put a landfill, the risk to people's health is not going to be detected as early as it would in a community where people are going to the doctor every year for physicals and checkups. The government didn't organize any health surveys in Warren County. Health studies are only done in the more affluent areas. Knowing all this, I was just infuriated.

There could have been some technology to treat those PCBs along the roadside, but it was a matter of money. It was a whole lot cheaper for them to bury it in Warren County. That really made me work night and day to try to keep them from doing it. For me it was really not a just an environmental situation. It was a justice issue. Because I've worked all my life around social justice, this was just another social justice issue.

I called all the civil rights organizations for help. The Commission for Racial Justice and SCLC were the major organizations that came in; at the time I served on boards for both of those organizations. There was a real shortage of people with the ability to get people to speak out against anything in Warren County. The general attitude of black people is, 'We're a poor county, we shouldn't expect anything.' You have to make people feel that they can make a difference, and I think for many of the people in Warren County, knowing what grew out of their struggle makes them feel empowered, that little people can make a difference.

What really started the whole thing was our civil disobedience campaign. Two weeks into the trucking of PCBs into Warren County, we were marching every day. I was one of those found guilty for impeding traffic. On the first day we had about one hundred people arrested when the trucks saw that people were already lying down on the road and causing them to stop. It wasn't as if the people walked out in front of them. The people were already there so they didn't actually impede the trucks.

That particular day I knew the trucks would be carrying PCBs and I didn't know whether a truck could turn over or would hit us. We were reminded that Dr. King said that if you have not found anything worth dying for, then you're not fit to live, and that's how we basically felt. Everybody who went out there to march knew they could lose their lives and that if that was what it took for them to stand against a powerful government, then that's what they were going to do.

Anytime you saw the state people, they were covered from head to toe in white gear, wearing breathing masks, but we didn't have that. If a truck had turned over and spilled stuff on us, we weren't equipped, so when I got up and got my daughter ready for school, I didn't want her there with me. I don't know if my husband would have allowed her to go with us. He left for work around seven that morning, and my daughter normally catches the bus about 7:30. I think to this day that she didn't say anything because she knew her daddy would have probably put his foot down. I dressed her, and when I said, 'Kim, you need to be getting out to catch the bus because the bus is going to be here in a few minutes,' she said, 'Mom, I'm going to go with you, I'm not going to school.' I told her, 'You know you need to go to school because this is very dangerous, we can get hurt. I know I'm going to jail and then you might be left by yourself.' I was a paralegal at that time, and she knew that juveniles were not going to be locked up in the cells but would be taken to Juvenile Hall where they could probably call somebody. So she said, 'Well, I have my aunt's telephone number, and if they lock me up they'll give me a phone call, won't they?' I said, 'Yes, I'm sure they'll give you a phone call.' She answered, 'If you're going to be alright, I'm going to be alright.'

She felt just as committed to doing it as I did. It shouldn't have mattered to me that she was a child because I was a child when my parents allowed me to become involved. So I said, 'Okay, we'll go.' After they had arrested me, I could see her talking to the press, and there were maybe one hundred people surrounding her. When the reporters saw her crying, they tried to get a story about this little girl who was afraid of going to jail, but she informed them that she was not afraid to go to jail, she was afraid that people were going to get cancer. By that time I was in tears. I wanted to get off the bus, and I didn't know why she was crying until about six that evening after I had gotten out of jail. Miss Austin, the jailer, came to me while I was in jail that afternoon to let me know that my sister had picked Kim up. When I got out of jail I stopped at a neighbor's house and watched the news. I saw her telling the news media why she was crying, so I felt better.

When we went to court we had about fifty attorneys who volunteered their time. The cases of all those people arrested the first day were dismissed because they were actually lying in the road; the trucks saw them and stopped on their own. The attorneys argued that these people didn't really impede traffic, so the judge dismissed all the cases.

The second day we were out there the highway patrol expected us to go all the way down to the entrance of the landfill, and they were all down there. We didn't go all the way down, and we actually stopped the trucks from going in. There were about five of us. Other people were on the sidelines unwilling to be arrested. When we saw the trucks coming, we stepped in front of them. An Episcopal minister was actually hit because the truck threw on its brakes and slid into him. We were standing up at the time we stopped the trucks, but then we sat down in the highway.

The troopers were way down near the entrance of the landfill, and the trucks were backed up for about four or five miles because they couldn't get past us. The troopers didn't know what had happened because they had no radios in the trucks, so they sent someone up to see what was going on at the church because they knew that the trucks should have been down at the landfill. When they sent the trucks up there everything was just in a panic, and we kept them off for about three or four hours. That was one of the reasons why I was found guilty.

As the demonstration kept going they kept trucking, so we had to be creative. We split up into little groups. We were putting people in cars or in vans and taking them to other counties they [the trucks] would have to pass to come into Warren County. Our people were all the way up in Vance County at one time, stopping the trucks even before they got to Warren County. The state called out the helicopters, notifying the police wherever we were blocking the trucks.

We had been marching for about two weeks when we had a special rally, inviting people from other counties and states to come in. There were buses from Alabama and everywhere that came in to march with us that day, including Walter Fauntroy (the District of Columbia's congressman), who chaired the board for the Southern Christian Leadership Conference. He was going to march with us for a little while that day and then he was going back because he needed to be on Capitol Hill, but I wanted to make sure he got arrested. I knew that we needed to do something to keep the media covering us, and so I convinced Walter that they would not arrest him because he had immunity as a congressman. He walked right out in front of the truck, kneeled down, and then other people surrounded him. Many important people joined Walter, and they started praying. Walter was telling the state troopers that he was a U.S. congressman and they couldn't arrest him. He was still hollering, 'You can't arrest me, I'm a U.S. congressman,' while they were taking him to the paddy wagon.

The troopers were really upset that day and charged everybody they arrested with impeding traffic and resisting arrest. They put Walter Fauntroy on a bus around nine in the morning and kept him in there all day. They had all these buses that they brought from the prison system to take us to jail. I think they arrested about fifty or sixty people that day, and they put Walter in the bus with all of these big fat people that they had to lift. They got so mad that they had to lift them that they charged them with resisting arrest because it took about eight or ten troopers to pick a person up. Walter's plane was still revved up at the local airport. They thought he would be back in an hour or two, but the troopers kept him in that bus until about seven that evening when the House representative from Durham came down and got Walter released. Walter was furious. The first thing he did when he returned to Washington was to order a congressional investigation into the siting of landfills.

Walter's congressional investigation was a fringe benefit for me because I just wanted the media. But when the congressional investigation was done it revealed that all of the hazardous and toxic waste facilities in the Southeastern region were located in predominantly black communities, where about 80 percent of the people lived below the poverty level. So Walter's investigation prompted the United Church of Christ's Commission for Racial Justice's study on toxic wastes and race.[7]

The media covered the whole story, not only about the siting but also about the cleanups, and that's when they discovered the EPA had been violating their own rules. Once the congressional report was completed, the civil rights organizations got angry, because they said, 'While we were fighting to ride in the front of the bus, the stuff they were putting in our communities was going to kill us off before we had a chance to enjoy riding in the front of the bus.' Once the civil rights organizations got involved, the Commission for Racial Justice, Ben Chavis, and others found congresspersons who would introduce legislation that promoted the signing of the Environmental Justice Act in 1992.

Until Warren County nobody recognized what was happening in the siting of hazardous or toxic waste facilities. People there really feel good about their struggle. Before Warren County we didn't have a board for hazardous and toxic waste management in North Carolina. No government agency had a toxic waste management board, and now we have a Southeast regional board on hazardous wastes. The government knew that it had to be more responsive now that people were aware of what was happening.

I think people in Warren County saw that even if you're poor and members of a minority, you can make a difference. It took the leadership of Ken Ferruccio and myself. Ken's not originally from Warren County, but he and his wife Deborah moved there a number of years ago. They liked Warren County because it was simple and the people were very nice. I thank God for them because it was hard enough for me. Ken is a very analytical person, and Deborah is a very emotional person. Just when you needed an outburst, Deborah would do it.

When I was in South Africa last year to help monitor the elections, we visited the University of the Witwatersrand. A professor there who was briefing our group mentioned that she had begun to do some work on the environment in South Africa and had heard about a study that was done in New York. I raised my hand and told her, 'I prompted that study. I'll make sure you get it.'

Every time I see any magazine, *Time* or even the *Southern Studies Magazine*, every article on the environment mentions the environmental justice office in Washington and refers to the demonstration in Warren County where more than five hundred people were arrested. I talk to other people in other counties where they've said to their people, if Warren County can do it, we can do it.

About two weeks after they had capped the landfill a parent called me because her child was nauseated and vomiting and complaining of stomach cramps. She told me that some other kids had been complaining about the same thing. I typed up a little notice and went to the school and asked the principal if he could give them to the kids to take home because I had called a meeting of all the parents. The principal, who was scared of the system, bless his heart, told me he had three more years before retirement and was afraid that the school would be closed if we said the children were getting sick. He didn't want to give the notes to the kids, so I stood outside of the school and as each child got on the bus, I handed them the note and told them to take it to their parents.

I requested the use of the school auditorium and set the meeting for that Tuesday night. I called the local media and told them that we were going to be meeting because some of the kids were sick. The media came out and started interviewing the kids, and the children told them, 'I am afraid, I don't drink the water.' Parents came and testified about how scared their kids were. As a result of that meeting, the state Health Department called in a doctor, who went to different schools and talked about PCBs. Even though she didn't tell them the truth, at least she relieved the children's fears that they were immediately going to get sick.

The state was supposed to be monitoring the landfill, but every time something happened we would always have to call their attention to it. When it rains in Warren County for four or five days, I know it raises the water table, and that really scares me. Four years after they capped the landfill, Ken Ferruccio happened to go down to the landfill because, like me, he worries about it. He saw it had ballooned up and called me. I went almost to the entrance and could actually feel the earth rumbling. We called the Department of Health and Human Services, and they sent out their safety people, who just cut a hole in the top of the landfill.

All the water in the landfill was creating methane gases. We didn't know what other chemicals were in the landfill at that time. When they put the PCBs there they told us that it was going to be a dry landfill, that it was supposed to have a pump that would force the water through this leach system to entrap any chemicals inside the lining. The pump is supposed to bring the water on top of the landfill, where the sun would evaporate it. But that system has not worked. When the PCBs were first placed in the landfill we had hired a scientist who worked pro bono because he knew we couldn't afford it. He told the state that the system was not going to work because of the slope of the site, the inadequate liner, and the sandy soil. When we saw that balloon in the fill, we asked the state to put filters into the vents to try to filter out some of the chemicals that may have been escaping in the air. The state of North Carolina refused to put filters on the vents. It may have cost $20,000, but what is $20,000?

Following that, my daughter Kim's fifth-grade teacher told me that she was always finding excuses for not going outside. She either had something that she wanted to read or something she wanted to do. I had a talk with Kim and some of the other kids who had been having problems going outside. Kim had told some of her good friends that she had read that methane gas travels in pockets, and that if you breathe a pocket of methane gas, it will kill you. So she had gone to school that year, afraid to go outside because she was afraid she would die before she even got out of fifth grade. We had another wave of demonstrations around then, trying to force them to put in filters, and they never did.

Pauline Ewall, the scientist we hired, said that the day they tried to test the contents of the landfill, they could hardly find soil dry enough to do any testing. It took them two days, instead of a few hours, to gather their samples because the methane gases were so strong in that landfill they were afraid it would burst. One of the things that Governor Jim Hunt said in 1982 was that technology was not available to detoxify the landfill at that time but that as soon as that would happen, he would assure the citizens of Warren County that he would work toward the detoxification of the landfill. Well, technology is available now (1994), and so what we are saying is that we don't want anything pumped out of that landfill, that we don't care how much it costs, that Warren County needs to be restored to where it was, that detoxification needs to happen.

The first day they were going to test we decided to hold a press conference because we wanted to let the media know that our goal is to hold the state to detoxification and that we want an on-site solution. When we told the state that we didn't want anything pumped out, the governor appointed a working group of about six or seven people from the state and about ten or twelve people from Warren County. That working group is jointly chaired by myself, Ken Ferruccio, and Henry Lancaster, who works with the Department of Health and Human Services. At a hearing, the Department of Health announced that they suspected there might be a million and a half gallons of water in that fill. I told them that I had been going all over this country talking to grass-roots groups and groups on environmental justice, and we know what has been happening and we don't want anything pumped. They were talking about pumping it out and sending it to Alabama, and I told them that people are already dying in Alabama because they're living with so many chemicals.

Bill Mayer, who was in charge of Health and Human Services, the Hazardous and Toxic Waste Division, said that before they could come up with a solution in terms of detoxification, they needed some scientific analysis. He told us that when the state is going to be paying a scientist, it has to put it out for bid. They always underestimate the intelligence of people in rural communities. So I said to him, 'As far as I'm concerned, that scientific expert has got to be someone who can translate highly technical things to grass-roots people in Warren County, and someone we can trust. If you have a scientist that's going to come and tell us nothing, and we don't trust him or believe him, the state will have thrown away its money because we're not going to accept what he may say.' We argued back and forth, and the people of Warren Country ended up hiring Pauline Ewall from Virginia.

The Warren County members of the committee wrote away for résumés from five scientists, asking them to explain their feelings about detoxification and whether they knew of any technologies that might be suitable for what was happening in Warren County.

Pauline's letter and her résumé were impressive, but what really mattered was that she was talking about highly technical matters in a way that we could understand.

While all this was taking place, you have to realize that I was poor, and I've become poorer since then because we have to pay for our phone calls and for our postage. Even when state people come to meetings, they are on salary. The last few meetings have been held in Warren County, but for the most part all the committee meetings have been held in Raleigh. When we drive to Raleigh we drive at our own expense. When they drive to Warren County they're getting mileage because they're working for the state. Ken and Deborah's telephone bill is astronomical. They are members of the Episcopal Church and I think one or two of the churches in the Episcopal diocese did give them some money to help with some of their phone bills, but basically you do this on your own.

The next hurdle was that the Department of Health wanted to use the state's lab because it was cheaper. We told them that if a test costs $1,500 and you do it in the state's lab and we have no confidence in the state testing, then they will have thrown away $1,500. A test done in another lab under Pauline's scrutiny that cost $2,000 is more valuable because at least we can have some confidence in that. So we were able to force them to do split sampling with Pauline, and she's going to use an independent lab.

Meanwhile, the state's tests revealed that dioxin might exist in the landfill, and they wanted to do further testing. But Pauline was not going to approve them retesting. Ken Ferruccio had called Vanderbilt University and talked with a professor who told him that the kind of test needed to determine that the dioxin came from the landfill would cost almost as much as detoxifying the landfill. We felt that rather than spending millions of dollars on trying to determine the presence of dioxin in the landfill, the state should spend that money on cleaning it up.

Pauline agreed with us. She believed the state knew that dioxin was coming from the landfill. She said the landfill was such a slushy mess, she would not approve further testing and advised us instead that we should try to clean it up. She views retesting as just another tactic the state is using. She is planning to call a press conference to reveal what she has actually found inside of the landfill and outside of the landfill and to explain her concern.

Some people don't want to believe that environmental racism exists and would rather say that environmental injustice is due to poverty rather than race. That may be because in 1994 people don't want to be reminded of the discrimination black people suffered in the past. I don't think it's any coincidence that toxic wastes are located in communities of black and Hispanic people. I don't think it's a coincidence that railroads run straight through the heart of black communities. It's a long-standing history that black folk live on the other side of the tracks. If you go into a community and you're looking for a black neighborhood, you find the railroad track and you cross it. There are not only hazardous industries located in black communities but also landfills and incinerators, and that's where the accidental spilling occurs. When you read about a train derailed that was carrying chemical waste, you can be sure that it is not in an affluent white community. Waste management companies looking for somewhere to put an incinerator or a landfill are not going to go in a country club area because the property values are so high. Property values are lower in black communities.

For me, the environment is where you work, where you play, and where you go to school. I think some environmentalists see the environment as being this place in space, or this place out on the ocean. It doesn't make any difference what you do for the whales if little children are dying of lead poisoning or dirty water and pesticides. You've got to save the people first.

I believe that environmental justice is a human right. Even though I live in a poor community where the land is cheap and the population is 85 percent black, I'm just as entitled to clean air and water. I'm just as entitled to be free of industry's pollutants and toxic waste incinerators sited in my community as those people who live near the country club. Their right to life is no greater than my right, their children are no more deserving of human life than my children, who are poor and have to live in Warren County. I believe that environmental justice as a human right is what we all ought to be demanding because the Bible says what you do to the least of these, you do to me. I think those of us who have clean environments ought to fight too because sooner or later we are going to run out of space, and of black and poor neighborhoods, and it's going to come back to the rich neighborhoods.

The county movement is going to link globally. The People of Color Environmental Summit that was called by the United Church of Christ's Commission for Racial Justice in 1992 really gave me hope of achieving that because there were people from Mexico and Third World countries that attended. For me, that redefined the movement. At that summit a set of environmental principles was adopted, and those principles were sent to all the traditional environmental groups. Those principles basically sought to ensure that as we fight for environmental laws, we must ensure that we protect the Third World countries.

I often say that if you could be a mother you could do anything because mothers have a special gift of intuition and sensitivity. Even when you have not won a victory, you have a sense that you have because you have inspired other women to speak out against something. I think women have a natural organizing ability, mothers especially, because raising children brings out gifts that men are not equipped with. If I'm trying to organize women I say that they could be on the city council, for instance. The women who were out there and supportive from the very beginning against the burial of PCBs may not have had any more than a fourth- or fifth-grade education, but they could see themselves being in that position, and, therefore, they could see me. You really have to make women appreciate what they do every day in their homes as mothers, and then they develop a greater appreciation for what they can do. When you have raised four or five children you have accomplished a great task.

I think being a mother enhances rather than conflicts with being an activist. I think you find the most dedication and commitment in women who are struggling from their mothers' example. Most of the five hundred people who went to jail protesting the placing of PCBs were women. I would say the majority of those women were mothers. I go to school board meetings and I fight with superintendents and teachers as if I had a child in the school system because I am a mother. Once you have a child, every child becomes your child. As I think about my children in the future, I think about all children in the future. I guess God decided, 'I'm going to give this woman a husband who's not going to conflict with what she's committed to doing.' I feel like God has special blessings for those of us who really dare to speak out and become committed. My husband has always been very supportive, and sometimes when people ask him why he's not as active as I am, he'll say, 'Well, somebody's got to pay the bills.'

I believe that the greatest thing you have to give is your service. I always tell my children the greatest thing you have to give doesn't cost any money. It's your service. I think that I could not be as compassionate about giving if I were not a mother. For the most part the people I work with on behalf of social justice are women. You don't find the egos. When you come together as women to get something done, you just do it, and you don't have to struggle with each other over who's going to speak to the media or who's going to do another task.

What I'd like to try to do is to pull together an environmental justice movement that overcomes racism, classism, and sexism. Though we need to recognize that environmental racism exists, we shouldn't let that separate us in working for environmental justice. A clean environment is a human right for every boy, girl, man, or woman; that realization alone can pull us together. There's a place in this movement for human rights and environmental justice for the wealthiest white affluent person. You don't have to be poor and black or female to work for human rights. We need not let those '-isms' prohibit us from coming together and working for justice.''

Notes

1. Jenny Labalme, *A Road to Walk: A Struggle for Environmental Justice* (Durham, NC: Regulator Press, 1987), 2–3.

2. Ibid., 3.

3. Robert D. Bullard, ed., *Unequal Protection: Environmental Justice and Communities of Color* (San Francisco: Sierra Club, 1993), 50–52.

4. Labalme, *A Road to Walk*, 5.

5. Adaora Lathan, "Dollie Burwell: Standing Up for What's Right," *Audubon Activist* 7, no. 8 (May 1993): 8.

6. Bullard, *Unequal Protection*, xi–xii.

7. Commission for Racial Justice, United Church of Christ, *Toxic Wastes and Race in the United States: A National Report on the Racial and Socio-Economic Characteristics of Communities with Hazardous Waste Sites* (New York: Commission for Racial Justice, 1987).

10 / Juana Beatrice Gutiérrez and the Mothers of East Los Angeles

JUANA BEATRICE GUTIÉRREZ, PRESIDENT OF the Mothers of East Los Angeles, Santa Isabel Chapter, was born in rural Mexico. In 1952 she moved to El Paso, Texas, where she met her future husband, Ricardo Gutiérrez, a U.S. Marine. They married in 1956 and moved to East Los Angeles, where they have lived for forty years. Juana is the mother of nine children, the grandmother of twelve, and a powerful political leader. In 1994 she received the National Association for Bilingual Education's President's Award as its Citizen of the Year for her achievements in her community, and the following year President Bill Clinton honored Juana and the Mothers of East Los Angeles (MELA) at a White House ceremony for winners of a yearly award for voluntary organizations. Juana was also nominated by Congresswoman Lucille Roybal-Allard (D-CA) for the Mujer Award, sponsored by the National Hispaña Leadership Institute, which she received in Washington, DC, in September 1995. Despite her age, Juana typically rises at 5 A.M. to begin a long day that intertwines political activity with household chores. Her face reveals a woman of courage and commitment as well as the trials of struggling for the dignity of her people.

The Gutiérrez house in Boyle Heights is adjacent to one of the largest freeways in the state and a reminder that Mexican-American neighborhoods have been the recipients of prisons and hazardous industries rather than social programs and infrastructure. East Los Angeles houses 75 percent of the city's prison inmates; Whittier Boulevard, which runs into their street, is the location of five hazardous waste sites; and the nearby community of Vernon is one of the city's worst polluters. These are injustices that Juana Beatrice Gutiérrez has worked to reverse.

Her home on South Mott Sreet in East Los Angeles is a hub of activity, with people typically gathered around the front yard deep in discussion. Upstairs hums the office of the Mothers of East Los Angeles, a highly effective political group that has battled against environmental and other injustices since 1985. This combination of home and work symbolizes the synthesis that Juana has made between the public and the private. The well-being of her family and the families within the district are the impetus for her political activities, and her overflowing house reflects the energy and agenda of a woman who has transformed the meaning of motherhood to include political activism. She is supported in this endeavor by Ricardo, who has participated in the Mothers' demonstrations and serves the movement in a number of different ways. However, while an active leader of the MELA, Juana does not wish to be singled out, and she continually stresses the collective aspect of the movement as well as its reliance on her Latino people. The clean, well-lit park directly across the street from her house is the setting for a variety of youth programs and proof of the Mothers' long-term efforts to create a safe, drug-free neighborhood. Walking the streets of Boyle Heights, one feels surrounded by a community that has fought to control its destiny and that actively participates in social improvement on an ongoing basis.

The Mothers of East Los Angeles was created in 1985 to oppose a proposed state prison on the Crown Coach site, near the heavily populated Boyle Heights and its thirty-three schools. Today, the organization includes about three hundred members, all longtime residents of East Los Angeles and of similar backgrounds. Most of them had been already active either within parishes, the schools, or labor support groups and were able to transform these traditional resources in order to address political issues.[1] They were, therefore, well prepared to respond to yet another threat to the well-being of their children. The community as a whole was outraged both by the selection of the site and the secrecy with which the project was handled. The Department of Corrections developed its proposal for the prison in 1984, violating its own policy by not seeking neighborhood input and by postponing an environmental impact report until after the purchase of the site.[2]

Juana was alerted to the proposed construction by a state assemblywoman, Gloría Molinas, who had a history of championing Latino causes. Father Juan Moretta of the Resurrection Church also contacted Juana because he knew that once the women were involved, the district would be mobilized. It was not difficult for her to respond to these calls because she long had been active and had organized a Neighborhood Watch Committee of Mothers, which successfully eliminated drug dealers and gangs from the area. She and her Neighborhood Watch captains responded with intense grassroots activity, going from door to door to inform people and gathering signatures for a petition. The Mothers' experiences as community workers and the networks they formed for the safety of their children provided both the core membership and the foundation for their foray into the political arena. They also availed themselves of their church affiliations, announcing their meetings in parish bulletins and holding gatherings in the churches after services.

Juana and the Mothers formed a coalition with a number of other organizations in the area, including the Central City Business Association and the Boyle Heights Kiwanis Club. They organized weekly Monday-night candlelight vigils and marches on the Olympic Boulevard Bridge that drew more than three thousand people and attracted media attention and support from other communities. At one demonstration they assembled seventy-five hundred people on the bridge. The leaders of the protest had to stop more supporters from coming to prevent the structure from collapsing under the weight of the demonstrators.[3] They traveled 350 miles by bus to lobby state assemblypersons in Sacramento and developed a research and information campaign so that all community members could participate and respond to the media.

Meanwhile, Juana and the Mothers confronted the state Department of Corrections and Governor George Deukemejian in state and local arenas. They would find out when he would be making appearances and then turn up unannounced, holding press conferences to keep their struggle before the governor and in the public eye. Because of the MELA's intense lobbying efforts and the media coverage they obtained, the state senate ultimately reversed its position of support for the construction of the prison.[4]

One year later they were faced with yet another challenge when the state planned to construct an incinerator in the nearby community of Vernon—already the county's worst polluter—disgorging twenty-seven million pounds of toxic chemicals into the air, land, and sewers. The projected facility would have burned 125,000 pounds of toxic wastes daily in the Mothers' backyards.[5] Three years previously, Cerrell Associates, a consulting firm, had prepared a report for the California Waste Management Board, advising government and industry to target "lower socioeconomic neighborhoods" for waste facilities.[6] The report also provided profiles to aid in the selection of sites, claiming that "middle and higher socioeconomic strata neighborhoods should not fall within the one-mile and five-mile radii of the proposed site. Conversely, older people, people with a high school education or less are least likely to oppose a facility."[7] By its actions the MELA would reveal the hollowness of that evaluation.

The South Coast Air Quality Management District and the state Department of Health Services insisted that the incinerator would have no impact on the community and that California Thermal Treatment Services (CTTS), which would carry out the project, was not required to file an environmental report, despite the fact that it had been cited on numerous occasions for health and safety violations at its incinerators in other locations.[8] While fighting against the prisons, the MELA took up the gauntlet against the incinerator and joined with a number of other groups, including Greenpeace and the Natural Resources Defense Council. In December 1987 the Mothers led a delegation of five hundred community members into a Department of Health Services hearing to demand an environmental impact report. They also maintained their contacts with state assemblypersons, especially with Lucille Roybal-Allard, who had replaced Gloría Molinas, and participated in a suit against California's Department of Health Services for approving the incinerator without an environmental impact report.

The Mothers were faced with yet another issue when, in 1987, the state announced a plan to build an oil pipeline from Santa Barbara County to Long Beach, bypassing the affluent coastline areas of Santa Monica and Pacific Palisades and detouring twenty miles inland near several schools in the Boyle Heights area before returning to the coast. Because the pipeline was to be located only three feet below ground, residents were concerned about gas leaks or a major explosion. Juana and the Mothers actively joined the Coalition against the Pipeline and spent weeks on the telephone, mobilizing more than one thousand people. They participated in a heated exchange with representatives of the oil companies, challenging the projected route for the oil pipeline and demanding to know why the coastline communities were not targeted. Ultimately, they were successful in defeating its construction as proposed.[9]

Confronting the problem of the incinerator transformed the MELA from a single-issue organization, expanding its agenda to include a clean environment, jobs in safe industries, and the promotion of the health and education of the community's children. The members wanted to prevent East Los Angeles from being the dumping ground for the waste resulting from the political and business elite's unchecked drive for profit that also left minority communities without educational or social resources. The following two years they blocked the construction of toxic waste incinerators and treatment plants on other sites, and their network expanded to different parts of the state as people began to hear about the MELA's work. They traveled to far-flung communities, lending their organizational skills; and, in turn, groups from Kettleman City [a mainly Hispanic area that houses the fifth-largest toxic landfill in the country],[10] Richmond, and Martínez, California, experiencing similar problems, came to march with the MELA.

The MELA's persistence against the prison and the incinerator bore fruit. On May 24, 1991, they were notified that CTTS had abandoned its plans to build the incinerator. The following year, on September 14, 1992, Governor Pete Wilson signed a bill terminating the prison proposal. Their political successes defied the characterization of Mexican Americans as locked into low political participation due to their religious traditionalism, cultural values, low income, and education. On the contrary, the MELA demonstrated how they could capitalize on their cultural attributes, including strong family, church, and neighborhood ties, to create an effective political force.

The Mothers then turned their attention to water conservation and to the elimination of lead paint. The water conservation program, initiated by Juana, joins the Metropolitan Water District with local water agencies, combining the goals of water conservation with community action. Responding to Boyle Heights residents' concerns about unemployment, the program creates new jobs for community members who are trained to install and distribute free ultra-low flush toilets. The revenue generated by this program has financed health insurance, medical assistance, immunization and lead testing, environmental awareness, and after-school programs. The Mothers are also active in bringing children to clinics to be tested for lead poisoning and to receive vaccinations. In 1994 the MELA initiated a number of new programs and services, including graffiti abatement, which reflected their view that the environment is all inclusive.

The MELA are supporters of Button Willow's and Kettleman City's battle against the placement of incinerators and are members of Women against Gun Violence, taking on the National Rifle Association.[11] They are also supporters of a number of environmental groups, including California Communities against Toxic Dumping, the Latino/Asian Coalition, and the Southwest Network for Environmental and Economic Justice. Moreover, they work closely with Concerned Citizens of Central Los Angeles on environmental issues.

Contrary to conventional political wisdom, the MELA have decided not to incorporate themselves or to create a bureaucratic structure, but rather to retain their organizational flexibility and spontaneity, scheduling meetings in response to crises. Refusing to accept funds from outside sources, they maintain their autonomy by holding parish breakfasts and founding their organization on broad community participation. Although the MELA is organized and led by women, it operates on the basis of family participation. Because their activism involves attending meetings, creating telephone chains, and conducting door-to-door visits, they have, out of necessity, included family members in these time-consuming efforts. While initially reluctant, many of the husbands have joined in the Mothers' political struggles and have become their ardent supporters. The Mothers also brought their children and grandchildren with them when they began to demonstrate, transforming the traditional definition of the family to include social and political work.

Juana Gutiérrez and the members of the MELA entered the environmental struggle with a rich historical legacy of community service. For these women, the environment, adequate housing, equal education, and economic and social justice are the foundation of human dignity. By their activism they reveal how human rights can be achieved through participatory democracy.

JUANA SPEAKS

There is no line between my family life, my work, and my community. I think that when we set out to do something because we believe in it and we work together, everything is possible. We are trying to stop the racial injustice of dumping toxic wastes in Latino communities.

"I was born in Zacatecas, Mexico, and grew up in Chihuahua and El Paso, Texas, and I've lived here in Los Angeles for forty years. I have nine children, four boys and five girls, all born here in East Los Angeles. All of them went to private schools, first Santa Isabel Catholic School, then the boys went to Cathedral High School and the girls to Sacred Heart of Jesus High School. Afterward, they all went to the universities. I have one in Loyola, one in Arizona State University, one in Pasadena State College, two in East Los Angeles College, two in Princeton University, and two in Santa Barbara State College. I also took care of three other children. I never worked outside of the house, but I made products to sell outside. Only my husband worked.

When my kids grew up and attended grammar school, I started to work in the community. I started in the PTA [Parent-Teacher Association], then I organized sports programs for the schools, sports programs in my playground, and summer programs to occupy the children. After this, I organized a Neighborhood Watch program in this area, because this area was dangerous when my children were growing up, and there were a lot of problems in the playground with drug dealers and gangs. I organized the watch because some of my neighbors said they wanted to leave, but I didn't want to, this is my home. I went door to door to talk to people and drew up a bilingual letter in English and Spanish for the whole area. Some families said, 'No, I don't want to sign any letter, because I'll have problems with the gangs,' and I answered, 'You won't have any problems because nobody knows who signed. I will bring the signatures to the city councilman.' He helped me a lot because I asked for more protection from the police and for lights on the playground because we had neither lights nor a playground director. After I had gathered all the signatures, we had a director, lights, and more police and cleaned up this area. I did this for all the children, not just for my kids.

I have organized Neighborhood Watch captains on every block. We have meetings and exchange information. We talk to the police and bring back information to the neighbors. We have a communication network, telephone numbers for all the neighbors, and all the members have my telephone number. When something happens, the telephones ring. When they see suspicious people, everybody comes out. Sometimes people come from other areas to buy and sell drugs, but when they see all of us coming out of our houses, they just leave. We don't have to call the police. Sometimes when I have meetings with the police chief, I tell him, 'I never saw that police car around the park. Why? Are you sick?'

In 1985, Assemblywoman Gloría Molina's assistant, Marta, called me and said, 'Gloría wants to have a meeting with you and the leaders of the community.' We settled on a day and time, and I called my Neighborhood Watch captains from Santa Isabel, Dolores Mission, and other parishes. I organized a meeting in my house and called the parish priest and my captains from the neighborhood. All these women, my husband, and the priest met with Marta, Gloría's assistant. She told us that Gloría found out that the governor's commission had plans to build a state prison in our neighborhood. Then Gloría addressed us. After she spoke, she said, 'Now you know the problem. What are you going to do about it?'

The first thing I did was to inform the community and our parish and different parishes in East Los Angeles. I asked our parish priest to let me talk to people on Sunday after Mass and he said, 'Yes, go talk to the people and inform the community.' I got people to collect signatures in the various parishes. My husband went to Santa María, I gathered them in Santa Isabel. Soon we assembled nine hundred people in church on a Sunday because nobody wanted a prison here. We need schools, not prisons. After four or six months, we were working in the community, and we were also working with Gloría.

She brought our signatures to Sacramento. Then, Father Moretta from the Resurrection Church came and asked me, 'Juana, what are you going to do against the prison?' I answered that we would try to do something, but we didn't have power. He said, 'Go to other parishes, Santa Isabel, Dolores Mission, Talpa Church, and Resurrection Church, and have meetings.' At the meetings he suggested the name 'Mothers of East Los Angeles.' We have Mothers of East Los Angeles in Talpa, Resurrection, Dolores Mission, and Santa Isabel. Everybody liked the name. He said it was like the Mothers of the Plaza de Mayo and suggested we use the white handkerchiefs like the Mothers of the Plaza de Mayo because that would make us look more like good mothers. However, I told him that when I'm mad, I'm not a good mother; when I have problems, I'm not a good mother.

I gathered a coalition against the prison, including the Chamber of Commerce and different clubs with the help of the priest. Everybody worked together, and we organized marches. Every Monday at 6 P.M., for more than a year, we marched with candles from the Resurrection Church to Olympia and Santa Fe Avenues. When we started we had only one hundred Mothers and some husbands, because our husbands support us, especially my husband. We had telephone committees, information committees, news and television committees, media committees, and communication committees. When we were facing the prison and incinerator problems we had more than four hundred members. Now we have around three hundred Mothers.

We fought for eight years against the prison and we fought for seven years against the construction of an incinerator in our area. We also opposed the construction of a Chemclear toxic plant three feet from a local high school, so we had three victories in the same year. I don't consider this only the Mothers' victory, but also a community victory because everyone worked together. We started with the Mothers, then the fathers, sons, daughters, the whole family joined. The Mothers were the leaders. My husband and another father made the posters and helped with the march. The first time the politicians and the governor said that the prison and the incinerator were going to be built here, only Gloría Molinas supported us. After we demonstrated our power, the politicians came to support us.

We work very hard on the environment. Since our success with the incinerator problem, everybody calls the Mothers to support them with their own environmental programs. We go from San Francisco to Richmond to support people who don't want incinerators in their communities. These people are also mothers with community support. We go and have meetings in Santa María and San Diego. We have a statewide network of Mothers. We are members of the labor committee of El Pueblo para el Agua y el Aire Limpio

(People for Clean Water and Air) of Carmen City and Fathers for a Better Environment of the North Side.

We talk to students in various universities: the University of California at Northridge, Loyola College, Pasadena and Claremont Colleges. We try to convince them to become involved, not only to attend classes but to become aware of the problems in the community. The environmental problems are the biggest ones we are facing now. The big corporations have a lot of money so they are able to get permits from the governor and the health department. The governor's commission has lawyers for all these corporations. We are trying to stop the racial injustice of dumping toxic wastes in Latino communities.

A half mile from where I live the city burns toxic wastes, and there are a lot of plans to dump toxic wastes in our communities. We have a lot of kids in the area with lead in their blood. I bring many children to the clinic to be tested. Once lead is in the blood, it's there forever, affecting the brain. It mainly affects children between two and six years old. Studies have recently shown that when these girls grow up, they are infertile. Also, children who have lead poisoning have no energy. We have ten high school girls working with us who go door to door with flyers and information about lead poisoning from the health department. These students convince parents to have their children get checkups.

We have a recycling plant for car batteries in our neighborhood, which we are fighting against. We don't want to shut it down or to create unemployment, but to make sure it obeys the laws protecting the environment. One of our biggest problems are the body shops where they repair cars. We may look at these garages and wonder how they affect us. We can't overlook all the toxic chemicals they use and the waste dumped into the area, affecting our people's lives. We have reported many owners of these shops, and they have started to comply with the law. They know it is the Mothers' work to look after this.

We also compile reports on the working conditions in these shops for a special agency that is supposed to protect workers. Students in UCLA who are studying urban planning or the environment conducted a joint study with us on body shops. They discovered that, in order to handle all the chemicals safely, workers need gloves and special equipment but the employers refuse to provide these. We report this. We requested that the warning signs be posted in Spanish and English because many workers can't read English. We also have an environmental engineer who volunteers his services and represents us in our meetings with the health department and EPA agencies because the employees of those agencies use very technical language which we cannot understand.

We now have a water conservation program, an immunization program, and a lead poisoning program. We have support from the health department for these. We have ten high school students working on the lead poisoning problem who are paid. We are financed by the water conservation program, which gives us $25.00 for each toilet we give to the community. For this we pay twenty-eight employees, with the adults receiving $8.80 an hour, the kids $7.00, and the supervisors $9.00, and everyone also gets insurance. We pay for all the office equipment and for the van rental because we need it to transport the employees in the community. After we take care of all these bills and workers and insurance, we have a little left in the bank, which is community money for our scholarship program.

We have raised $70,000 for scholarships. Students get scholarships on the basis of need, not because of their grades. Then, they come back and stay in the community. We have sent students to Harvard. We give scholarships to high school students to keep them in school. We had a student whose father is very sick and whose mother is going to school. He told me he was going to quit school because his family didn't have money, although he is a very good student. We got him a $1,000 grant recently. Some of the high school kids get $300 for books and clothes. We don't want to give money to the schools because then the kids don't get anything. I made a buffet for one hundred and fifty people to raise scholarship money. The money we have after we pay all the bills and workers stays in the bank and is for the scholarships and programs for the future.

Now we are getting help from the health department. They have grants for salaries for young people to work with us, and we recently received a grant for $10,000. It's the first money we ever got from the governor because we never got money from any government. We made our own money by cooking breakfasts and dinners in the parish and having dances. This is the first and also the last. I don't want any money from the governor because when you get the money from another organization, you have to do what they want. I don't sell myself.

Most of the women in our organization were housewives and mothers. We have a lot who are working outside of the house, but their primary focus is their children. When we started, some of the husbands didn't want their wives to go out because they thought it would be a bad example. After these husbands saw how powerful we became, they came to the group too. I'm lucky because my husband and my sons and daughters help me a lot. The coordinator for the scholarship program is Beatrice, my daughter. The coordinator for the environmental program, Elsa López, is also my daughter.

When we have some issues, I ask the parish priest to let me use the church after Mass on Sunday. I tell him we have a problem or an event, and I want to talk to the people after Mass. We have a newsletter that our young people put together and a brochure. When we have meetings I put the notices in the parish newsletter. We meet every month and hold a general get-together every two months. When we have a problem we call emergency gatherings for the organizers, and I get on the phone. I have a secretary who sends out letters for the meetings, and we have a lot of volunteers from the community, but the responsibility is mine. I am the president. We have a vice president, a secretary, a treasurer, and coordinators for the projects. The board members are volunteers, but the coordinators get a salary. I ask people to join who I know are active in the community.

The project manager who works on water conservation is my daughter, Elsa. We have a manager for the lead poison program and the scholarship program. The graffiti program will have two college students, one to clean up the graffiti, one to paint murals for the walls, not only for here but for other areas.

In the graffiti program we have a girl from the Sacred Heart of Jesus, who is fifteen going on sixteen, and a young college student from the community to help us. People just come to me, especially from the universities, because I go to classes to talk and then the students ask if they can work with me. Right now, we are going to have two young people from Occidental College for the graffiti program because we had a conference there. We have applications to check people out because we want to know who really needs the work. This time we will have twenty slots for the summer program, and I have supervisors for them. These girls who work with us take a block a day, cleaning the streets and the sidewalks. They never stay by themselves. We go with them and bring them sodas and lemonade. I try and stay with them as much as possible so they don't have problems with the gang members. The other Mothers on the board come to make sure that everything is all right. We paint the Mothers' logo on every wall that we clean. People ask me how we dare to put this on walls around the gangs. I do it anyway, but I have also talked to the mothers and grandmothers of gang members, telling them that if I see the name of their son or grandson on the wall, I'll report them.

I would like to do more, but I can't because I don't have the money. I would like to do something for the senior citizens, too. Sometimes we take them in the van and bring them to Las Vegas or Santa Barbara because some of these people have never left Los Angeles. They've gone only from their home to church and back again. Next month [July 1994] we are bringing twenty-five students to Mono Lake for one week of camping. My husband and I are going with them. Another group will bring more children, seventy-five in all, for a summer camp.

I never stop. Sometimes I have two or three meetings a day. I am a member of the Mexican Mothers of the Year, and they are having a meeting, but I can't go because I am going to Santa Barbara to take care of my grandson while my son takes his exams. There is no line between my family life, my work, and my community. The Mothers' office is upstairs in my home, and the reason I can do all this is because I have a lot of support from my family. My son Martin brings me a lot of ideas. Gabriel in Santa Barbara helps me out. I write my letters in Spanish and José, my secretary, translates my letters into English. José graduated from college and couldn't find a job, so he asked me if he could work for me.

Before I married I liked to work, but my parents never let me do anything for the community, especially my father. Often, when I saw so much injustice, I got mad and I wanted to do something about it, but my father said, 'That's none of your business. You stay in the house.' Some of the women have difficulty with their husbands, but not all of them. Some husbands tell their wives that they can go to the meetings as long as they leave the house clean and food on the stove. My husband never asks me for something like this. He drives me to meetings that are far away. We'll stop to eat on the way or we come home and make sandwiches. He works in the community, too, and loves this work.

Our real name is Madres del Estero de Los Angeles contra Todas las Injusticias (Mothers of East Los Angeles against All Injustices). We have a lot of veterans here in Los Angeles. You see these people right here on the freeways because this area has more freeways than others. A lot of people live under bridges, families with children and no jobs and no food. Some people come and knock on my door and ask me for food, and there was one man who came to ask for coffee every day for months. I asked him where he lived and he answered, 'Under the bridge.' I asked him why he lived there and he answered, 'I am a veteran; I get one hundred dollars a month.' This is one of the injustices I don't want to see.

Right now, Governor Wilson is saying that all these immigrants are taking jobs and are a drain on social services. That's not true. I have been living here for forty years. When people go to get welfare, the receptionist asks for a Social Security number, a green card, or an I.D. Illegal immigrants who don't have these things don't get anything, so this is not true. Our people came here to work, especially the farm workers who toil from three in the morning to six in the evening for less than the minimum wage. Helicopters come to spray pesticides on top of these people. I saw all of them very sick with skin problems. I have always been a supporter of César Chávez and the farm workers.

Right here in the community the injustice we see is police behavior against the community. Education is another injustice we suffer. I know the state has money for education, but in this area the grammar schools don't have any cafeterias and the kids have to eat outside. The people in the valley and the schools over there have wonderful cafeterias. We never get any money; it all goes to the rich neighborhoods. I wanted to change this, but the governor never listens to us.

One of these days the governor will be sorry that he treated us this way. I would like to start a boycott; all Latinos would stop working and buying for one day, and they'd see the economy go down. They always blame Latin immigrants for economic problems. It's their own fault, but they are always looking for a scapegoat, like Governor Pete Wilson pointing to illegal immigrants. People like Gloría Molinas are working for the community and are not for sale. They work with the whole community, but Diane Feinstein and Barbara Baxter, who came to the community to ask for support, promised to help the Latinos, but they didn't say how. Then, they turned around and began talking against the immigrants, but they couldn't do without us because Latinos work the hardest and receive the lowest pay.

Sometimes I get tired, but I can't stop this work, especially when somebody attacks me because of what I do. When somebody says something against me, that's like gas in my motor to go on. My daughters will take over from me when I can no longer keep up, especially Elsa and Beatrice. We would like to have more young Mothers in the group. We are having a membership drive right now. We have about three hundred members of just Mothers. I have Mothers from all different areas, not just from East Los Angeles. Pretty soon we will be a citywide organization. All the groups need women, especially mothers, because without women, men are worth nothing.

I think that when we set out to do something because we believe in it and we work together, everything is possible. I speak with many students in California, and many of them think that the Latino woman is only there to clean the house and take care of the children. This is not true these days. I am very proud of my Latino women. We have many professional women, and we have many young people who go out to study and then come back to the community to fight against environmental issues. This is one of the biggest issues in the community. We talk and fight, but the problem cannot be resolved in one day. In the past the EPA didn't pay any attention to us. Now, they want to meet with us and to hear us talk about the problems. When you want to accomplish something, if you work together, anything is possible.

We work with many people who are fighting on behalf of the environment, not only with Latino people. We belong to the Southwest Network in New Mexico, a national network that works against environmental problems. We learn from each others' situations. For instance, we have a terrible problem in the Coachilla Valley, where there are Native American reservations. Indians and Latino and Chinese farm workers live there. The counties of Los Angeles and San Diego dump all their drainage and waste in the valley. We couldn't understand how these people could live there because we could hardly spend an hour in that place. The residents asked us for help because they wished to protest this dumping, and hundreds of us came to support them. Environmental racism is especially acute in California. We also work with an African-American organization in East Los Angeles, Anglo Mothers, and Mothers of Santa Monica, and with people in Chinatown. We are not racists, and everyone is welcome in our organization. We cooperate with people suffering from environmental problems in northern and southern California. Southern California is one of the most toxic areas in this country. Through our work with other ethnic groups, I have come to realize that environmental racism exists everywhere, and we must all guard against it.”

ELSA LÓPEZ SPEAKS

"We used to have the meetings here in the house, but when the group got too big, we starting having them in the parish hall. We have different speakers on various topics. We had one on the environment, one on domestic violence, one on water conservation, and a student from the University of California at Santa Barbara came and spoke about federal assistance for college. We also help students with their applications for colleges, grants, and financial aid.

I am managing the project for the water conservation program. We work with the DWP (Department of Water Program) and give out free flushless toilets to the community for the DWP area. People install them and have seven days to return the old ones. Those are then crushed and mixed with old tires, which are used for roadways to cover potholes and for freeways damaged by earthquakes.

I will have been involved in the water conservation program for two years on August 1 [1994]. We've given out over thirty-two thousand toilets. Not only does it conserve water and save people money, but it's also bringing employment to the community. It's brought insurance for the employees. It's brought other work, such as the immunization program. We just continue developing more projects. We were able to get the lead poison program on the basis of our record.

We have various committees for different projects, for scholarships, for water conservation, for the environment. The environmental committees are organized according to specific issues. For example, we have committees that go up north to Kettleman City or wherever they ask us to go. Those groups help other areas get to the media and to various members of the government in order to help bring the issues out. We function spontaneously. As problems arise we deal with them.

I was born into this. I didn't have a choice. After I got married I moved close by, to Monto Bello. When my kids were small I used to drive my mother to the marches, but I didn't tend to get too involved. Then, once my kids started growing up and I began working with the school district, my mother babysat my youngest son. So my youngest son is very aware of political and environmental issues. I used to ask him when I picked him up, 'What did you do with Grandma today?' and he would answer, 'Oh, today, we went to City Hall and we sat in the city council.' Even his vocabulary is more advanced than the kids in his grade. When he was in preschool, they would ask him what he did, and he would tell them,

'Well, I went and marched against the prison in East Los Angeles,' Or, 'I marched against Malathion [insecticide].' The small children didn't understand him, but the teachers did. He's very wise.

In the future we are aiming for toxic removal from residential areas. That will be our next big project. We will have the walkers educated about different types of toxics and then go door to door to inform people that there will be a pickup. The County of Los Angeles will bring in special pickup trucks to remove the wastes. A lot of people don't want to put these things in their cars and just leave them in their garages. This way, the walkers will get out and educate the people on the dangers and inform them about a pickup date when they can actually place the toxic wastes on the curbside. We'll clean up this community one way or another."

RICARDO GUTIÉRREZ SPEAKS

"We try to get things done for the benefit of the community. This community has been pushed around too much already. We ourselves had to move twice when they were building the freeways. One thing we discovered since we have been involved in all this is that the government will override the community if it's just a community protesting, but if the community has outside friends that join the struggle, it has more power. When we started demonstrating against the prison and the incinerator, it was not just the Mothers and the community; it was the people that we brought from all over.

When we started the fight against the prison, it was the first time that there was an organized protest against the government, and people were very surprised that these old women out there demonstrating knew what they were talking about. Before, organizers would come in, get the community out there, and say, 'You do what we tell you to do.' Our people didn't have a voice. When the prison issue started, we felt that everyone had to be told what their prerogatives were. So we instructed old ladies, everybody.

The newspapermen would come over and talk to different people, and they were so surprised that everybody knew what they were there for. Whenever there is a demonstration, marchers usually point to someone that will answer the questions: 'I don't know, he'll tell you about it.' We got our community involved in the whole process. When we first told them that we didn't want the prison there because of all the schools, people picked it up and said, 'We don't want it because we have schoolchildren there, and we have so many schools within a two-mile radius. The governor says that there is not a single house within a mile; we'll prove him wrong because the houses are right there on the street where they planned to put the prison.' The media came over and said, 'Hey, this is something different. It's a community really at work.' At first, only Channel Thirty-four, the Spanish channel, began covering us. Later on, we were having these marches every Monday, and we had all the channels in Los Angeles here, from Two to Thirteen. We had people come in from the north and south of California. We had the farmers come over and join us. César Chávez was here because we were very close to him before. We had movie stars coming over, the actor that played Baretta [Robert Blake], and Miss Moretta [of the television series]. The archbishop marched with us. All these people marched with us on the bridge.

We were not involved in the project for the oil pipeline in the beginning. The community asked for our support and Juana, Mrs. Robles and Mr. Robles, myself, and another man, went over there to help because they were having problems getting organized. They wanted lots of people, and I told them it wouldn't help to gather people if they didn't know what they were fighting for. We contacted people all along the projected sites for the pipeline in the different cities and talked to them. That's how we did it the first time. The second time, we contacted people with knowledge, and we learned from them. A number of white people and retired engineers joined us. We told them that the more they educated us about the problem, the easier it would be for us to come out and talk about it. That's the way to win.

Later on, another pipeline was going to come through here from another direction, and they were very surprised that our community knew so much. We had our discussions and informed everyone. Old ladies were coming up to members of the media and telling them, 'Oh, you cannot come through there, because in this area there is a rupture, and it is very likely that there will be an earthquake there, so you cannot do that in that location.' Then they would say, 'You cannot do that over there because if it leaks, it will go into that creek, and that creek goes into the river. The river has a kind of fish that is unique to the area.' We did a massive education in the area, and I feel that this is one of the reasons that we won.

When we had the fight against the incinerator, we went out and did our work. A newspaperman went up to an old lady and asked, 'How come you don't want the incinerator over here?' and she answered, 'Because it's going to affect you as much as it's going to affect me. Most of the food processing plants are right there. Do you want an incinerator half a mile from the food processing plant? I cannot afford to buy that food but you can. It's going to be contaminated. Do you want that to happen?' "

Notes

1. Mary Pardo, "Mexican-American Women Grass-Roots Community Activists: Mothers of East Los Angeles," *Frontiers: A Journal of Women's Studies* 11, no. 1 (1990): 1–8.

2. Gabriel Gutiérrez, "The Mothers of East Los Angeles Strike Back," in Robert D. Bullard, ed., *Unequal Protection: Environmental Justice and Communities of Color* (San Francisco: Sierra Club, 1993), 220–34.

3. Earl Shorris, *Latinos: A Biography of the People* (New York: W. W. Norton & Company, 1992), 353.

4. Ibid., 224–25.

5. Rodolfo Acuna, "The Armageddon in Our Backyard," *Los Angeles Herald Examiner*, July 7, 1989.

6. Gutiérrez, "The Mothers of East Los Angeles," 228.

7. Pardo, "Mexican-American Women," 4.

8. Gutiérrez, "The Mothers of East Los Angeles," 229.

9. Pardo, "Mexican-American Women," 4.

10. The population of Kettleman City is 78.4 percent Hispanic, and it is the site of the country's fifth-largest landfill. See Commission for Racial Justice, United Church of Christ, *Toxic Wastes and Race in the United States: A National Report on the Racial and Socio-Economic Characteristics of Communities with Hazardous Waste Sites* (New York: Commission for Racial Justice, 1987).

11. Jill Stewart, "Society Matrons and South-Central Moms Take on the Gun Lobby," *Los Angeles Weekly* 18, no. 24 (May 12–18, 1994).

11 / *Grace Thorpe*

ALTHOUGH GRACE THORPE HAD TO turn down an invitation as guest speaker at the National Conference of American Indians' Nuclear Waste Forum in December 1993 because of triple bypass heart surgery, she nevertheless delivered a powerful statement to the forum from her hospital bed. The name "No Teno Quah," or Wind Woman, as she is known among her Sauk and Fox people, reflects Grace herself. Her brothers call her Big Windy Woman, and indeed she stands over six feet tall and exudes an intensity that can intimidate her most formidable opponents. The fact that she is a seventy-three-year-old grandmother enhances her distinction and her tactical skills. Grace has been an activist on behalf of Native Americans for several decades and has been on the front lines of Indian politics, beginning with the American Indian Movement's occupation of

Alcatraz Island in November 1969, when she arranged visits for Jane Fonda and Candice Bergen. This was just one episode in a series of Native American attempts to occupy surplus federal property, such as Fort Lawton in Seattle and Roswell, New Mexico; Grace took part in all of these, working with the news media and supportive celebrities, including Marlon Brando and Dick Gregory. While she was concerned with generating publicity for her people's cause, she also sought to protect the participants from brutal reprisals and imprisonment at the hands of government authorities. Grace helped Indians to acquire a number of sites, assisting them in incorporating and establishing tribal headquarters, community centers, and even a university, known as Deganawidah-Quetzalcoatl University, near Davis, California.

In the 1970s, Grace began lobbying in Washington on behalf of the National Congress of American Indians and continued supporting that association throughout her career. She has also acted as part-time judge and health commissioner for her Nation. Grace is the president of the National Environmental Coalition of Native Americans (NECONA) and the 1994 recipient of the Lifetime Achievement Award from the National Youth Council. She serves on the Greenpeace Advisory Council for Native American Affairs and on the board of directors of the Nuclear Information and Research Service. She is the daughter of 1912 Olympic decathlon and pentathlon medal winner Jim Thorpe.

In 1992, Grace was retired from the political and working world and was absorbed in making pottery when she learned that her Sauk and Fox tribe had accepted a federal grant to study the placement of radioactive waste on tribal land without consulting the members. Galvanized into action by her outrage, she became a full-time environmental activist, fighting against what Winona LaDuke, the Anishinabe activist, has referred to as "radioactive colonialism."[1] The previous autumn, the federal government had sent letters to fifty state governments, some county governments, and American Indian tribes, offering a $100,000-grant to study the possibility of temporarily storing spent nuclear rods, the highly radioactive steel rods produced in creating nuclear energy. The Department of Energy planned to bury the radioactive waste produced in the 112 nuclear plants around the country in monitored retrievable storage (MRS) facilities before it would be shipped to a proposed permanent repository in Yucca Mountain, Nevada.[2] All of the state governments turned down the proposal, while seventeen tribes sent in applications, including the Sauk and Fox, believing that the grant money would lower the high rates of unemployment and poverty among their members.

Grace immediately began to research the dangers of nuclear energy and to study the proposals for government grants with a keen sense that there were important strings attached to the innocent-sounding bids. She discovered that the funds for the initial studies typically went to lawyers and people outside of the tribes and that such programs would not improve the economic situation of Native Americans. As did other Native American environmental activists, Grace viewed the schools, jobs, and services promised for having MRS facilities as a form of economic blackmail, claiming that the government is supposed to provide these benefits according to treaties made in exchange for land concessions.[3] She also found that radioactive waste is extremely hazardous to human health and vowed to actively oppose the desecration of Indian lands.

Her method has been a tireless grass-roots activism and relentless networking despite access to minimum resources. Her travels are financed by environmental organizations and her many public presentations. She works out of her own home in Prague, Oklahoma, which she shares with her daughter and granddaughter. Her few pieces of equipment, including an answering machine and a fax, have been donated, and she has no assistant to answer the flood of mail that she receives. Typically, she uses the local bank to photocopy information. Compared with the office of the nuclear waste negotiator and the Department of Energy's glossy videos, information packets, energy forums, and hefty budget, this approach may seem futile, but it has been far from that. Grace's considerable knowledge of the dangers of nuclear residue and her profound belief in individual and grass-roots efforts have had a powerful impact in her battle against the government. Regarding the media as an important educator, she has tried to pass as much information as possible to writers and editors around the nation. Armed with her expertise, Grace has crisscrossed the country, informing Native peoples of the hazards of storing radioactive residue and persuading tribal councils to turn down the lure of government funds for studying and establishing monitored retrievable storage sites.

In the process, she has also helped return power to the people by influencing individual tribes to revise their constitutions and reclaim the democracy that they enjoyed before the U.S. government's Bureau of Indian Affairs established tribal councils in 1934. The councils are often more amenable to pressures from the federal government than are full democracies. Grace persuaded a number of tribes to revert to their original form of government by visiting their members and talking to as many people as possible. Once these transformations occurred, the people expressed their refusal to accept lethal wastes. As of March 1995 fifteen out of seventeen Native American tribes had turned down MRS because of the outrage of an angry grandmother.

In February 1995 the Mescalero Apaches of southern New Mexico, one of the strongest supporters of storing spent nuclear fuel, voted against the tribal council. Turning out in record numbers, three-quarters of the reservation's eligible voters defeated the proposal and their leader of thirty-eight years, Wendell Chino, who had long advocated at the national level the storing of nuclear residue on his tribal lands and whom Grace had confronted on many occasions. The Mescaleros were the furthest along of any tribe in the MRS process, having applied for the third and last phase that required tribal governments to publicly identify an MRS site and begin formal talks with the nuclear waste negotiator to actually build a receptacle. They thus were expecting to receive tens of millions of dollars. That vote was especially significant because tribal members who opposed Wendell Chino in the past on the MRS had lost jobs and had suffered intimidation.[4] Unfortunately, a few weeks later, lured by the prospect of so much money, the tribe reversed its decision and decided to go ahead with the plan, although it is opposed by New Mexico's legislature and by the state's congressional delegation.[5] That decision also goes against a January 1995 ruling by the U.S. Court of Appeals for the Sixth Circuit that utilities will build de facto permanent repositories for nuclear waste near their plants, thus ending the drive to create storage facilities on Native American lands.[6] If the first vote had carried, it would have fulfilled one of Grace's three main aims in seeking environmental justice—to leave the radioactive residue at the site of nuclear plants. Her other goals are developing safe storage of hazardous wastes and creating alternative sources of energy.

One of the secrets of Grace's success is her ability to network not only within the Native American nations but also with groups within the dominant culture. In 1993, Grace helped found the National Environmental Coalition of Native Americans, which was instrumental in helping to sway tribes against the adoption of MRS on their lands. That same year, the NECONA linked up with Nuclear

Free America, an international clearinghouse for information about nuclear free zones. Together they created the nuclear free Indian lands project to promote the passage of nuclear free zone laws by tribal governments and to prevent the acceptance of high-level radioactive waste in Indian country. That effort brought together Native American activists, local environmentalists, and local tribal and neighboring non-Indian governmental officials to counter the nuclear industry. The project emphasizes the link between the creation of nuclear waste and its disposal, claiming that ending production is the only safe alternative. In the future the combined groups intend to work with the media to publicize local nuclear free zones, make presentations at energy conferences, and support efforts in Congress to eliminate programs seeking to place nuclear residue on Indian lands.

Grace's political style reflects the Native American way, using persuasion and negotiation to build consensus and providing information so that each person can participate in managing his or her own destiny as well as working for the good of the nation. While her years in Washington have given her a keen sense of the reality of politics, and although she understands the difficult choices tribal councils must make, Grace is more comfortable acting on behalf of a positive goal than engaging in confrontation with either the tribal or the federal governments. Her outrage at the injustices suffered by her people has not clouded her vision of a healthy future for all peoples on this planet.

As a mother and grandmother, Grace Thorpe brings a special perspective to her environmental work. Most Native American nations regard their older women as important sources of wisdom and political counsel, although Grace admits with a wry smile that her work as a tribal judge has diminished as a result of her activism. She demonstrates the capability, fire, and courage developed by years of struggle. It is a lesson the dominant culture could well learn as it ridicules older women and continues to despoil Indian lands. Grace operates with the insight of her years, understanding that problems are not solved overnight but over time. She knows how to plant seeds for future efforts—that keeping in touch with a *New York Times* reporter, for instance, will eventually result in a story that could reach millions. She believes fervently in the power of individuals working together to effect change. Her directness and her passion have proven a significant source of moral strength in the Native American struggle against environmental racism.

GRACE SPEAKS

It is wrong to say that it is natural that we, as Native Americans, should accept radioactive waste on our lands, as the U.S. Department of Energy has said. It is a perversion of our beliefs and an insult to our intelligence to say that we are "natural stewards" of these wastes. The real intent of the U.S. government and the nuclear industry is to get rid of this extremely hazardous garbage on Indian lands so they can go and generate more of it. They are poisoning the earth for short-term financial profit. They try to flatter us about our ability as "earth stewards." They tell us, when our non-Indian neighbors object to living near substances poisonous for thousands of years, that this is an issue of "sovereignty." It is an issue of the earth's preservation and our survival.

[Statement of Grace Thorpe to the National Congress of American Indians, December 1, 1993, Sparks, Nevada.]

"I joined the service during World War II; I was a corporal, Corp. Thorpe. While I was serving in New Guinea, I fell in love with an Anglo paratrooper. We met again in Japan, where I worked with the occupation forces from 1945 to 1950, got married, and had two children.

When I came back with my children, I wanted to establish ties with my tribe, so I got them enrolled. Then, through the years, I wanted even stronger connections, so I investigated how we got our Indian names because I very much wanted to have one. I contacted Mary Mack, north of Shawnee, and asked how to go about getting one. She told me, 'Well, we have a fast that goes on all day. The elders meet and go over the old names of people that have passed on; they give those names to the new children that are born or the people that want names in the tribe.'

So I got the Indian name of 'No Teno Quah.' Quah is woman, and it means woman with the power of the wind that blows up before a storm hits. My brothers call me Big Windy Woman, which has some truth in it, I guess. At any rate, that was my Aunt Mary's, one of my Dad's younger sisters, and it was Dad's grandmother's name, so it's also my great-grandmother's name. It's shortened down to Wind Woman.

Shortly after, my marriage wasn't working out, so I went to visit my mother-in-law. She didn't know that we were breaking up but sensed it, so she just plain asked me if I would consider moving my family nearby. She said she'd do what she could to help me get settled.

We bought a little house in Pearl River, New York, which is right on the borderline between Bergen County and New Jersey, on the other side of the Hudson. It was a small town then, with about ten thousand people. I went to work for the Reuben H. Donnelly Corporation as an outside field representative, selling the Yellow Pages for the New York telephone book and making a very good living for my kids.

I lost my son in an automobile accident when he was sixteen. At the time, I was advised by many people that I considered wise to just stay where I was, at least for a year, so that I could think more clearly. My daughter had just graduated from high school and gone off to college. After she had done that, I felt that I was free to do as I pleased.

We've often heard, be careful what you dream because it's going to come true. My dream had always been to do what I could for the Indian situation, the Indian problem, as they like to call us in Washington, DC. Then I thought, well now I can do whatever I want to do. I almost heard voices one morning real early, before it got light, saying, 'Hey, Grace, you can do whatever you want to do now. You no longer have the responsibility of the children, and your daughter's away; go and do whatever you please.' I answered, 'Yes, but what am I going to do for money?' The voices replied, 'Well, you can sell your house. It's a nice house in a nice neighborhood, real estate prices are high, and you could sell that to hold you over and you could go to work for the Indians.' I replied, 'I sell advertising, how do you know that they're going to be able to use anybody like me?' 'Well, you don't know if you don't try.'

I sold my house and my furniture and took off for California, where my mother lived. I used her telephone number and address, phoning in once a week. I visited Indian reservations along the way, and began collecting rocks and beachcombing to just heal the wound from the loss of my son. It used to embarrass my mother to tell people that I was out collecting rocks and she would say, 'My daughter is on one of her gem expeditions.'

Then I worked for the Bureau of Indian Affairs and the Association on American Indian Affairs that does a fine job of lobbying in New York City. I came across the Association on American Indian Affairs when I lived in Pearl River, and I used to attend their meetings.

After that I was hired by the National Congress of American Indians to organize conferences to invite manufacturers into Indian areas. The Congress was established fifty years ago and is the oldest, largest, and most prestigious Indian organization in the United States. They needed somebody that could coordinate these conferences, that knew promotion and publicity. I had done a tremendous amount of coordination and community organizing all my life. When I was in Japan, I created the Engineer Officers' Wives Club and became the president. Then, in Pearl River, I started a Parent-Teacher Association, a Junior Women's Club, and I ran the March of Dimes, so I thought I was suited perfectly for this job. I coordinated two very successful conferences, one in the West and one in the East.

I did get a couple of college degrees after that. Matter of fact, I didn't even have a high school degree. I got a GED, and then I went to the Antioch School of Law and took the first two years of law school. I worked on a paralegal degree because they couldn't give me a degree since I had to have the undergraduate degree first. So I did everything backwards. After I earned my paralegal degree I went to MIT (Massachusetts Institute of Technology) on an urban fellowship.

I did my internship for the law degree working with the U.S. Senate Subcommittee on Indian Affairs. The work was overwhelming, and so I was advised to just pick whatever issues I was interested in and work on two or three. One of my interests was Indian preference for jobs financed by the Bureau of Indian Affairs. I would check to make sure that the Bureau tried to find Indian people for contracts with the Indian Health Service and for the Bureau of Indian Affairs.

I also worked on the Community Action Program, training people on Indian reservations to do construction and whatever needed to be done there. When the program was on the verge of being cancelled by the Appropriations Committee in the Senate, I lobbied with the senators and members of the House to keep it going. I was off and on in Washington for eight years, from 1968 to 1976.

I retired in 1976. I had been working again for the U.S. Senate Subcommittee on Indian Affairs, and my sister was on the American Indian Policy Review Commission. We had been hired for a two-and-a-half-year period. When we finished, we decided to go back to Oklahoma and try to start a museum for our Dad. We have this very famous father, James [Jim] Thorpe, who was a quite well-known athlete.

We went back to Tahlequah, Oklahoma, where Northeastern Oklahoma State University was located. We'd heard about the Native American Studies program there, and we enrolled in that. From there, we went to the University of Tennessee, where we both got bachelor of arts degrees. I had always been interested in art as a kid so I took a lot of art courses. I was having a great time drawing pictures of wild flowers around Oklahoma, sketching people and scenes, learning how to throw a pot on a wheel, and the old-fashioned methods of working with coils in clay, as well as the modern methods of high fire.

Then, in January 1992, I read an article in the *Daily Oklahoman* about my tribe, the Sauk and Fox, putting in for a feasibility study with the Department of Energy for burying nuclear waste in our land in exchange for a $100,000 grant. Well, I was shocked. Incidentally, the Sauk and Fox were the last tribe of Indians to fight for their lands east of the Mississippi River, and that's known in history books as the Black Hawk War. Our land was along the Mississippi River, starting with what is now southern Wisconsin going all the way down to St. Louis. Our hunting grounds and our territories were about five or six hundred miles on either side of the Mississippi River, which is pretty lush land, and, incidentally, some of the best farming area in the world. Many of our people were massacred during the Black Hawk War. I thought that war was in 1832; this was 1992. What on earth has happened that we're now considering putting nuclear waste on the few acres that we have left? We've only got about fifteen hundred acres in Oklahoma.

I didn't like the idea one bit; I called the tribe and asked, 'What on earth are you attempting to do here?' The tribal administrator told me, 'Oh, Grace, we're not going to put nuclear waste here, we just want to use that money. Wendell Chino, Mescalero Apache chairman, said that there's no strings to it, we can get the $100,000. We just figured this is another way to get some easy money.' I didn't like that answer. I felt that it was like prostituting ourselves and selling our name on an issue. I replied that I didn't think it was a good idea for us even to be associated in the same sentence with nuclear waste. I didn't know a heck of a lot about it, and so I started doing some research. I was located near Oklahoma State University in Stillwater, so I was able to get as much material as I could about the radioactivity in nuclear waste. I didn't like what I read.

I don't have a chemistry degree and I'm not a physicist; the more I read, the more complicated it got.

I did read that you can't see radioactivity, you can't smell it, you can't feel it, but it's the most lethal poison known in the history of man. I didn't need to know much more than that. So, I checked to see what I could do to get my tribe to withdraw from this program. I proceeded to just talk to people in the tribe about nuclear waste. I didn't find anybody that liked it. Fortunately for me, there were some other issues that people were upset about. These people had called me in to advise them on the technicalities involved, so I met with them and approached the issue.

First, I got a copy of the constitution of the Sauk and Fox tribe and found that in order to call a special meeting—we had meetings annually—or if the people wanted to have a special meeting, there was a procedure to follow. I had to get a petition signed by over fifty tribal members stating that they wanted to call a special meeting. I contacted as many tribal members as I could and found that none of them liked the idea of accepting nuclear waste. I ran across only one person that did. I'd see them at the clinic, I'd see them at the powwows, and I'd see them at various places around tribal gatherings, so I chatted with the people. We formed a coalition and got about eighty signatures.

We called a special meeting on February 18, 1992. I stood on the floor and made the motion that we withdraw from the MRS, which is an acronym for the Monitored Retrievable Storage program that the Department of Energy was fostering at the time. There were seventy-five people there, and we overwhelmingly voted to withdraw from the program. There were seventy people, all on the floor, that wanted to withdraw; the only ones that voted for it were the tribal council members.

Shortly after that I started getting calls. I remember getting a call from the Indigenous Environmental Network that was having a conference in June in Dallas, Oregon. They wanted me to be a keynote speaker. This was about their second or third conference. I said, 'Why do you want me as a keynote speaker? I'm not involved in national Indian affairs anymore and haven't been since 1976. I'm retired.' The coordinator replied, 'Aren't you the one that got your tribe to withdraw from that MRS program to study nuclear waste? That's what we want you to do; we want you to come and tell us how you did it.' Since then I've been overwhelmed with calls, and I'm giving talks all over the nation to Indian and non-Indian environmental groups.

When I got involved with that, I just started doing whatever I could. First, let's get a little history of what the MRS is. The federal government is responsible for nuclear spent fuel rods that they use to operate the commercial reactor plants, generally in the East. There are about 112 of these plants. Now, the waste that this produces is the responsibility of the federal government, according to the law. These reactor plants produce fuel rods about the size of my thumb. The rods would last for only about two or three years, then they'd have to be removed and placed in water. They're radioactive for from 10,000 to 250,000 years, so they have to be stored away.

The government believes that the best place to dispose of this radioactive waste is to place it deep in the ground. There is a contract that obligates the federal government to permanently store these rods in 1996. In the meantime, the government has to make arrangements to put this nuclear waste someplace until it can permanently deposit it in Yucca Mountain in Nevada. Somebody in Washington had the bright idea to get contact communities that needed economic development, jobs, and some money to come into their areas. The government couldn't put the waste where there was too much resistance. They tried to do it in Tennessee, and it didn't work because the people refused. So they thought they'd give $100,000 a year to study the feasibility of burying nuclear residue, then the second phase of it would be $250,000, again for the tribes and consultants to come in and study the area to see if it's suitable, and then the third phase would involve a $3.5-million grant.

The MRS was in phase one at that point and they (the federal government, the office of the nuclear waste negotiator, it's also tied in to the Office of Civilian Waste) sent out a packet about an inch-and-a-half thick to all the municipalities in the United States and to all the states, to the governors of all the states, and to the Indian tribes. This actually started in the fall of 1991.

Not one out of the fifty states wanted to have anything to do with it. There were four counties and seventeen Indian tribes that applied for it. The counties all resigned. Eleven of the seventeen Indian tribes that applied for it were in Oklahoma. The others were in various states. There are only three left now. We were able to get them all to withdraw from Oklahoma. The last one just withdrew in August of this year [1994], just a couple of months ago.

Among the ones that are left are the Mescaleros, who, incidentally, were the first ones that applied for it. Unfortunately, Wendell Chino from the Mescaleros spoke about this at a gathering of the

National Congress of American Indians in San Francisco in 1991, telling the Indians that this was an easy way for them to get $100,000 with virtually no strings attached. Actually, most of the $100,000 went for consultants and lawyers; the tribe didn't get any of it. The Ponca tribe in Oklahoma, for example, put in for this first $100,000 grant; then, when they were asked if they wanted to go into phase two, they analyzed how the money was spent and said, 'Hey, we didn't get any of that money, so why do we need to do this just to supply money to somebody else?'

I went over and talked to the Eastern Shawnee in Miami, Oklahoma, and the Miami tribe itself. I spoke to the senior citizens at the Indian center there, and I spoke at the local high school, where I was sponsored by the Indian Club. I would try to find a member of the tribes that had applied for these grants who could coordinate an effort to do the same thing that I had done: read the constitution, get a petition signed, get the people to withdraw. I also encouraged the media in Oklahoma to talk about the issue. There were articles in *Oklahoma Today*, in *Tulsa World*, and in Indian publications. I thought that it was my job to get as much information out to writers as I could against the placement of nuclear waste on our Indian lands.

I then began to speak to groups about the issue. I worked with the Tonkawa tribe. There were five tribes located around the Chilocco Indian School that I went to as a kid. That land was then broken up and each tribe got eight hundred acres. The Tonkawa tribe was contemplating putting in a nuclear research facility that would not only take the waste from all over the nation but would also process the residue from irradiating meats and isolate plutonium. It was a very dangerous process, and nobody does it now.

I am still researching the problem. Because it is such a broad subject, I have found that I need to narrow in. That is how I've been able to accomplish anything. If I just spent all my time reading and trying to learn about the whole situation throughout the world, then I wouldn't be able to accomplish what I want to do, which is to keep this nuclear waste off Indian land.

Now we've got it narrowed down to three tribes. I was at Fort McDermitt, which is one of the groups that wants it (I can't say they all want it, it's the business council that wants it). Fort McDermitt is in northern Nevada and southern Oregon. Then, there are the Goshuts in Utah; the Fort McDermitts and the Goshuts are both Paiutes. I can understand why they want them because there is no industry at Fort McDermitt. All they have there are two little motels, a small casino with a restaurant, and a gas station.

The local people are kind of half and half on wanting it, and so are the Indians. I'm not so sure about the feasibility. They have high mountains above the desert that get really severe snowstorms in the winter. I'm not sure whether they have to worry about earthquakes and heavy storms if anything goes wrong. The railroad is seventy miles away. New roads would have to be built to get in there.

The government is trying to sell all the great jobs and the economic benefits that would come in the area, kind of like the siren song of money, promised money, promised economic benefits, of course. But within the siren song there are also the current health risks: leukemia, thyroid cancer, other forms of cancer that we're not even aware of, and the potential damage to our genetic structure, which could result in the birth of deformed children in future generations.

Because of these risks, it doesn't seem worthwhile even producing nuclear waste. It's just too dangerous. I'm trying to find a senator right now, or a member of the House, that would sponsor a bill that nothing is produced or manufactured in the United States that cannot safely be disposed of. We should be spending a lot of money on researching solar methods. President [Jimmy] Carter had some good programs going on solar energy, subsidizing the construction of new homes with solar panels. When President [Ronald] Reagan took office that program was discontinued, so now we practically have to start all over again encouraging alternative types of energy. My ultimate goal is, again, to stop the production of nuclear energy because we can't dispose of the waste.

A gathering was called of American Indian environmental activists about what to do with the Mescalero situation in New Mexico and the other Indian tribes that had signed up to study the feasibility of putting nuclear waste on the land. So we formed an organization called the National Environmental Coalition of Native Americans. I was elected the president, and Lance Hughes, who's with the Native Americans for a Clean Environment in Tahlequah, became the treasurer, and Vivian Jake, who kept a waste incinerator away from the northern rim of the Grand Canyon, is the secretary. We also included Rafina Logs from the Mescaleros, my daughter, Dagmar Thorpe, who is involved in environmental issues, David Platero from the Western Shoshoni, and Dr. Argen Makhijani, a nuclear physicist from Baltimore and a member of the Institute for Energy and Environmental Research. The goal of the organization is to stop the federal government from putting nuclear residue on our Indian lands. I concentrated on that for just about a year, and we were able to stop the funding and actually slow down the process among the tribes that were eager to go ahead with the government grant.

Then, I ran across Chuck Johnson of Nuclear Free America and created an informal alliance with that group to establish nuclear free zones. I think that having a positive effort is much more effective than pursuing a negative effort. To fight for something I think is right just plain makes me feel better. I really don't like the idea of fighting against tribes that are wanting to get this nuclear waste, but sometimes you just have to do it.

The nuclear free zones would mean that no nuclear waste can be dumped on the land or in any building, nor can any trucks carrying nuclear residue cross property or cities in that area. Many cities throughout the United States have accomplished this. Chicago, for example, is nuclear free, and there are about four hundred such locations around the world. Some countries are completely nuclear free.

It just made sense to me to establish these zones on our tribal reservations and our tribal lands. It could be challenged in court, of course, but in that case you just go to court. I think the publicity it would generate would do us a lot of good. The legal aspect of it might be a gray area, because of the interstate commerce clause. However, it seemed a really good way to go, and so about a year ago I formed an alliance with Nuclear Free America and have persuaded thirteen tribes to join so far. The first one was the Flathead in Montana, then the Kaw, the Kenaitze, the White Mountain Apache in Arizona, the Red Cliff Band Lake Superior Chippewa, the Devil's Lake Sioux in North Dakota, the Kickapoos in Kansas, and, just recently, the Shoalwater, the Ponca, the Pawnee, and my tribe, the Sauk and Fox. They keep joining. All of a sudden another tribe will contact me and say they voted for it.

My efforts in the year ahead are to establish more nuclear free zones because it does really give a strong message. I don't know what the government's going to be doing as far as funding. People are very quiet about it in Washington right now, but they're going to be slipping in some kind of amendment at the last minute allowing them to do things. They are working on it right now, and they're going to call it something different. It's not going to be Monitored Retrievable Storage any more.

I'm on the board of directors of the Nuclear Information and Research Service in Washington, DC. They keep up on what's going on in the nuclear energy field and publish an excellent newsletter, which is very much up-to-date. Many people contact me, writers and students that want to do essays, and I steer them to the research service.

One hundred and twenty-five years ago, there was an outbreak of smallpox all around the world and in the military. The military hospitals in the United States had army blankets that were used for the smallpox victims. They gave all of those to the Indian tribes. It almost completely wiped out the Mandan and the Hidatsas and the Arikara. Then, they formed a group of the survivors up at Fort Berthold, but it almost wiped them out. As a matter of fact some of the history books will tell you the Mandan tribe is extinct because of this. What I'm saying now, this nuclear waste is like giving the smallpox blankets.

When I give talks, I try to call on Indian tribes if there are any within the area. When I gave a presentation at the Indigenous Environmental Network in Minnesota last month [October 1994], I went two days early and called on the Sisseton Sioux in northern South Dakota and on the Devil's Lake Sioux in Fort Totten, North Dakota.

If I have money, I put up a booth at the national Indian gatherings where I have information on keeping nuclear residue off Indian lands. A lot of people come up and talk to me. When I went to Minnesota with Nuclear Free America's Chuck Johnson and we visited various tribes, I spoke with a chief I had met at one of the previous gatherings. He said, 'Well, Grace, I didn't tell you, but as soon as I got back after meeting with you, I established a nuclear free zone.' Then he told me, 'I am sick to death of all these people wanting to dump their trash, their sludge, their human waste, their low-level nuclear waste on our reservation.' There may be other tribes that have done this too that I'm not even aware of.

All those tribal councils who were so interested in MRS were established under the Indian Reorganization Act [IRA] by the Bureau of Indian Affairs. It is difficult for the federal government to do business with a traditional form of tribal government. That form of government is based on consensus among the people; you take issues to the people and then they decide what to do. As a result, the government created the Indian Reorganization Act in the 1930s.

It takes the power away from the people and puts it in the representatives, much as the government does in the United States today.

The elected tribal officials aren't any different than the elected officials in the federal government. You've got people that are in and people that are out, who are against the people that are in. If there are representatives that are elected by just a few votes it's even worse, because you've got half of the people in the opposition and half who are in power. You always have that friction. It's not unusual in Indian tribes; it's not unusual in any form of democracy.

One of the tribal councils' main goals is to get money to keep the tribe operating. If they can't have an office with a phone and electricity, then they can't take advantage of a lot of federal programs. So it is their job to see that they get grants and that they are aware of which ones are coming in; it is important that they know, for example, if they're housing grants, or if they're other types of funds coming for other areas. The council members probably just didn't think when they accepted the grant for nuclear waste because Wendell Chino was telling them there were no strings attached.

But our tribe amended our constitution. It wasn't easy to do and took about three years to complete. The power is once again in the people, and anything that relates to the land or that's considered important has to come back to all the tribal members. This is unusual among the IRA tribes because in order to make an amendment to a constitution, you first have to introduce it; then the people on the floor have to agree to do it by a vote. Afterwards, it goes to the business committee, and maybe they'll push it or maybe they won't. If they do, they have to take it to the Bureau of Indian Affairs through the Department of the Interior. It has to be approved, and if there are problems with it, it comes back to the business committee.

The government would still prefer to deal with the elected officials on the tribal council. It makes it easier for them to operate, but of course it takes the power away from the people. That is what has been happening with the nuclear waste issue. The people that are the elected officials can make a decision that will affect all the people of the tribe, without bringing it to them for a vote.

Another thing that I'm attempting to do is to reform these IRA constitutions and make tribes aware of the kind of constitution they're operating under. When I talk to the Indian people, I tell them exactly how they have to get their constitution changed, what they need to do, what they need to say, how to have everything all lined up before they go into it. I even ask them to send me copies of their constitution and to keep in touch with me.

The government doesn't bother me. I stand up against all the industrialists; it doesn't bother me a bit. Well, I don't always let on who I am or what my work is, but I know I look like my Dad—I'm big so I'm easy to spot in a crowd. I was a spy at a high-level nuclear waste conference in Las Vegas several months ago. I went because I wanted to find out what they were talking about. I really feel that if we are trying to bring about change, we need to know who our enemy is and what they're doing. I thought, well, I'll just go and sit in on their conferences. They had about a $500 registration fee, but I didn't pay any attention to it. I just went on in and sat myself down and listened to what they had to say.

I sat next to this Swiss engineer and asked him what he did and where he was from. He told me that he represented a Swiss company, and that it was negotiating with some European countries to bring nuclear waste into the granite pits in the Alps. He was just so serious because he said the granite is the safest place to put this nuclear waste. Dear me, dear me.

Then I also heard the Mescalero members of the tribal council get up there and talk to these people, trying to show them that they were really serious in wanting their nuclear waste. They said that it was their duty to accept it because they were protectors of the land. Well, when I heard Freddy Peso say that, I almost vomited. At any rate, when old Freddy got up there to talk, he looked over the crowd and all of a sudden he spotted me. He stopped for a second or so before he continued speaking.

There's another conference coming up in Las Vegas where they'll be discussing the transporting of nuclear waste and the hazards involved on the highway and on the trains. I want to go because I'd like to be able to have more knowledge when I give my talks and to be able to tell people who interview me where to get more information on the transportation issue. I have found that when you want to accomplish something, you must learn as much as possible, even when you're not quite sure how you're going to use this material. Then, try to figure out what you can do with it and hit as many different places as you can. For example, I call on the Indian tribal members, trying to encourage them to combat what their tribal council has done.

I also try to get information into the newspapers, television, and radio, so I cooperate as much as possible with all free-lance writers, media people, and Nuclear Free America. I'm on the phone practically all the time when I'm home. In order to accomplish something, you hit the media, which, in turn, educates the public. I try to educate the public personally but I can reach only two hundred people if I give a talk, whereas I can reach two million through the *New York Times*.

Then you also try to change the laws, which means you have to lobby Washington. So you need to know Washington, what's going on there, who's the one that pushes the button, which committee makes the decisions covering your issue. In your talks with these people you need to have knowledge. I try to keep myself as much informed as possible, but I have found that it's so complicated that I do not pursue the technical aspects of atomic energy. Once in a while somebody in an audience will ask me these kinds of questions, and I reply, 'Look, I'm not a nuclear physicist; I don't know the technicalities. All I know is what I read about the hazards.'

I think we women are probably more concerned about the health of our families. We make sure we wash our hands before cooking, that things are boiled, that the water supply isn't contaminated. Perhaps men don't pay as much attention to these matters. I think that our role as women is to bring up healthy children, so, of course, that all ties in with the environment.

I'm concerned about what's going to be happening with the next generation. I'm worried about my granddaughter, who is eleven years old and will get married and have children some day. She's Western Shoshoni, and she might be living out in Nevada with the fallout from the bombs and the hazards from the nuclear waste that they're trying to put in the Yucca Mountain. That's old Western Shoshoni land.

I sit on the tribal health commission; we supervise the health of the tribe and are responsible for the operation of our clinic, so I know how to work all these different things. You just don't go into something without the proper experience. Fortunately, because of my age, I have been involved in many kinds of work; and so even though I'm limited in money, I'm still not limited mentally or in my resources. Even though I operate on my Social Security income, that doesn't mean that I'm not streetwise or smartwise or whatever you want to call it. I know how to get things done.”

Notes

1. Winona LaDuke and Churchill Ward, "Native America: The Political Economy of Radioactive Colonialism," *The Insurgent Sociologist* 13, no. 3 (Spring 1986): 51–78.

2. Barbara Reuben, "Saying No to Nuclear Waste," *Environmental Action Magazine* 25, no. 3 (Fall 1993): 16–18.

3. Ibid., 17.

4. Ibid.

5. "Deadly Nuclear Waste Piles Up with No Clear Solution at Hand," *New York Times*, March 14, 1995.

6. "70 Nuclear Plants on Route to Being Radioactive Dumps," ibid., February 15, 1995.

Part IV

Upholding Women's Rights as Human Rights

12 / Gertrude Mongella

GERTRUDE MONGELLA, ASSISTANT SECRETARY-GENERAL of the United Nations, director of the UN Fourth World Conference on Women, of the Conference Secretariat, and of the Division for the Advancement of Women, was born in a village on a small island in Lake Victoria, Tanzania, in 1945. She married in 1969 and has three boys and one girl who range in age from twelve to twenty-five. The way her family functions reflects Mrs. Mongella's belief in equality and democracy at all levels of women's lives; her husband continues to work in Tanzania and commutes to New York periodically, and both spouses share in the rearing of their children.

She has never lost sight of the richness and significance of growing up in a small village; and therefore, as secretary-general of the Beijing Conference on Women, Mrs. Mongella has focused on the pressing concerns of ordinary women around the world. She regards her role as providing them with a forum and a voice. Although she is quiet and courteous, her message is radical, and she has pronounced it with great courage throughout her varied career: women need to become first-class citizens throughout the world, and they should not have to wait until the established structures are ready to grant them entrance.

Mrs. Mongella came to this conclusion as a young student and incorporated that conviction into the various phases of her career, beginning with her years as a teacher and an inspector of secondary and teacher-training colleges. In 1975 she became one of the few women to be elected to the parliament. Working in a male-dominated environment, she had many obstacles to overcome but faced them with strength and determination. She continued to open the way for women by later entering the executive branch of the government, where she held a number of ministerial positions including the Minister of State for Women's Affairs; Minister of Lands, Natural Resources, and Tourism from 1985 to 1987; and Minister without Portfolio in the president's office from 1987 to 1991. She was also a member of the Central and National Executive Committees of the ruling party in Tanzania, and from 1982 to 1991 served as director of the Social Services Department for the party. Relying on her skills as a teacher, she approached these political positions with a view to educating government officials and the public about women's needs.

Between 1981 and 1991, Mrs. Mongella also worked at the international level, representing her country at global meetings and conferences on issues concerning women, development, and the environment. During that period, women's concerns received increasing attention within the UN system; in 1981 the Convention on the Elimination of All Forms of Discrimination against Women entered into force, and in 1984 the UN World Survey on the Role of Women in Development constituted the first official recognition of women's major interest in issues of development at all levels. Mrs. Mongella was an active participant in these events. In 1985 she served as chairperson of the African Group and vice chair of the Nairobi Conference to Review and Appraise the Achievement of the UN Decade for Women, which was initiated in 1976 and evaluated by that conference.[1] The strategies adopted for the advancement of women by the conference represented an important milestone, signaling the beginning of a new sensitivity to women's issues within the United Nations. Mrs. Mongella's role in the conference and afterward led to her new responsibilities in 1993; the forward-looking strategies adopted at the time were further developed at the Beijing Conference.

In 1989, Mrs. Mongella was appointed Tanzania's representative to the UN Commission on the Status of Women, a body that was established in 1946, along with a branch for the advancement of women, responsible for servicing the commission. The latter, which Mrs. Mongella now directs, was given division status in 1988 and moved to New York City from Vienna in 1993, serving as the central UN unit for all matters concerning women. It acts as the secretariat for world conferences on women and for the Committee on the Elimination of Discrimination against Women, as a source of policy analysis on gender issues for the Economic and Social Council and the General Assembly, and as a human rights treaty-monitoring body.

Mrs. Mongella led her country's delegation to the Committee on the Elimination of Discrimination against Women in 1990. She also participated in an expert group meeting on women in political and decision making positions held in Vienna, and she served from 1990 to 1993 on the board of trustees of the UN International Research and Training Institute for the Advancement of Women, a body that was permanently established in 1983 and endorsed by the General Assembly in 1985. She was then appointed secretary-general of the Fourth Conference on Women, which was held in Beijing from August 30 to September 8, 1995, reflecting the fact that some of the strongest voices on behalf of women's human rights are coming from Africa and other regions of the developing world.

In preparation for that conference, Mrs. Mongella consulted with heads of state and senior government officials to elicit their support and cooperation. She also met regularly with Supatra Masdit of Thailand, who led the parallel forum of nongovernmental organizations (NGOs), and with members of the NGOs. The theme of the Beijing Conference was "Action for Equality, Development, and Peace." Equality was targeted as the key to improving women's conditions throughout the world, given the fact that they are denied adequate participation in political, economic, and social decision making.

The conference also focused on development within the entire lifespan of women and the interdependence of different age groups, as well as the linkage of the problems affecting women of all ages. For example, female children in developing countries typically suffer unequal opportunities for nourishment, health services, and education, all of which impact their lives as adults. Given the male-dominated power structure at the international, national, regional, and local levels and within cultures, women have lacked opportunities to participate in defining economic and social structures and policies that affect them so deeply. Hence, they suffer an excessive share of the burdens of poverty around the world, coupled with unequal access to employment and training programs. The conference questioned both the goals and processes of development and sought to put together a definition that represents women's needs and their important role in economic production.

Mrs. Mongella points out that peace, while crucial for all human progress, is especially critical for women because it is the women and children who suffer the most from wars and who have been excluded from decisions to enter conflicts. Whether in Bosnia, Rwanda, or Somalia, women have been victims of torture, *disappearance*, and systematic rape as a weapon of war, and they are disproportionately represented among refugees and displaced persons. Nevertheless, they have been able to build bridges across conflicting nations and within warring countries and regions, including Sri Lanka, Bosnia, and the Middle East. They represent a majority of the membership of various peace groups around the world, often acting in leadership positions. However, the conference stressed that they have yet to carve out an official space for themselves in this important endeavor or to be included in the process of international conflict resolution.

Although women's rights as inalienable human rights have been recognized at the international level, the problems suffered inordinately by women, such as violence, have yet to be systematically addressed within nations because these issues are linked to male power, privilege, and control. Mrs. Mongella has always been impatient with the unwillingness of nations to address this issue and believes that once officially perceived as a problem, domestic abuse will abate. The conference focused on the violence against women that occurs not only in the public sphere but also within the family, reflecting women's lower social status and the lack of legislation to protect them as well as the unwillingness of some public authorities to enforce laws where they do exist.

The conference considered remedies for these issues as well as mechanisms to promote the advancement of women and an awareness of and commitment to their human rights. Some of the proposed solutions included the use of the mass media and education to promote women's contributions to society, the economy, and protection of the environment. It was also suggested that because women tend to be relegated to limited and low-paid occupations, their productive capacities are undervalued; instead, they should be a strong presence in financial and key economic institutions as well as gain increased access to credit, technology, and training.

As Mrs. Mongella has always pointed out and the conference participants stressed, the path to women's equality lies in the transformation of all the structures that govern our lives. Although this may seem like a daunting task, women have created highly effective networks of international, national, and grass-roots efforts to work toward the many dimensions of achieving women's rights as human rights. These organizations not only supported the Beijing Conference but also will continue working to achieve its goals.

Meanwhile, women such as Mrs. Mongella are working to increase their numbers within the United Nations, given that females are systematically excluded from major decision making within such key institutions as the Economic and Social Council, the World Health Organization, and the World Bank, to name just a few. Recent studies reveal that only 15 percent of executive jobs are held by women, in violation of the United Nations' pledge to be an equal opportunity employer. Guidelines and goals for assuring equality are set by the secretary-general and the General Assembly, but they are not enforced. The world organization's highest appeal board, the Administrative Tribunal, has no women among its membership.[2] Mrs. Mongella believes that adjusting this imbalance and allowing scope for women's natural leadership talents within the United Nations will make the world more hospitable to their needs.

GERTRUDE MONGELLA SPEAKS

One of the biggest problems for women is the issue of equality. This is the mother of all the problems.

"Let's say I began to work for women's rights because I am a woman. I'm a woman, and being born a woman was not a mistake. I sometimes wonder if some women think they should be men, but I've always been comfortable with who I am, and I've always achieved what I wanted to achieve as a woman. Sometimes I say I was lucky to be born a woman. There's nothing wrong with being a woman. The problem is with the obstacles imposed by society. We have to work on the obstacles.

I was working on behalf of women even while I was in primary school and in the middle schools. Sometimes I wasn't that conscious of this; I mean the situation wasn't as structured as it is today. I did discover in primary school, where the boys were the class leaders, that they were not as talented as we thought. So it really motivated me to say, 'I have a potential, I have a right as a person.' I think the other thing is family. I was born the second of four children. I grew up in a traditional [culture], where boys were the ones that mattered because they kept up the family line, and girls were expected to marry and join another family. My parents never treated us that way. We girls felt we belonged to the family and that we had equal rights. That's why my parents struggled to send us to the university after high school. It was a big sacrifice; the family grew cash crops, used the most rudimentary tools, and often lost crops because of natural disasters. My parents sacrificed and tilled the land to send us to school. They didn't drink local beer like other people. My father could have said, 'Let the oldest son go to school, I don't have the money or the energy to send the girls,' but he gave us equal opportunities. That was a big contribution. He was committed to this because I remember once one of my uncles asked, 'Why are you sending the girls to school?' and my father replied, 'Why not?'; so he was doing it quite consciously. My mother was also very supportive because she could have said, 'Why are you going to college when everybody is getting married, why don't you stay home and get married?' That was also important. Most of us bring up our children without knowing that by our actions we can either discourage or encourage them.

I went to a secondary school run by the Marianist Sisters. I liked them because my teachers in the middle school were traditional nuns, the types who would help you to go to Heaven. These nuns were more balanced in developing the talents of people. They would look at you and see what your talents were and help to draw them out. In secondary school, apart from the normal classes, I was very good in drama and art. I liked to be in everything and joined in games such as netball, but really, I wasn't much of an athlete. I was interested in everything around me, especially in dancing. I used to learn almost every dance from every tribe.

I went to high school for two years. Then, I moved from the nunnery to the government secular school. I thought it would be more free, but I found out that, in bringing out talents, the church school was much better. They cared more about you as a total person. After that, I qualified for the university. I had always wanted to be a teacher, so I studied for that and also to be a trainer of teachers.

After I finished university I immediately went into teacher training. I didn't stay long because I went into politics and branched out to become a member of parliament. However, since I did train to be a teacher, whenever I have an opportunity, I still become more of a teacher rather than anything else. I've been speaking on behalf of women throughout my career, especially when I entered parliament, because there were very few women there. I realized that you can't wait until you have a critical mass in parliament, and the few women who get into the decision-making bodies must give themselves the responsibility and appoint ourselves because there is no one else to take on that role. You say to yourself, 'Okay, I'm here on behalf of the majority who can never be here,' so you appoint yourself as a spokesperson for women.

I was not only in parliament but also in the cabinet and in the central committee of the party. These are the most important decision-making bodies in my country, Tanzania. You have to carry your message forward and not be intimidated when people frown at you. If you make that mistake, then you will never have another chance; so you must be consistent on this issue. You also have to make people understand the issues. In the beginning you find that people won't support you if you say that we need more women in parliament. You have to keep on saying it and building up a convincing argument. You have to develop strong arguments about why women should not be second-class citizens. These things need a lot of repetition. I always tell people that, once you start on a hard topic, don't step back. If you step back, you will find yourself ten steps behind. You just have to keep on moving. People always say, 'Mama Mongella can never finish a statement without putting in women.' Every time I spoke on industries, I would end up with women; when I talked about education or other things, I would speak about women. You end up being identified with the subject and people say, 'Oh, there she goes again.'

I think that in this job I am very much a student. This is one of the times when I really had to sit down and learn. I am meeting so many people from different backgrounds, coming in contact with so many ideas, many of which are conflicting. One of the things I am learning very fast is tolerance. I have always been talking about tolerance, but this job is going to take a lot of it. I often see people talking in very different ways and with very different approaches about the same issue. There is everything to gain from various groups of people if you can just watch and listen and look. Sometimes there are people speaking the same language, but they are using a different vocabulary. These are some of the things I am finding out.

I'm learning more and more that men's attitudes are not only the result of a certain culture or a certain level of development, but that they are a worldwide problem. The situation has been bad for many centuries. People are getting discouraged and asking what have we achieved since Mexico. I say that it's only been twenty years and that what we have to deal with today has been there for centuries. What miracle do you want to perform?

I'm not after small steps as such. I'm saying, let us take the big steps without discouraging ourselves about the timing. If you look for what we've done in twenty years, as a teacher I know societies have been performing below the pass mark. But not women, who have always had to excel, otherwise they would not have survived. Given the problems women go through, you can say they are the strongest species on this planet. They are survivors. They solve problems which are so difficult to solve. I will give you an example from Africa. You are in your house and there's no water, let alone cold water. Maybe the closest place to get water is a kilometer or more away. There's no electricity either, and the food is not in the supermarket. Still you must lead the same life as the person who has all these things. You get up in the morning, there is no fuel, there is nothing at hand; but at lunchtime, people have something to eat. It's only women who can make that happen. You make the fire, you get the water, you bring the food, and you put it on the table; people eat. You still take care of the sick, you take care of the children, you take care of everything. Then, you still find time to dance.

People say because women have always worked in this way, they have to keep on doing so. This is where I become impatient. If people would only say, 'This is wrong,' full stop. Why don't people say, 'Violence against women is wrong'? I mean, there are certain things we don't need to say, 'By the year 2000.' I say there is a difference between appreciating that certain matters have been there for a long time and everywhere and, at the same time, being able to say that they are wrong. We must say they are wrong. Maybe we cannot change the roads overnight or construct hospitals and water systems and so on, or revise the laws, but there are many areas where it's just a matter of even saying it, and you have it. If everyone agreed that to allow violence against women is wrong, then it's wrong now. You don't need to wait until the year 2000. If we say that in the United Nations the number of women in decision making is low, we don't need to put that in the program. You just need to say that when an appointment is going to be made, look for the right woman and appoint that woman. That's what Sweden did. After the last elections the Swedish government didn't wait and make a twenty-year program, but just said, 'We are making a cabinet, and there will be eleven men and eleven women.' Sweden is not going to collapse. So there are things which can be done. You can increase the number of women in parliament. We don't need to program until the year 2000. If we are going for elections, let us give a chance to the women.

There is so much we can do. For instance, there are many banks which require the husband's signature for a woman to obtain a loan, and it should just be a matter of changing the form and striking that out. Whether it's credit or getting into the laws or getting into whatever, some of the things we think are big are really not that difficult. It's more a matter of a psychological approach. Attitude is a big obstacle, and that is the problem. Women are being deprived because the attitudes have been wrong. A woman doesn't know she has value because she has been told so many times that she has none. She has not been lucky enough to have someone like my father, who said, 'You are equal to your brother, you can just do it, and even do it better.' They have never been fortunate enough to hear that.

One of the areas of concern is with the mass media. How do we make sure that the mass media do not devalue women? The mass media are like a knife. You use it to harm yourself or to be useful. We want to turn it into a useful knife, not to cut women, but to show these things we have spoken about. If that woman we have spoken about who gets up in the morning to fetch water, who has not been thought of as being any good, who has been able to feed the whole family so they can survive, how do you turn and portray her as a weakling? She is the strong one.

I don't really want to peg my effectiveness to motherhood, because not all women are mothers. I think that motherhood is only complete with fatherhood. I am able to do what I do because of my husband, because he has accepted being a father. Sometimes we refer to motherhood and it means mother-father combined. That's not mothering, that's just suffering. That's what has kept women pegged to the children in the wrong context. I am often asked, 'How do you balance the family and your work?' and I answer, 'How does my husband balance?' It's because, as a spouse, I am ready to share the responsibility with him. We are always excusing the fathers and letting them off, instead of saying that we are complementary and that I have to play my part and leave the other part for the other partner. He's the father, let him act like a father.

Many people are trying to promote motherhood at the expense of the woman. We should promote it saying, 'This mother has been overworked, where is the father?' If he does his work, I would love to be a mother. I would love to be a mother, where I play my part and the father plays his. Most of the time we find motherhood bitter. When I first came here, there was someone from UNICEF who said that during this conference, we might help women from the north to breast-feed. I was reluctant. I told him, 'Look here, if I were in this place, I wouldn't even produce one child because of the problems women go through.' We are poor (in Africa) but being a mother is such a blessing there. That's why it is so difficult to talk about abortion there; when you get pregnant, your father is expecting, your mother is expecting, your in-laws are expecting, your husband is expecting, your neighbors are expecting. They are just waiting. That makes being a mother a pleasure. In this country, people don't even look at a pregnant woman. You can be pregnant and deliver before anyone notices it. It's especially difficult when a woman is busy. She says to herself, 'How can I do that to myself twice?' There is no backup system in this country (USA) for mothers. In our societies someone can say, 'Your child can come and stay with us for a year or two.' It's mutual. When I am sick, my children will never go hungry. My neighbors, not even my relatives, will step in until I come back from the hospital. In this place, who steps in? There is no one.

In developed countries women are rebelling. They are left too much to themselves, and that's why they say, 'Only one child! Why should I suffer so much?' This is another matter which I learned about. I have realized that I had to adopt a wider view of these issues because here there is no social structure which will allow women to enjoy being mothers. You need material benefits and social support.

One of the biggest problems for women is the issue of equality. If everybody thinks women are not equal, then they will be treated unequally everywhere, in the community, in the nation, and at the international level. This is the mother of all the problems. I think, if we are to succeed, we must get to a level where the only differences between a man and a woman are their capacities as people, not because one is a woman and one is a man. If we get to that point, then we will solve a lot of problems because that is behind the issue of accessibility and of laws discriminating against women.

If you talk to the young people, they don't mention politics. That's what I have learned while preparing for the world conference. I have an expert colleague who has begun working with young people. We have never really listened to the young. But we must, because the Beijing platform is for the future. How much do we allow them to speak? Whom are we planning for? By the year 2000, the young people who are now in primary school will be almost getting out of college. They are telling us today that they need employment, that you can't get into politics without a job. They need to be in good health, and they need access to housing. When they get out of college, they are the ones who suffer the most because they are just beginning their lives. Sometimes, they experience more violence than us grownups. Political power is not yet one of their goals. It's we who have lived and known what political power really is who have put it at the top of the agenda. But it is important for us. If some of us do not get into political decision making, the world will never change.

We would be happy to see the conference taking action to assist women with their needs and their concerns throughout the life cycle. The young child has her own needs and requirements, and so do the youth, the elderly, and the adults. You can't include the sharing of political power on the agenda for children. Even my daughter and myself don't have the same attitude toward power. Elderly people are not interested in getting into power. They are interested in their retirement and in the services available to them as they age, so that, while each section of the life cycle has its own needs, there is dependence at each stage.

I have to place equality in context. In some developing countries, there's no use in asking for equality alone. Take the example of countries where there are no schools or health facilities for either sex. Does any woman want to be equal to a man who is also disadvantaged? You mustn't forget the development concept. It must be a development that takes into account the women's needs. This is what I have learned from my work on this conference. Coming from a developing country, I used to say that if we reach a certain level of development, these problems will disappear. Now, I find that if you look at the statistics, that some of the issues women face in economically developed countries are more severe than those found in developing countries. You ask, Well, what is development for? Maybe it's time to redefine the concept. Development which does not eradicate violence against women is not development. Development which does not guarantee equality for women, or which does not bring peace, is not development. These are some of the questions we are now asking ourselves.

We also have to ask, Who defines development? Does it only refer to material gains, or do you go beyond that and see how it affects men and women? We must look at the goals as well as the consequences. Take the question of polluting the environment as part of development. Development which has pushed us to consumption that depletes the environment, that increases the violence in civil society, that increases the manufacture of deadly weapons, is not development. It does, however, balance the books because these weapons are sold for money, and leaders can say this year our economy has grown. In some nations, if you take out the money from drugs and weapons, they would be the least-developed countries. Sometimes development takes place at the expense of other things. If we don't take care of the environment, and we destroy the planet, what's the point of talking about equality between men and women? If we destroy the planet, we can never undo what we have done. If you cut a tree, you see it going, you see it gone. If we pollute the rivers, the rivers will die.

Women have a special feeling for the environment because women interact with the environment directly, particularly in developing countries. It may be more obvious in these countries, where there is still interaction with the natural environment. But even in developed countries, women are in constant touch with the environment. Women care because they are the ones who are left to pick up the pieces. Women don't want to sacrifice the environment for other things. They don't want to compromise to obtain social or economic benefits.

This is what I think about peace. If there is something that is man made, it is war. Often, we try to make words gender neutral, to apply a word to men and women, but I think that this one is man made. If you look at television, you see old men discussing how to go to war, or pretending to stop the war by warring. Then, you see young men waging war. The picture of women and children is one of suffering, crying, dying. These are the pictures I see all the time. There are three of them: the men sitting there trying to discuss whether to go to war or to stop the war by warring; and handing over the guns to young people to go and kill themselves; and the women suffering. This is one of man's activities which has never made any sense to me.

Another disturbing issue is the statistics: $3 trillion being spent on arms, and no more resources for development. I can never understand that. There is money for guns, to kill people, but there's no money for schools or for social programs. Also, we never see women in negotiations. The teams which go to Somalia or to Bosnia and other such places are all male. That is why the women are now saying, 'Enough is enough.' We want peace because there is no point in beginning to talk about equality if you are in a situation where you are not sure whether you will survive the next moment. That's why women have chosen these three goals, which should be maintained—peace, equality, and development. This is what we want to say in the conference. When we went to Nairobi, we were worried about the Cold War. Now we are having hot wars. If mothers and other women do not bring the wisdom which is lacking in this process, then we are in serious trouble. We have to encourage women to act, and we have to demand that we take part in all discussions concerning war. We should no longer say that it is a man's business to go to war. When people used to go out and fight on a battlefield, it was entirely men's business. Now, with technology, whether you are in the house or involved in a war or not, you can get killed. So women can now say, 'This is our business.'

We cannot change things by women feeling that there are some powers above who will come and bring about changes. We are the ones to create them. We have to be determined because it's not easy. Changing the situation is akin to calling for revolution. Sometimes when you say that, people get frightened. But if there is no revolution in our human society, there is not going to be any change. We are not talking about a revolution in which people lose their lives, but about revolutionary attitudes to transform our political and social development structures so that the women don't remain the outsiders in this system. It's sort of a rejection by those who control the structures of the status quo. That's why I say that my contribution is very small and is insignificant. We need international commitment and accountability. Nothing can be done if resources and people are not committed to taking action in order to have a change.

If you look at the concepts we have been talking about, we can't get anything accomplished without working at the grass roots. With regard to the peace question, if you do not socialize your people to live in a peaceful culture, then you can't get away from war. This means reaching everybody. We all have to work together and to reach out to the grass roots. Everyone has a part to play.

If you really want to bring about change, you cannot separate the grass roots from national and international action. International action is there to set the standards, but all people belong to nations, and they all have special characteristics. Sometimes I wonder how we even define 'grass-roots women.' Who are they? They are ordinary people living ordinary lives. They are not in official positions. These are the people who are often ignored. We tend to talk very much about them and talk as if we all belonged to institutions. I think the NGOs have an important role to play because they have a very special linkage with grass-roots people, and their work is focused on the interests of these people. One of my hopes is that, after Beijing, there will be a very strong role for the NGOs. We have recognized their role in preparing for the conference. They have been responsible for articulating views, for example, on the issue of violence, mobilizing support, sensitizing the public about it, and helping to eliminate it.

The NGOs are in a better position to reach out to poor people and work with them to achieve solutions. In the preparations for the conference, we have required that national preliminary meetings should involve both governments and nongovernmental organizations in order to include people who will not be able to go to Beijing. These people are very important. Going to Beijing matters, but bringing the voices of the majority of people is equally important. Those who are coming to Beijing are not mainly grass-roots people. Our aim is to work with societies as they are organized. I think it is important to ensure that people are involved in their different structures. This is a conference for people—men and women. It is different from other conferences because the topic has been focused on women and on people in their diversity.''

Notes

1. United Nations, Commission on the Status of Women, *The Nairobi Forward-Looking Strategies for the Advancement of Women. Adopted by the World Conference to Review and Appraise the Achievements of the United Nations Decade for Women: Equality, Development, and Peace, Nairobi, Kenya, July 15–26, 1985* (DPI/926-4176–September 1993-10M).

2. "UN Said to Deny Equal Employment to Women," *New York Times*, April 10, 1995.

13 / Jessica Neuwirth and Equality Now

JESSICA NEUWIRTH, PRO-BONO DIRECTOR OF Equality Now, exudes a sense of purpose and inner strength. She is a quiet person who rarely speaks of herself and who has an engaging simplicity of manner. Her ability to listen to and understand diverse voices enhances the powerful intelligence she brings to her work. Jessica has devoted her talents, her organizing skills, and her unwavering vision to securing human rights rather than to a lucrative profession. Born in New York City in 1961, she became active in Amnesty International while in high school, an undertaking that would define her future career. She continued this work throughout her undergraduate years at Yale University and was advised by the executive director of Amnesty International to go to law school if she wished to pursue her human rights efforts. As a result, she attended Harvard Law School while acting as coordinator for the

Soviet work of Amnesty. She graduated in 1985 and since then has devoted herself to human rights, alternating with periods of working in the field of international law.

Jessica's years of experience with Amnesty International were varied and included serving as policy adviser for the United States, working closely with the board of directors, and, later, spending two years helping to organize the international concert tour celebrating the fortieth anniversary of the Declaration of Human Rights. Subsequently, she chaired an Amnesty task force on women and human rights that transformed her perception of rights and led to her passionate commitment to the issue of women's human rights. After filling in for the deputy executive director of Amnesty International USA while he was on a field mission for several months, Jessica left the organization and began practicing law at an international law firm in order to expand her areas of expertise.

While pursuing her legal career, she continued to devote herself to women's rights. As a result, in 1992, Jessica, Navanethem Pillay, and Feryal Gharahi, a Muslim lawyer, created Equality Now, an organization devoted to securing women's rights and founded on the unique perspective of its directors. Jessica was then thirty-one years old, at the peak of a career in human rights that had begun at age fourteen.

The office of Equality Now is right near Jessica's apartment, enabling her to combine the many aspects of her life. Each of the directors of the organization correlates professional and human rights work, revealing women's unique abilities to pursue a number of endeavors simultaneously. Equality Now operates on an almost entirely voluntary basis and works closely with grass-roots women's groups around the world, receiving and sharing information on the status of women and violations of their rights and responding to their needs and particular styles of operation. These tasks are accomplished through the Women's Action Network, composed of almost two thousand groups and individuals in sixty-five countries around the world, which organizes appeals on behalf of specific cases and campaigns on women's issues. The creation of the network reflects a desire to acknowledge the problems and resources of different nations; the founders themselves are from the Muslim world and the black South African community as well as from Western culture. Each of the six board members is active in various aspects of law in addition to volunteering time to the organization. The fact that they represent manifold cultures and outlooks enhances the organization's effectiveness in dealing with women's human rights issues in areas such as the rape of Muslim women in Bosnia. While it makes reaching agreement more challenging, ultimately, cultural diversity has helped create a more relevant and sensitive organization.

Jessica and the members of Equality Now have sought to raise the public's consciousness regarding women's rights as human rights. While most abuses against women fall within the purview of the Universal Declaration of Human Rights, adopted in 1948, such violations have tended to be ignored by the member governments. This is because human rights abuses, such as domestic violence, occur within what typically has been defined as "the private sphere" and are therefore not recognized as legal offenses. Public authorities thus have been unable and, often, unwilling to prosecute offenders, even where legislative provisions are available. Domestic violence, rape, the trafficking of women, genital mutilation, female infanticide, sexual harassment, pornography, and reproductive rights have not been included within the agenda of the more established human rights organizations because these crimes are not perpetrated by public authorities, the usual target of these groups, and because often these organizations fear the charge of "cultural imperialism" from more traditional nations.

In contrast to the centralized and Western-oriented groups such as Amnesty International and Human Rights Watch, the founders of Equality Now wished to create an organization that is democratic and decentralized, combining the work of professionals with that of laypersons around the world. They sought to take the best of these organizations, such as their sponsorship of specific cases of abuse and the subsequent gathering of international support for action, and use these techniques to combat human rights violations of women on the local, national, and international level.

Since creating Equality Now, Jessica and her colleagues have undertaken five actions on behalf of women's human rights, beginning with a worldwide protest on behalf of reproductive rights in Poland. Soon after the fall of the Communist government, the Polish medical society revised its code of ethics to prohibit doctors from performing abortions, despite the legality of this procedure in that country. Members of Equality Now contacted doctors and medical associations around the world to express opposition to the medical society for imposing sanctions on doctors performing abortions. Despite national and international pressure, the Polish legislature passed a law criminalizing abortion, with a two-year prison sentence for doctors who perform abortions except when pregnancy results from rape or incest, when the fetus is damaged, or the mother's health is threatened. Undaunted, Equality Now has been working with the Polish Federation for Women and Planned Parenthood as well as with the International Planned Parenthood Federation to address the new situation in Poland, emphasizing that women's reproductive rights are a worldwide problem.[1]

Equality Now's second action was initiated in October 1992 on behalf of a Saudi Arabian woman known as "Nada," who had sought asylum in Canada in 1991 on the basis of the gender discrimination she faced in her country. That same year the Canadian Immigration and Refugee Board ruled that Nada was not a refugee and issued a deportation order and warrant for her arrest, forcing her into hiding. Working with Nada's lawyer and women's rights groups in Canada, Equality Now added an international dimension to the Canadian campaign on her behalf. It also generated international publicity on the case, including an op-ed published in the *Christian Science Monitor* that came to the attention of several Canadian parliamentarians. Concern for Canada's international reputation was cited as a factor in the government's decision in January 1993 to allow Nada to remain in the country and to introduce national guidelines to facilitate the consideration of gender-based claims to political asylum.[2] This achievement revealed the success of concerted action in transforming hitherto male-dominated concepts of rights developed in the mainstream human rights organizations.

The third action on behalf of a specific case concerned the death of Maricris Sioson, a twenty-two-year-old Filipino dancer who went to Japan to work in the entertainment industry in 1991 and died there on September 14 of that year. Although Japanese doctors listed her cause of death as hepatitis, when Maricris's family opened her coffin they discovered that she had been beaten and repeatedly stabbed. Autopsy findings revealed that a double-edged blade had been thrust into her genitalia and identified the cause of death as traumatic head injuries and not hepatitis. The Japanese police insisted that Maricris died as the result of natural causes, and thus no one was charged or tried in connection with her death. Equality Now board member Surita Sandosham met with the Filipino doctor who had performed the autopsy; the organization also enlisted Dr. Fred Jordan, chief medical examiner of the state of Oklahoma, as an independent expert. After the review of the medical records, Dr. Jordan concluded that the death should have been classified as a homicide. Equality Now has worked with the BATIS Center for Women in the Philippines and the HELP Asian Women's Center in Japan, seeking to investigate the death and prosecute those responsible. It wishes to publicize the vulnerability of the thousands of Filipino women working in Japan's entertainment industry.[3]

Equality Now also has undertaken campaigns related to the problems of mass rape and forced pregnancy among refugee women and girls in Bosnia-Herzegovina, and to UNICEF's failure to fund efforts to stop genital mutilation. Studies estimate that 100 million girls and women globally have undergone such mutilation. The lifelong health consequences of this practice include chronic infection; pain during urination, menstruation, sexual intercourse, and childbirth; and psychological trauma. Although this practice occurs in the name of tradition and culture, Equality Now has found that many grass-roots women's organizations within these very cultures are fighting to eradicate it. Building on the efforts of groups that have long campaigned against female genital mutilation, Equality Now called upon UNICEF to provide more funding to help stop this practice. It also enlisted the help of American television, initiating a campaign to increase awareness of the problem.[4]

The many letters from high officials, professionals, and ordinary people around the world in support of these actions have demonstrated that local initiatives can be channeled on behalf of international efforts, and that people from widely differing cultures can find common ground on behalf of women's human rights. In its brief history the organization has helped empower women around the world, thereby demonstrating the ability of dedicated individuals to elicit public awareness of abuse and to inspire the broad participation of ordinary people in human rights work. Jessica Neuwirth and Equality Now have enlarged the discourse and concepts of human rights, establishing a clear linkage between local, national, and international efforts to achieve a more inclusive definition of human dignity.

JESSICA SPEAKS

I don't like the idea of human rights of women as a new wave or a new generation. The rights of women are set forth in the Universal Declaration of Human Rights, and they have been there all along in international law. It's the human rights movement that has neglected them. To date, the movement has concentrated on one corner of the original spectrum of human rights law. It's a very important corner, but other areas are equally important. What we're trying to do is broaden the human rights movement to cover more of the original range of these rights.

"I was in the first Amnesty International high school group, which was formed in 1977. We just did the usual campaigning on behalf of prisoners of conscience and against torture and the death penalty. I continued my involvement in Amnesty during college and spent a summer as an intern in the national office. During law school I joined the coordination group of Amnesty that was focusing on the USSR, and shortly thereafter I became the USSR Coordinator, responsible for the Soviet work of Amnesty in the United States during a very interesting time, before glasnost. Acting as coordinator was a volunteer position, but I probably spent twenty to thirty hours a week doing it. The USSR coordination office was based in my home in Cambridge, Massachusetts, and we had a group of about five or six people sharing the work. The human rights situation was really very dire at the time: long sentences in labor camps, where prisoners were severely beaten and routinely deprived of essential food and medicine. I will never forget the day I learned that Vladimir Marchenko had died in a labor camp—the intense feeling of anger and frustration over our inability to have prevented his death. He was a young Ukrainian activist whom I had met in the Soviet Union just a few months before, while he was in between prison terms. There were several deaths in labor camps around that time. Conditions were extremely harsh, and treatment of prisoners, especially political prisoners, was brutal.

For my first summer in law school, I was granted a Harvard Law School human rights fellowship to travel to the Soviet Union, where I met with a number of dissidents and recently released prisoners, including Vladimir Marchenko. I went in on a guided tour organized by Intourist, the Soviet state travel agency, which was the only way to go. I picked the longest tour I could find and went to Moscow, Kiev, Minsk, Kishinev, Odessa, and Leningrad. In each of those cities I just managed to slip away from the tour and find the human rights activists and the released prisoners. There was such a climate of fear at the time that you couldn't write down names, addresses, or phone numbers. I remember one woman who was so afraid that she wrote her name on a slip of paper, which she then set on fire as soon as I had read it. I knew I would be searched on the way out, and I was thoroughly frisked, but fortunately I have an excellent memory.

The next summer, in 1984, I went to South Africa, funded by another human rights fellowship from Harvard. After several delays caused by the South African government, which couldn't decide whether or not to give me a visa, I finally made it to Durban, where I met Navi Pillay, interning for her law firm. Navi was doing political trials at that time and, in particular, a case involving a number of children who had been detained for over a year, tortured, and then tried as conspirators with the ANC [African National Congress]. I worked with her on the appeal in that case, which focused on torture, and spent a lot of time talking to many lawyers in South Africa about what was going on generally, and also more specifically, in terms of the legal system and torture. It was in a hospital, talking to a young doctor, Bob Dyer, who had been fighting to keep a torture victim from being hauled back into incommunicado detention, that I first saw the security police in action. While I was talking to Dr. Dyer about this particular case, the police burst into the room and dragged him off. They forced him to release the patient to their custody. Watching this doctor put so much at risk, watching Navi relentlessly pursuing justice at all costs, I came to appreciate the courage of human rights activists on the front lines and the tremendous personal sacrifices they make. It was very humbling.

In 1985 I graduated from law school and took the bar. I then immediately went to work for Amnesty International, organizing lawyers and health professionals to do human rights work. I found it very interesting because there were a lot of forensic issues that involved law and medicine, and I had a chance to work with some of the best human rights lawyers and health professionals in the country. I got a much broader sense of the issues internationally, and since then I have retained a profound sense of the importance of professionals in the struggle for human rights—lawyers, judges, doctors, and their professional associations.

I stayed at Amnesty International for six years, moving through quite a number of different positions that gave me a very good overview of the organization. I did campaigning, research, administration, concerts—a little bit of everything. I mostly worked in the United States section and, for a short while, at the International Secretariat in London, and I also had the chance to visit many Amnesty sections around the world.

For a long period of time I served as legal and policy adviser to Amnesty International USA (AIUSA), but by far the biggest project I worked on was the Human Rights Now! tour. That tour consisted of a series of concerts in September/October 1988 to celebrate the fortieth anniversary of the Universal Declaration of Human Rights. It was conceived and masterminded by Jack Healey, the executive director of AIUSA, and traveled to fifteen countries, staging twenty-one concerts in the course of six weeks. Bruce Springsteen, Sting, Peter Gabriel, Tracy Chapman, and Youssou N'Dour were the headliners, with other bands joining them in each country. Many of the countries, such as Zimbabwe, the Ivory Coast, and India, had never had rock concerts on such a large scale. It was a very complex project, which could never have succeeded without Jack Healey's vision and courage. Jack served as executive producer, and I was his special assistant, with particular responsibility for legal and policy issues and more general responsibility for overall coordination of information. Preparing the tour took two years, and it was the most intensive period I have ever experienced. I don't think I slept at all for the six weeks of the tour. When we weren't on airplanes or in stadiums, we were usually on the phone or in meetings dealing with unbelievable crises. We were in high gear almost twenty-four hours a day.

I came back to New York after the last concert of Human Rights Now! in Argentina. I was exhausted but almost immediately had to fill in for the deputy executive director of AIUSA, who had gone on a field mission for several months. There were a number of factors which made me think about moving at that point. I was troubled by some of the internal discussions we had had in the context of the Human Rights Now! campaign, with regard to the Universal Declaration of Human Rights and the positioning of the organization, not only on rights within the Declaration but outside the more limited mandate of Amnesty. Watching governments like Argentina, Uruguay, or the Philippines go through political transitions made me question Amnesty's approach. The torture and *disappearances* that took place in Argentina were classic human rights violations. But as a new government emerged, facing all the difficult questions about dealing with the past, dealing with a dire financial situation and a crushing debt, Amnesty played a much less helpful role. Watching this process unfold, I began thinking about questions such as how one not only protects civil and political rights but also deals with the debt crisis. The debt crisis seemed to me like a really important factor in human rights.

At that time, I was not thinking specifically in terms of gender but more about economic and social rights. However, if you look at the human rights concerns of women, there's a mingling of political, economic, and social issues. Maybe you can isolate torture and political imprisonment and not look too much at other issues, but you can't isolate the violations against women that are the most pressing and not look at economic and social as well as civil issues.

But at that time I wasn't looking at women's issues particularly. I was looking at new governments, and it seemed as if the watchdog role that Amnesty International had always played was not that useful because governments needed an interactive and positive kind of assistance that was beyond the scope of Amnesty International. There was a sense of Amnesty's message to governments as, 'We don't care what you do, just don't do x, y, and z violations.' However, there was Argentina, with hyperinflation and people facing serious problems such as keeping up with the cost of living while their pension was evaporating. Those were pressing problems, and people might end up marching in the streets over them. Then, the soldiers might come out and create a human rights crisis of concern to Amnesty International. However, Amnesty would not address the underlying issues of Argentina's economy and its debt, which was the more pressing human rights issue to those pensioners marching in the streets.

Thinking about all these issues, I became less interested in Amnesty International's work and more concerned with learning about international finance. I considered going back to get a degree in economics but preferred the idea of getting more practical experience related to the debt crisis. I ended up where most of my Harvard Law School classmates had started out five years earlier—on Wall Street. For almost three years I worked at Cleary, Gottlieb, Steen, and Hamilton, an international law firm based in New York and representing various sovereign nations such as Argentina in their negotiations with commercial banks on the refinancing or restructuring of their external indebtedness. I thought that helping to represent such countries would be a good way to learn about and understand the issues involved.

If someone had told me while I was in law school that one day I would work for a Wall Street firm, I would have laughed it off. But at the time, five years later, it seemed a completely natural next step in my career. At Cleary, Gottlieb I had a great opportunity to work on sovereign debt issues and other financial transactions that were being undertaken by developing countries. At the same time, I was lucky enough to get fine legal training from one of the best law firms. I had the privilege to work with Roger Thomas, who is the consummate lawyer and for me the embodiment of professional excellence. What surprised me the most was that I met some wonderful people and really enjoyed my work.

While I was at Cleary, Gottlieb, I started to think more about women and human rights. One of the last projects I had undertaken at Amnesty International, at Jack Healey's request, was to form a task force to look at women and human rights work within Amnesty International. We did some research, which ultimately led to a report on issues relating to women, within the Amnesty International mandate, such as rape in prison, rape by military forces, and imprisonment of activists who advocated gender equality. In the course of this work for the task force, it became clear to me that what I saw as the most pressing problems for women were not going to fit so readily into Amnesty International's mandate, at least not the way Amnesty interpreted it. Amnesty International is very prisoner oriented, and most prisoners in the world are men. Most violence against women takes place on the street or in the home.

Every two years Amnesty has an international meeting of its governing body. I was a delegate at the 1989 gathering in Dublin, where we organized the first international meeting on women and human rights, chaired by Goler Butcher, a wonderful activist and board member of Amnesty International USA, whose recent death was a great loss to the human rights movement. Goler's diplomacy and skill in chairing the international meeting were a godsend because there really wasn't any consensus on what Amnesty should be doing, even among those who came to the meeting and presumably thought Amnesty should be doing more for women. Some people felt that the issues were outside of the mandate and that the mandate should not be changed. One of the bones of contention was abortion, where the question was, If a woman is imprisoned for having an abortion, is she a prisoner of conscience? I think so, but it's not a matter that Amnesty has ever been forced to face. It's not something everyone agrees on. After that meeting, I realized that Amnesty International wouldn't expand its mandate to include the central human rights issues for women—it seemed politically unrealistic.

A few years later, at Cleary, Gottlieb, I suddenly found myself making more money than I had ever dreamed of, and in 1991 I decided to take a vacation. With Jacqui Hunt, a friend of mine from

Amnesty International and subsequently a board member of Equality Now, I went back to South Africa to visit Navi Pillay. The ANC had just been legalized, and I wanted to see firsthand the euphoria I had been hearing about. So much had changed in such a short time. In 1984 I had had the sense that activists in South Africa didn't really expect to see change in their lifetimes. In 1991 there was an explosion of energy, and everything seemed possible, including the end of apartheid. I found Navi, who had been focused entirely on traditional human rights areas such as torture and prison conditions when I first worked with her, now doing innovative legal work on issues relating to domestic violence, an area which was pretty well unknown in South Africa.

I talked to Navi quite a lot about her work, and we started thinking together about international activism for women's rights. There was something practical and effective about Amnesty International's techniques and about its concepts of human rights that we thought could be used to address human rights violations against women. The first component was detailed and accurate case-specific documentation of the violations. The issues for women were clear, but the individual cases and concrete information weren't being researched systematically at the international level. The second component was international activism, the idea of building an international grass-roots campaigning force for the human rights of women. There were many groups already working on a whole range of women's issues, and it seemed that there was great potential for action based on global solidarity—even more so, I think, than in other contexts. In the women's movement, groups that work on specific issues understand the connections among all the issues. The fight for reproductive rights, to counter violence against women, for economic rights, and for political empowerment all relate to the underlying struggle for equality.

With all these thoughts in mind, in the winter of 1992 I went with Kate Lauer, a friend of mine from Cleary, Gottlieb, to Thailand and Cambodia. We went to visit the refugee camps on the Thai-Cambodian border and we went into Phnom Penh, just after the peace accords had been signed and the UN was setting up its advance mission in Cambodia (UNAMIC). En route, we spent a couple of days in Bangkok and took the opportunity to visit a group whose work on the trafficking of women I had become familiar with, the Foundation for Women. We spent a morning in their offices, hearing story after story of young girls being bought and sold into prostitution. What was going on seemed like a major human rights violation, and yet it was neglected in the mainstream media and human rights efforts.

After I returned to New York, and in between offering circulars and closings at Cleary, Gottlieb, I started to think more seriously about the legal issues involving the human rights of women. I reread the Universal Declaration of Human Rights and rediscovered certain articles that had always been there but which I had never really focused on before. All of the violations against women that I was concerned about were violations of the fundamental human rights guarantees in that document. It is really an amazing document. The Universal Declaration of Human Rights captured in 1948 a vision of rights which is broader and more comprehensive than anything since then in international law. Amnesty International has taken a few articles from the Declaration and called them 'human rights,' but they are only part of the vision set forth in the Declaration. There are very specific provisions, such as the right to choose your own marriage partner, which is in Article 16. More generally, 'Everyone has the right to life, liberty and security of person,' according to Article 3. What is security of person if it's not the right to be free from rape? The Declaration doesn't specify security of person only from acts committed by state agents. It is true that governments have the responsibility, under international law, to implement this document. But I've come to feel very strongly about the argument that governments fundamentally have a responsibility under international law to protect their citizens from violence. That must be one of the main purposes of government. Moreover, there is a specific obligation under international law for governments to protect their citizens equally. Article 7 provides that 'all are equal before the law and entitled without any discrimination to equal protection of the law.' If women systematically remain unprotected by the police from domestic violence, for example, that's a human rights violation under international law.

There are many other provisions in the Universal Declaration of Human Rights which are particularly relevant to women. Article 4 provides that 'no-one shall be held in slavery or servitude, slavery and the slave trade shall be prohibited in all their forms.' Yet girls are being sold into sex slavery every day. Article 13 provides that 'everyone has the right to freedom of movement and residence within the borders of each state.' How many countries do not allow women to leave the home? The right to own property is in Article 17, which says that 'everyone has the right to own property alone as well as in association with others.' It doesn't say, 'only men,' it says 'everyone,' and yet there are countries where women are not allowed to own property. I don't like the idea of human rights of women as a new wave or a new generation. The rights of women are set forth in the Universal Declaration of Human Rights, and they have been there all along in international law. It's the human rights movement that has neglected them. To date, the movement has concentrated on one corner of the original spectrum of human rights law. It's a very important corner, but other areas are equally important. What we're trying to do is broaden the human rights movement to cover more of the original range of these rights.

Think about it in the context of South Africa. What is the difference between race and gender discrimination? South Africa was a pariah in the international community because of its institutionalized discrimination. That's a model we look to. Why don't we make Kuwait a pariah because women don't have the right to vote? People say, 'Well, that's cultural.' What does that mean? There are women in Kuwait who want to vote. Kuwaiti women demonstrated during the last election. Wanting control over your own life isn't some Western idea. I think it's a universal aspiration. It's true that women get socialized into certain roles and a certain consciousness, so that sometimes we don't fully appreciate the extent of our own second-class status. That happens everywhere. At the same time, in any country in the world, you will find women who want equality.

The human rights movement has shied away from women's issues on the grounds that they are 'cultural.' Well, if it was any group other than women, that movement probably wouldn't feel so comfortable with this line of argument because rights are supposed to be universal. Governments often try to make the case that human rights are a matter of internal affairs, and the human rights movement has strongly opposed this position. Why is it acceptable to say such a thing about human rights violations against women?

I think the human rights community hasn't asked itself that question seriously enough. Look at the practice of female genital mutilation, which the human rights movement is so afraid of condemning. One hundred million women around the world have undergone some form of genital mutilation. It's a very dangerous practice, and many girls have died in the course of it. Others have been severely afflicted with lifelong medical complications and psychological effects. I don't want to spend a lot of time talking about whether or not this is a human rights violation. When you tie a little girl down and slice off a part of her body and that little girl has no legal protection, that has to be a violation of her rights. We can go through the legal arguments of why it is a violation, but I think it's just a question of acknowledgment.

When we started Equality Now, it was because we had been looking at issues like trafficking in women and female genital mutilation, and we knew that people would care about these violations if they only knew more about what was happening. Our target wasn't really the human rights community of fulltime activists. It was ordinary people, women and men who would be willing to do something to help stop these violations—just write a letter of protest, or make a contribution, or volunteer to help in some other way. We contacted all the women's rights groups we could find, and it seemed that there wasn't any organization focused on bringing in members of the general public to address these international women's rights issues. Navi Pillay, Feryal Gharahi, and I were the three official founders of Equality Now. We incorporated in April 1992, and the organization just took off because there was such a strong response to the idea. From a few newspaper articles, we received hundreds of letters and thousands of dollars. The Women's Action Network we created now has almost two thousand members in more than sixty-five countries around the world.

We try to keep the work simple, and we try to avoid ideological debate and rhetoric. We want to focus on the facts, on the girls and women who are being bought and sold, beaten, raped, mutilated, killed. Our hope is that anybody with a conscience and a sense of decency will agree that this is wrong, and that equality is a fundamental right. That's our starting point. I have to confess that I wasn't born a feminist. We are fortunate to have Taina Bien-Aimé on our board now, a lawyer from Cleary, Gottlieb, who has more of that background and outlook. Sometimes I get a bit lost in the ideology, and Taina can always interpret the concepts in a way that makes sense to me.

Our initial board of directors was very small, just Navi, Feryal, and I. I met Feryal through Jack Healey, and she did all our initial work on Bosnia-Herzegovina. Jacqui Hunt, who joined the board soon after we started, has also been very involved in our work on Bosnia and on other projects. Surita Sandosham, another board member and a lawyer trained in Singaporean as well as British and American law, took time from her maternity leave, just months after she had had a baby, to represent Equality Now at a week-long meeting on trafficking in women in Thailand. One thing all our board members have in common is that they are very busy. They all have a similar work style, just focusing on getting things done. We consult a lot, but we hate meetings.

Equality Now also has an advisory council. Jack Healey was the first person on the advisory council. In fact, Jack was one of the inspirations for Equality Now, and he has been tremendously helpful. Gloria Steinem, Rose Styron, and Veronica De Negri also joined the advisory council from the beginning and have lent their support to the organization from its first days. More recent additions to the advisory council include Liz Young, Jewelle Taylor Gibbs, and Maurine Rothschild.

Organizationally, we're trying to do things a bit differently. Our first paid staff person is an office manager, who provides volunteers, board members, and others with the administrative support they need to make the best use of their time. All of our major projects have been spearheaded by different volunteers. We had a team of two, Sophie Hahn, a lawyer, and Bonnie Greenfield, a graphic designer, who produced our brochure. Each of our events to date, in New York and Los Angeles, was organized by a different volunteer who came in and took on the coordination responsibility with the help of the office.

If we could afford program staff, we would set up small offices in each region of the world to do the research and coordinate campaigning efforts. We are hoping in the next few years to have enough funding to try this model, starting with a small office in Africa. There's been a very great centralization of international human rights work, mostly in the United States and Western Europe, but that's not where most of the work is focused. To me that makes little sense. It seems inefficient. We want to have people based close to where their work is. Another tradition from Amnesty International we've abandoned is the 'work in own country' rule, the idea that members from the country you are researching shouldn't be centrally involved in the research work. Not only do we feel that they should take the lead on matters of research, but we feel that they should direct matters of strategy. They know their countries better than we do, and they know what will be most likely to have an impact or, alternatively, what might be counterproductive.

We try to find groups that match where we are in the human rights spectrum and then see how we can support their work. We want to reinforce the priorities they've established and the actions they've already undertaken in their countries. What we can add is an international overlay to their work, so that other people outside the country know what they're doing and know best how to help them. We try to be open minded and creative in our work with these groups. We give them some idea of what we think the resources are and let them play with various strategies. We try not to assume that just because something works well here it'll work well somewhere else, and vice versa.

We don't have the resources to visit groups in other countries systematically, but we're getting in touch with them. We send them all of our Women's Actions as a matter of course, and many groups and individual activists write letters regarding those Actions. We've gotten petitions from women in Sudan on behalf of women who have been raped in Bosnia, letters from Latin American groups concerned about female genital mutilation in Africa, letters from South Africa about reproductive rights in Poland. There's a lot of solidarity.

We are very committed to using this solidarity for issues in North America and Europe as well as other parts of the world. We think that pressure from other parts of the world would be very helpful on problems here. Last year we took up the case of a Saudi Arabian woman who was denied political asylum by a judge in Canada who rejected her claim and said she would 'do well' to comply with the laws she was criticizing and that she should show more respect for her father and her family. Women and groups from all around the world started protesting in response to our Women's Action, and I think it made the Canadians a bit nervous and had an impact. There's no reason to think that the United States is impervious to international public pressure, and we have plenty of problems here that could be highlighted.

When I come into contact with the reality of what's happening to women, I still get shocked. I wonder how I could have been in the human rights movement so long and yet have no understanding of the extent of human rights violations against women around the world or even in my own country. When I first started getting the numbers on domestic violence in the United States, I was really taken aback. Even a conservative body like the American Medical Association estimates that several million women every year are getting beaten severely enough to require medical attention. It's statistically impossible that I wouldn't know some of these women. I thought I didn't until I started talking about it. As with all human rights violations, breaking the silence is the first step. I was truly amazed by the stories friends of mine started to tell me about their own lives. I would go to a meeting to talk to someone about something like not-for-profit tax exemption, and we would end up talking about how it feels to be stalked. It was really a revelation.

We have a video that we use to try to show the range of human rights violations against women. It includes a segment on domestic violence, with a clip from South Africa where a woman describes her experience of having been hacked with a bush knife by her husband. I have never seen anyone watch that testimony and not cry, men and women alike. It is the same experience as watching the testimony of torture—the sense of degradation, and the powerlessness of having nowhere to turn. Next on the video is the story of Tracey Thurman in Connecticut, right next to the South African segment so that people can see this isn't a problem just 'out there' but also right here in the United States. Tracey Thurman called the police many times because she knew her husband was going to try and kill her. Even after she was stabbed repeatedly, the policeman was on the scene for forty minutes before the would-be killer was arrested. In that time, while the policeman was standing there, this man jumped on Tracey Thurman's neck. All I can think is that if you just turn the clock back and have the police immediately arrest and restrain this man, in other words do their job properly, Tracey Thurman's spine wouldn't have been broken. You have to ask yourself, When does inaction become action, and what difference does it make from Tracey Thurman's point of view? She had a right to protection from the police, and they violated that right by ignoring her repeated calls for help and then by minimizing the nature of the crime that was occurring when they arrived at her house; in other circumstances, they would have taken a more assertive course of action in the face of an assault with intent to kill. We have to make it clear that this kind of devaluing is not going to be tolerated.

It's a great disappointment to me when people in the human rights movement don't embrace activism on issues such as domestic violence or reproductive rights. The great human rights leaders are very strong on women: they understand that women's rights constitute an equality issue just like racism or any other form of discrimination. It's hard for us to admit that just as there is sexism everywhere, there is sexism in the human rights movement. I don't even think everyone is conscious of it, and that's a big part of the problem.

Equality Now relies on attention from the media because we don't have enough funds to do systematic outreach; we don't do advertising, and we don't do direct mail. We've grown pretty much by word of mouth. The Women's Action Network of Equality Now has several thousand members in sixty-five countries. What we find is that there is one really active person and all of a sudden there's a flurry of new membership. Equality Now grows in fits and starts, but it keeps growing. We don't always know what happens to the Women's Actions. We may get a copy of a press clipping months after it appeared in a country where we didn't know anyone had heard of Equality Now. One day we got in the mail a copy of our Bosnia Women's Action poster, 'WANTED: RADOVAN KARADZIC, FOR MASS RAPE AND MURDER,' in Turkish. We have no idea how that poster got to Turkey, but a group had translated it and sent it out through their whole trade union.

Interest in Equality Now seems particularly strong among young people. Thanks to a leap of faith by Bob Guccione, Jr., the editor and publisher of *SPIN* magazine, Equality Now has had a monthly letter-writing column since January 1994. *SPIN* is a music magazine with a readership that is primarily in the thirteen- to twenty-five-year-old age group. We get a lot of mail from these readers, and they write many letters of protest in response to the monthly columns. Kids tell us that they look forward to the column. One girl wrote to us that she cried every month when she read the column. These kids are really great organizers and activists. I don't think anyone is too young to care about human rights. I first got involved in Amnesty when I was fourteen, thanks to Lee Stearns, who was my high school history teacher. That's the age when you're beginning to figure things out and find yourself. It's a great time for these young people to know what's happening in the world because then they learn to care about it. I remember a letter from a *SPIN* reader which started out, 'I'm only twelve, but I can see what's coming, and I don't like what I see.' Lee Stearns, who became a very close friend of mine, died in a tragic accident just a few months after we founded Equality Now. She had long since started a women's studies program in the high school and was in the process of getting her students organized to begin an Equality Now group.

Equality Now is a volunteer movement, and I've really put a lot of time into it. There are many people right there with me putting huge chunks of their lives into this, just because they feel it is important. When I left Cleary, Gottlieb, it was only because Equality Now was growing so fast that I felt we had to take advantage of this momentum, and I just didn't have enough time to keep up with all the opportunities. Now, of course, I had worked for years at Amnesty International so I knew how to live on less money, but you get spoiled. It's fun to go up in income, and it's not that easy to come back down. But the work is so rewarding, it's well worthwhile. Watching the organization grow from an idea in my living room to an office with staff, interns, and volunteers has been a very moving experience. I have been working part time and expect in the future to go back to work full time. People come in to fill the gap, and that's what we need, a broad-based movement of leadership.

Lawyers are so used to hands-on coordination and the control resulting from that. We do have certain skills that are helpful, although many people would argue the opposite. But I have learned so much from my interaction with women's rights activists around the world, and humility is the first lesson. It's a hard lesson for a person like me, who comes from a background of privilege, but you keep learning it. I have an ever-increasing respect for other ways of approaching human rights and different ways of thinking about activism. I find myself awed by the women around the world who are doing so much to promote human rights. They deserve so much more support than they get, and they're doing so much with so little.

The fundamental issues that we are dealing with, like equality, are everywhere. I think there are different stages of consciousness in the spectrum of discussion, and we make the mistake of thinking that other countries are monolithic in their opinions; if you find one woman who says she wants to circumcise her daughter, then somehow that translates into the assumption that all women in that country support circumcision. There are a lot of women in this country whom I would not want to represent the opinion of American women. Yet, on the other hand, when women do come out with retrogressive views, I don't think they should become primary targets. Those outlooks are just the result of environment and circumstances beyond their control. It is often difficult to follow your heart or some small inner voice because from the time you are born you're subjected to so much pressure not to. We should focus on the socialization but, instead, we tend to focus on the victims of social forces.

How do we fight this pressure? I think the bottom line is equality in the power structure. That's the only real solution. There's no way to systematically win battles on sexual harassment and discrimination unless there is equality at the top, because we're always going to be asking people to see a perspective that's not their own. There are many good, progressive people who will make the effort and see it that way, but it's just not the same as identifying with it and understanding it from a personal vantage point. I don't know if I will live to see real power sharing at the top. I hope so.''

Notes

1. Equality Now, *1992–93 Report*, 2.
2. Ibid., 5.
3. Ibid., 7–9.
4. Ibid., 6–7, 10–11.

14 / Navanethem Pillay

AFTER YEARS OF WORK FOR political prisoners in the struggle against apartheid, Navi Pillay began to focus on the legal and political status of women in South Africa. This involvement led her to create the Advice Desk for Abused Women at the University of Durban and to coauthor *Violence against Women: Rights and Remedies*. The Advice Desk is one of the few organizations in South Africa that specializes in domestic violence and related issues; since it opened its doors in 1986, it has assisted over seven thousand women and their families. Navi also has written numerous articles about women's issues, and in 1992 she helped found and now chairs Equality Now, an international human rights organization for action on women's rights.

Navi and her husband adopted two girls while she was in the throes of some of her most difficult cases. Like many women involved in human rights work, Navi believes that there must be continuity between practices in the home and the profession of one's beliefs in the public arena. She has created a home environment that allows for freedom of expression as well as honoring the values of mutual respect and dignity. When the children reached their teens, they were encouraged to choose whatever religion appealed to them. "The practice in our home is that you don't hurt a single person's feelings. You try and help as much as possible. You have moral values. You have a sense of what is good. The children said to me that they like my values."

Although Navi had always combined her political work, her career as a lawyer, and her life as a mother while at the same time coping with a dangerous political situation, she only began focusing on women's rights as human rights in the 1980s, when she spent time in the United States working on an advanced degree at Harvard. Since then, Navi has become more and more deeply involved in trying to gain recognition for women's rights.

As many people welcome the coming of a new government in South Africa, women such as Navi Pillay are aware that they face many years of hard work to ensure their rights despite their active participation in the struggle against apartheid. While all people of color suffered flagrant injustices under that system, rural women were particularly vulnerable as their husbands and fathers were forced into the migratory labor system, leaving them as heads of households in the poor agricultural regions or as servants in urban areas where they were separated from their children by discriminatory residency laws. Black women suffered doubly under apartheid, subject to discriminatory laws imposed by the Afrikaner government and also caught in the web of male-dominated traditional law.

The Women's National Coalition in South Africa, which has been conducting research on women's rights, has noted that despite their racial diversity and differing economic and social backgrounds, there are some key concerns common to all women in South Africa. These points include their legal status; their general social and familial status; their economic position; the issues of violence, intimidation, and rape; and finally, the pressing need for both political awareness and political participation at all levels within South Africa.[1]

As Navi Pillay stresses, discriminatory practices are largely based on the legal system. She sees the rationale for unequal treatment for women as grounded in the origins of South African law,

English common law, Roman Dutch law, African customary law, Indian social systems, and Bantu law, all of which regard women as legal minors under the authority of a husband or guardian. In addition, women are under the tutelage of the *kraalhead* (political leader of the community), according to the customary law of Bantu and Zulu systems.[2] Women in South Africa are also subject to varying civil, customary, and religious laws. There are only three old statutes that deal specifically with their rights. These laws allowed the admission of women as attorneys, gave the vote to white women, and allowed white women to sit on white juries.[3] All South African women suffer from prejudice; they are systematically devalued and viewed as existing for the convenience of their husbands or partners. Changes in the legal system guarantee community property to African women married after December 1988 and white, colored, and Indian women married after November 1984.[4] However, the law does not cover African women in existing marriages, who still fall under customary law. Despite some small areas of progress the legal system neglects women's changing circumstances.

Navi Pillay explains that the law discriminates against women in crucial areas of their lives. For instance, although women have always been important participants in the labor force, they are unable to sign contracts or purchase property and goods without a male guarantor. This makes them wards of either their husbands or sons and is a form of humiliation. Furthermore, despite the social havoc created by apartheid with its migratory labor system, urbanization, and the disruption of the family, traditional practices still remain in effect, including polygamy, the power of chiefs over the everyday life of women, and the inability of women to own land. Women of color have noted that tradition-conscious men typically use the concept of culture to maintain their dominant positions.

Women from all walks of life suffer inequality in the workplace and are seeking equal pay for equal work as well as due consideration when applying for positions or for promotions. They are also demanding access to jobs traditionally reserved for men in the professions as well as in heavy industry, such as mining or construction, where the pay is higher. As in many other societies, women are relegated to socially ascribed positions in which both the pay and the social status is much lower than those in jobs reserved for men. While women represent an important percentage of heads of household, employers, banks, and credit agencies have failed to make provision for their growing responsibility and still require male sponsorship to obtain credit and to complete financial transactions. For those women who are financially dependent on men, unpaid work in agriculture and in the home is another source of grievance.[5]

Working women complain of widespread sexual harassment by male coworkers and by their employers. This problem has yet to be regarded as a social problem stemming from male dominance in politics and the economy. It is typically treated as the wayward behavior of a single individual rather than the problem of a male perspective in all areas of life, especially in the courts.

As in many societies, violence against women in South Africa is a national problem and affects all racial and socioeconomic groups. Navi Pillay has written that domestic violence is the primary area in which women encounter difficulties in the courts.[6] Currently, such violence is not a specific criminal act, and family violence is commonly viewed as a private matter. Unlike their counterparts in the United States, South African courts rarely order the removal of the abuser from the home. In both black and white communities, wife abuse is typically ignored by family members, neighbors, and traditional leaders.

Similarly, in this male-dominated legal system, the widespread occurrence of rape remains unpunished; when a case is actually brought to trial, the offender typically gets a very light sentence, which hardly serves as a deterrent. Women who testify in court experience renewed trauma but, as yet, there is no counselling or psychiatric care provided for the victims.

The status of women in the broader society is generally one of subservience, buttressed by an educational system that steers females away from higher education and the professions. Concerned South African women see a direct connection between improving their condition and addressing pressing social problems such as poverty, unwanted and teenage pregnancies, and the spread of AIDS. They have also noted a significant gap between legal theory guaranteeing equal treatment and accepted practice, which reinforces a man's power in a marriage.

Male dominance within the family, the economy, the legal system, and society impinge heavily upon women's political rights and participation. Within the home, wives are expected to follow the politics preferred by their husbands or risk a confrontation with family, religious leaders, chiefs, or employers.[7] While political parties often express concern for women's rights, their statements are rarely followed by practical steps. Women wish to address this situation by acquiring the education, skills, and political awareness that will enable them to participate at all political levels, from municipal councils to regional authorities to the national parliament.

Navi Pillay has dedicated herself to the achievement of women's human rights at all of these levels. Because of the pressing problems that women face in South Africa, the Advice Desk she founded recently expanded its mission to assure social change through partnership with women's community and grass-roots organizations. It now seeks to help redress the long history of discrimination against women and to guarantee them equal access to society's political, economic, and social resources.

NAVI SPEAKS

We see women's rights as human rights because women have been systematically disadvantaged as a group. Only the male perspective has been validated as the norm, in literature, law, and religion.

["Equal Rights for Women," *African Law Review* 3 (April 1992): 24.]

"I learned about the problems of African women when I was a patient at the public hospital, King Edward VIII. There, every Friday evening, a ward for twenty patients would be filled with sixty patients. I would get out of bed and help the nurses pull down extra mattresses, which were stained with blood and urine. They would put the mattresses under the beds and along the corridors for the extra weekend patients. The women would come in on a Friday night and all be discharged on Sunday night. They were people who had attempted illegal abortions on the street. Abortion is a crime in South Africa, and both the doctors and the women could get charged if they were caught. The doctors would do what they could to save the women. They told me that if they reported these women, the women wouldn't come to the hospitals. The women told me that because abortion was illegal, they had tried with the 'back street' abortionists to carry out the procedure. I asked details of what went on and learned about piercing with a sharp needle and injections with soapy water. As a result, these women developed infections and risked death. They were women who had to work to support themselves and their families. I learned so much from what was going on around me in the hospital about the neglect of women's health, what oppression meant to black women in this country. I emerged from this experience as a women's rights lawyer.

Soon after I returned from Harvard in 1982, I became involved in work for women's rights. Up to that point, I had seen myself differently. I hadn't concerned myself with matters traditionally regarded as domestic matters because I was a professional lawyer and I felt had to be the same as men and treat these issues as unimportant. I was completely in a male world, doing political trials. I was taught about women's perspectives relatively late, and by other women. I used to think that the struggle should be for political freedom and that then everything else, including women's empowerment, would come into place. Not so. Now the women are saying in the ANC [African National Congress] that they don't expect the men in the ANC will automatically grant women their rights or their proper position.

There are the laws which declare women as minors and prevent them from inheriting or owning property. In terms of the law there are various rules which treat women differently. Two months ago [December 1993] many changes were made, but we are talking about three hundred years where the man is the head of the household and the woman can neither buy anything nor get credit without her husband's consent. She can't sue or start a case without his consent. If she is giving evidence in any sexual offense, rape, or sexual assault, her single evidence is not accepted. It has to be corroborated by some other evidence. She can't have a bank account or a business of her own. Changes are now taking place, but it's going to take many years for women to understand that they have these rights. African women could not own property before. They came under the tutelage of first their father, then their husband, then their son. They were minors subject to these legal restrictions. Traditional and cultural practices, such as polygamous marriages and payment of bride price or *lobola*, discriminated against and disempowered women.

There is violence against women in the homes and in the community. Family violence is rampant, and there is little legal protection. The police say to the women, 'Kiss and make up.' We hold workshops in the townships, and we suggest standard remedies like telephoning the police, but the women answer that they have no phone and that there is no police station.

I am involved in many organizations working for women's rights. A lecturer in criminology at the University of Durban, Dr. Anshu Padayachee, and I set up the Advice Desk for Abused

Women. This organization has grown and has many networks which focus on the general development of women as well as issues of violence. I am also founder, with American lawyer Jessica Neuwirth, of Equality Now, an international women's rights organization. I used to belong to women's groups where you learned about flower arrangement and such and collected money to build nursery schools. Women were supposed to be concerned with crèches and welfare. These groups marginalize women, and they marginalize the issues of greatest importance for women.

We started this Advice Desk in 1986. We included social workers and welfare bodies, functioning as a coalition that provided referral and support services. We were working from our homes, taking telephone calls at any hour of the day or night. As we became known in the community, more and more people started phoning us. Now the Advice Desk is housed in the university and to date we've seen more than seven thousand women. Mainly women phone. Volunteers assess their needs and refer them to a psychologist, a shelter, or a lawyer. We have a team of lawyers, also mainly women, all giving their services free of charge.

It's hard to do all of this together with the day's work. I get all of these calls during my regular working hours. Sometimes the women calling don't need a lawyer, but I only gather that after spending half an hour talking to them. As the volume has grown so much, now I try to channel some of these calls to the attorneys who work with me. I've always had women attorneys working with me. They like being in a human rights firm, and they say they find ordinary commercial work boring. At first they criticize me for giving so much free time and advice, but then they start doing exactly what I am doing because you have a woman sitting in front of you with a black eye or a pregnant woman who has been kicked in the stomach, and she needs to talk. Mainly, we instruct women on their legal rights.

We make efforts to ensure that violations of women's rights receive constant media attention. We have done excellent videos on family violence, one of which has been aired on national television. In South Africa now there is a move to place more women in positions of power. I have received calls asking me to run for office. But I am unusual in that I am not even planning to vote. I don't know how I can vote. I am wary of this compromised settlement. Certainly, if one has to choose between the ANC and the Afrikaans government, one would chose the ANC as representative of the majority's aspirations. I do think that women should be involved in the political process and could make a difference, but I have no personal interest in political positions of power.

In preparation for the elections and the drawing up of an interim constitution, the women of South Africa formed a national coalition. It was very historic. The men have not been able to do that. I was at the very first meeting and recall reporting from one of the workshops back to the plenary, saying, 'You white women don't understand our problems as black women and, once again, we don't want you speaking for us.' I was reporting as a spokesperson, and at that stage I thought that it would not be possible for such disparate groups of women to work together. Afterward, I received a number of calls from other women telling me that I had an important role to play and should stay with the effort. So, I joined the legal working group at the national level of the Women's National Coalition. The coalition has about 108 regional bodies and organizations. The regional body in Durban has about 700 women's organizations affiliated with it. The coalition lasted for almost two years. In fact, I've just come from the national meeting, which was held on February 27, 1994, in Johannesburg, where the women presented a draft charter of women's rights. We have unity and diversity. I sat with Nationalist Party women, Inkata women, church groups, rural women's groups, lawyers, and other professional women. It was really something.

The role of the Women's National Coalition was to influence the new constitution, especially to include an equality clause in the charter for fundamental rights. The negotiated settlement which took place meant that there will have to be an interim constitution. The new government will then have the next five years to come up with a permanent constitution, which most probably will follow the draft or interim constitution. There was input from women, not only from women from the National Coalition but also from women in the various political parties, including ANC women and Nationalist Party women. Women were united on the need for a comprehensive equality clause in the constitution. We also have a special statute for the very first time on the prevention of family violence, a statute which removes discriminatory clauses against women in about thirteen laws, guaranteeing that both parents are now equal guardians and that the father is no longer head of the family. The same marriage laws now apply to all race groups, although customary law governing traditional marriages is recognized as well.

Having made provision for a guarantee of equality, the constitution also enforces the right to freedom of religion and culture. In some parts of South Africa, traditional society and cultural law are prevalent and are actively enforced, to the detriment of women. The traditional chiefs at these constitutional talks have said that the concept of equality between men and women is foreign to customary law. The rural men have met and said that they want traditional law retained because it is intrinsic to their culture. Black male students on university campuses have been polled and have said that, in their culture, if they want to sleep with a woman, she just has to agree, and they don't want her coming with Western ideas. The Advice Desk that we set up has come across these problems on the campuses. We are very hopeful that the equality clause, which provides specifically for gender equality as well as for different sexual orientations, will outweigh everything else in the future South Africa.

We see women's rights as human rights because women have been systematically disadvantaged as a group under the laws of apartheid, enduring customs, family violence, and lack of government action to protect women. There are no shelters provided by the state. The authorities have said that welfare is not the state's responsibility. Women have been disadvantaged as a group, and we see this as an imbalance of power. The lowest-paying jobs are held by women. There's no point in having a bare clause saying everyone is equal when you have a historically disadvantaged group. So the equality clause in the interim constitution is accompanied by an affirmative action clause, which we hope will be a great asset in the struggle for genuine equality.

I see the difference between men and women working for human rights all the time. The men make a profession out of it as if it were a corporate job. They do not have the experiences that women have. I think women add their own dimension to the work based on their personal experience. For example, we cannot walk on the street at night or be alone in public places without feeling afraid and threatened by violence from men. Men take these things for granted. We do not make men the object of physical attack or even of sexual jokes. Men look at women as sexual objects all the time. Even in my position and at my age, when I walk into a group of male lawyers, they invariably say something that stereotypes me as a woman. Both women and men need to be socialized into greater respect for gender differences and gender equality.

If I merely functioned as a lawyer committed to change through the political system, then I would be promoting a charter drawn up with a comprehensive equality clause that covers everything and that incorporates the lessons we have learned from mistakes made in other countries, such as the United States. Then I would sit back, feeling a sense of accomplishment with all of these legal documents in place. But in actual practice, these documents don't reach women at the grass-roots level. I have been drawn into the organized women's movement, nationally through the Advice Desk and the Women's National Coalition, and internationally through Equality Now. These organizations represent a commitment to translate legal rights for women into the actual empowerment of women in terms of real changes in their lives. In my opinion, the women's movement is just now getting off the ground, and this is a time of great opportunity for us to make a significant difference."

Notes

1. Women's National Coalition, Johannesburg, "Women's National Coalition Research Issues" (Convenor: Frene Ginwala, n.d.).
2. Navanethem Pillay, "Equal Rights for Women," *African Law Review* 3 (April 1992): 14–25.
3. Ibid.
4. Ibid., 21.
5. Women's National Coalition, "Women's National Coalition Research Issues."
6. Pillay, "Equal Rights for Women," 23.
7. Women's National Coalition, "Women's National Coalition Research Issues."

15 / Zhu Hong

As a noted researcher and a teacher of Victorian literature in China, Zhu Hong has used her position to combat censorship and sexism and to promote humane values. In a society in which sociological studies and political activism are dangerous and often life threatening, she has found that literature can serve as the voice of the oppressed and as a vehicle for change. Zhu Hong regards literature as a mirror, revealing social structures and practices that deny women political, social, and economic rights. For the past fourteen years she has translated fiction by women writers, revealing the oppression they endure and thereby breaking the code of silence blanketing women's conditions.

Born in 1933 as the daughter of a second wife and a Western-educated father, Zhu was exposed to the English language and, later, to English literature, at an early age. Although her father resided in a large compound with his other wives, he would periodically visit her and her mother, and he taught Zhu English when she was very young.

When the Japanese invaded China in 1937, Zhu's parents, who were newly divorced, sent her to a convent school run by Franciscan nuns to avoid the effects of the Japanese occupation on education. There, Zhu became fluent in English and began her long love affair with Victorian fiction and the works of Charles Dickens, Jane Austen, George Eliot, and the Brontës. While this education set her apart from her contemporaries and the other students at the convent, it ultimately provided her with a frame of reference with which to evaluate political events. It also gave her an inner strength that enabled her to retain her convictions through the most searing political and personal experiences.

Zhu was fifteen years old when the Communists took over mainland China in 1949. The convent was closed and the nuns deported as spies. Her parents were in deep trouble because both her father and stepfather had links to the Kuomintang. Suddenly left to her own devices, she decided to take entrance exams for the Catholic university because she feared that no other university would accept her unconventional education. Coming from a convent school, Zhu was regarded as an alien by the other students at a time when all foreigners were considered to be enemies. As a result, she was not allowed to join the Youth League, an organization that guaranteed its members not only jobs but also social acceptance. Spurred by a lifetime of rejection by her parents and of not fully belonging either in the convent society or in her family, she sought to join the Communists, believing that the revolution would mean regeneration for her country.

Soon after the revolution it became impossible for the Catholic university to stay open, and Zhu transferred to Beijing University. There, she finally had a stroke of good luck when the head of her class helped her to join the Youth League just before her graduation in 1953. However, because of her "bourgeois" background, Zhu's career possibilities were severely limited. While her classmates were entering the Ministry of Foreign Affairs and taking other positions in the diplomatic field or in the army, Zhu was assigned to the Institute of Social Sciences, where she conducted research in foreign literature and where she has remained throughout her life. Although this may seem like a worthy career to outside observers, at the time it was a source of great shame and an indication of her "bad origins." Her background was to haunt her throughout her life, both personally and politically.

Zhu married at a young age and had a daughter by her first husband. She later divorced, then married a colleague at the Institute of Social Sciences, and bore a son. However, she was unable to concentrate on rearing her children because, as a young cadre, Zhu was expected to spend frequent periods of time in the countryside without her family, engaging in manual labor and, especially, in thought reform. Beginning in the late 1950s, at the time of the Great Leap Forward,* academics periodically were forced to spend time in the country, where they led a highly regimented and impoverished life that also involved engaging in self-criticism. On many occasions, Zhu was told to pack up immediately and go to the countryside. There were no provisions for bringing her family with her, and she was forced to make last-minute arrangements for her children's care with her mother and, later, when her mother had died, with her second husband's mother. The various periods that Zhu spent on collective farms added up to more than five years.

The 1950s were followed by the socialist education movement, which Mao launched in late 1963 and which ended in 1965. Although limited to rural areas, it was a precursor of the Cultural Revolution. Like her fellow cadres, Zhu was sent down to the villages to conduct socialist education, which involved ensuring the continuance of the class struggle and so-called purity of thought and spending a whole year working on a collective farm. Ultimately, she came to regard these times as reverse indoctrination as she witnessed firsthand the poverty and misery of the countryside and what communism actually meant for the average peasant.

Despite these interruptions in her career and her personal life, Zhu was able to grow as a scholar and thinker. She was given the opportunity to study William Shakespeare and other Elizabethan and Jacobean writers and to write papers on them, soon learning how to use these assignments to promote her personal beliefs. For instance, one of her papers on Charlotte Brontë's *Jane Eyre* included statements on the importance of personal integrity, a controversial position in a society that demanded active conformity.

*The Great Leap Forward was an industrialization campaign in which the entire working population was made to produce steel, even in hospitals, schools, backyards, and in the countryside. The ultimate result was widespread famine as the crops went untended and production in other areas was neglected.

Zhu wanted to help people stop living the double lives that they endured in China, characterized by the thoughts that they kept secret for fear of reprisal and the public behavior closely monitored by the Communist Party.

The most difficult period that Zhu experienced was the time of the Cultural Revolution. As a result of the political turmoil, she was forced in July 1970 to leave her young children, one of whom she was nursing, and again was sent to work on a collective farm. Suggested by Lin Biao and carried out by Chairman Mao, the Cultural Revolution was part of a campaign to reform intellectuals and was referred to as "rolling in the mud to get the feel of grass roots." Because Zhu's husband also worked at the Institute of Social Sciences, the family had to give up its apartment, which was only guaranteed while they were employed. She remembers that she did not even have time to feel pain, given the fatigue of clearing out her home and arranging for the care of her children. She brought her children to her mother-in-law's home and gave her mother-in-law part of her very meager savings for their care. She also sent a portion of her small salary to help her mother, who was sent to live in the country.

The entire staff of the Institute was spread over several villages, with husbands and wives separated, the men living in one huge former cattle shed and the women living in peasants' houses. The intellectuals were divided into different groups depending upon their strength: some planted beans and wheat, while the elderly tended the garden and worked in the kitchen. Zhu was given the dirtiest and most unpleasant job, that of tending pigs. Typical of her genius for making the best of a situation and of her passion for learning, she read voraciously about pigs and managed to train them with a whistle that she procured so that they developed regular eating hours and flourished into healthy animals.

Besides experiencing hunger and deprivation, Zhu was made to confess publicly to supposedly antirevolutionary transgressions. One of her most painful memories of this period was her own husband's denunciation of her. However, as she explained, in China this is insufficient grounds for divorce, especially given the fact that she came from a bourgeois background and her husband was a true proletarian and therefore in good political standing. Despite these sufferings, and even during the most trying times, she knew that there were many people who were worse off. For example, one of her primary school classmates had been sent to Zinjiang to be a teacher in a middle school. Once there, she became the main target of the Red Guards because of her education and her family connections. After being "struggled against" while stripped naked, she hung herself in humiliation. Zhu realized that because of her skills in English, she also would have been a target in the same situation.

Zhu was released in 1972 at a time when many of those caught up in the Cultural Revolution were being rehabilitated. Rather than silencing her, this experience inspired her to continue working toward personal integrity and freedom of expression. However, she remains haunted by the impact of so many years of disruption on her children's well-being, and even though she had little control over her destiny, she feels guilty about the difficulties they endured.

In the late 1980s, Zhu Hong began translating contemporary Chinese writers, including the dissident author Liu Binyan, despite the fact that this was a dangerous undertaking. She also devoted herself to translating Chinese women writers, ensuring that their voices would be heard around in the world as well as in their own country. She wanted the plight of women in China to have as wide an audience as possible; and in turn she tried to make the literature of the women's movement in the West available to Chinese women.

Zhu does not necessarily focus on better-known writers for translation but aims to provide opportunities for as wide a range of writers as possible. She believes fervently in her efforts but insists that her contributions are minor compared to those of her contemporaries in China. Her goal is to use her knowledge and love of literature as a way to unearth the truth about the condition of women in her own country and to promote understanding between cultures. For Zhu Hong, women's rights are a matter of universal concern and can only be achieved by international efforts.

Zhu has published in English as well as in Chinese, and her works include: *The Evil Wife in Contemporary Chinese Fiction: Images of Women in Chinese Fiction*, vol. 1 (1994); *Women, Illness, and Hospitalization: Images of Women in Chinese Fiction,* vol. II (1994); and *The Serenity of Whiteness: Contemporary Short Stories from China by and about Women* (1992). Her critical essays cover many subjects that are taboo in China, such as divorce and the human rights abuses suffered by women. She has compiled a general introduction and one hundred entries for Chinese writers for the *Bloomsbury Guide to World Women Writers* (1992). These examples represent a very small sampling of a lifetime of dedicated work.

ZHU SPEAKS

I feel that even by definition fiction is a deeper truth (than sociology). As a critic I try to bring out the message in the fiction that women writers themselves are not aware of. I bring out how women suffer under communism.

"I was only nineteen years old when I started working at the Institute of Social Sciences because I was fifteen years old when I went to the university. However, I told the administrators that I was eighteen when I registered for entrance exams because that was the minimum age. We were a very small group in the Institute at first, less than ten people. We were required to read leftist literature and forbidden to read anything else. I read Howard Fast from cover to cover and some of the other leftist writers like Arthur Miller; Gywn Thomas, a Welsh writer; Jack Lindsey, an English Communist writer; and American writers like Belton Trembeau, a black writer; and Meridel Le Sueur, a poet. One of my first successes was a paper I was assigned on Howard Fast. Raised as I was in a convent and reading Charles Dickens, my reading tastes were formed, and I didn't like Howard Fast. When I handed in that paper, my superiors thought their worst suspicions of me were confirmed. That was already in 1954 because I started working in late 1953.

In 1955, [Nikita] Khrushchev's secret report to the Twentieth Party Congress came out.* As a consequence, there were waves of retreat from the Party abroad, and Howard Fast wrote a book denouncing the Party, *The Naked God*. My superiors had to make a turnabout because there had been so many articles praising Howard Fast that now they had to publish something negative. My paper was fished out from the art and literature desk and, after some refurbishing, was published. It was a satisfaction to see myself in print in my early twenties, but I also felt used. This was just my independent opinion, and I didn't want it to become part of a denunciation. At the time, I didn't even feel negative about him because he was a leftist but because he failed my literary test. Later, my article was made part of the refrain denouncing him.

I had read Khrushchev's secret report from the U.S. newspaper, the *Daily Worker*, when nobody had access to these documents. I was able to because the Institute subscribed to foreign magazines.

*The secret report documented the existence of the wide network of labor camps and the terror under Joseph Stalin's rule.

I had already had my doubts about communism very early on. When I read that article, I immediately thought of China. I knew something about terror because both my father and stepfather had been in prison, so I knew about prison conditions in China and that there had been wave upon wave of arrests and executions. There were many campaigns that are not so widely known outside of China, and I lived through all of them. When I was young, I tried to identify with the Party, but after I was rejected, my vision became clearer. I suppose it was all the books that I read, not because I was wiser than anyone else. I was just more detached. Because my entire family, our relatives, and friends were labeled enemies of the revolution, we had firsthand knowledge of the terror of living under the revolution rather than recalling it as what some people now say was the idealism of the 1950s. That idealism was an illusion—underneath there was fear. Reading Khrushchev's report, I felt this is like China, and I was not terribly surprised because of what I had experienced. I felt that I was carrying a secret knowledge inside myself, but I didn't tell a single person. It was a gauge of how lonely I was. I had no friend or lover. The satisfaction I had is that I knew that my instincts were right about the regime. It didn't mean that I was going to be a dissident. I conformed. I raised my hands and did what was expected. The only thing I felt that was special about myself was the inner knowledge I retained.

It was the same during the Cultural Revolution, when my parents were hounded, had their heads shaved, were assaulted by Red Guards, and their house was confiscated with everything in it. When my father was released from prison and working in a medical school library, the students seized on him as prey. He threw himself down from a four-story building and killed himself because he just couldn't bear it anymore.

Once I was taking a walk with a former classmate, and we were seeing all these people standing there with shaved heads and people made to stand on tables outside on the pavement because somebody was found in their house who was not right. We walked a very short stretch before we were caught for no reason and hauled to a place where we had to stand in front of Chairman Mao's picture. We were then asked what our family origin was. We were both bourgeoisie and afraid to tell a lie, although in that confusion no one would have known the difference. We were made to bow in front of Chairman Mao's picture and to say, 'I am the son of a dog.' We had to say it three times and then we were allowed to go. Our tormentors said to each of us, 'Son of a dog, you stay home and behave and learn the words of Chairman Mao. Why are you gallivanting about?' My friend was from a newspaper. We met outside, and he asked me, 'What do you think of the situation?' This was August 1966. I replied, 'This is the Middle Ages, and this little book is the new bible.' At the time, he wouldn't accept this and claimed my views were a result of my bad education. Much later, he wrote me a letter telling me how right I had been. I didn't really have any moral courage like the man I translated, Liu Binyan, who stood up and criticized the Party, although I could see what was going on. It's because of my reading that I have some standards. I was always carrying my own thoughts with me, and I carried my judgments of other people also. I could be very respectful to someone, but in my heart I thought, 'He is a son of a dog, a real scoundrel or a hypocrite.' It's not purely political, but moral.

After the Cultural Revolution, in the 1980s, when all the stories of intellectuals being martyrs came up, I felt differently, even though I was really a victim, too. From the beginning I was a victim of communism, but I felt that there was another aspect to consider. We were moral cowards, too, and should have faced up to it because we were guilty of betraying each other. I didn't do it, but many intellectuals, especially Party activists, had betrayed and preyed upon other people. I felt that the intellectuals, especially if they had had an education and had read in the humanities, should have had standards. They should have been ashamed of themselves and not only whine, asking for pity. Of course, nobody really agreed with me. I always had a fantasy of writing a novel about it, of showing up these victimized intellectuals as moral cowards and wimps. I was going to use my own material, make the village a Victorian setting so that nobody could say I was using them and accuse me of libel. I even have a title for it—'I'm No Angel.'

Today the writers are rehabilitated, all the enemies are rehabilitated, but one section of the population is not properly rehabilitated (this is something I kept to myself), and these are the so-called landlords. They are pitiful because their children are outcasts and, therefore, nobody will marry them. The worst kind of man, with a limp or too old to marry, will take a landlord's daughter and then bully her for life. I sympathize with them terribly. I always remember a little boy with a red scarf because he was so hard working. Then, because of the intensification of the class struggle, his red scarf was ripped off from his neck in a ceremony, not because he had done anything wrong but because his father had been labeled a rich peasant. This scarred him for life. These people were stamped out like ants and worms and nobody cares. Even today the world doesn't know how many landlords and so-called landlords have perished. I'm sure there must have been some evil landlords but, according to international standards, they are better than most. In the early years of the land reform, in the fifties, they were literally killed with their babies because the assumption was that the children would try to avenge their parents. Later, they were always outcasts. Even today the most liberal-minded intellectuals do not talk about it. That was all right because they were labeled landlords. Everything is relative. They could own something no bigger than the palm of your hand, but it was more than the peasants. In the country we really learned something about China.

We were returned from the collective farms to the Institute of Social Sciences in 1972. The Cultural Revolution was not over. There was the 'criticize Confucius' movement, the 'criticize Lin Biao' movement because Lin Biao had died. But it was petering out. It had lost its spirit, and Mao and his wife were terribly discredited. Still, we were afraid to say anything.

In the 1980s, despite the liberalization, the Bureau of Publications was still exercising censorship and control. I called a meeting, and I not only invited many scholars and arranged beforehand with a daily paper to publish all of the proceedings, I also invited one of the heads of the Publication Bureau. I was not afraid. We talked about sex and violence in literature, but then the unspoken subject was censorship. We wanted to open up the debate and not have the Bureau censor us. We used many examples because there were people working in all areas of foreign literature who were participating in the conference. We wanted to bring up the problem of how hard it is to pronounce judgment.

At the time there was already one newly concocted word which the government coined, a term the authorities used to exercise censorship. They called it 'social effect.' This was progress because it was not damning the person who was writing for what was going on in his or her head but the social effect, which was not good. My main talk was on the social effect, how to judge the effect of a book on a person in his or her childhood, youth, or old age. Also, different nations and races would experience different results. What I was doing was to contest the idea that any authority could pronounce a judgment on what is a good or a bad social effect. I had already published articles on the issue even before that in 1984. I had quoted Harry Levine, whose article 'Literary Criticism Is Not an Exact Science' I had translated. This meeting created quite a stir. Every speech was printed, including my own. After Tiananmen, when there was a checkup on bourgeois liberalization, this meeting was brought up as an example. Other colleagues raised related issues. I also raised the example of the *Vatican Index*. The *Index* is huge and sometimes is changing. I said it's impossible for any authority to take judgment upon itself. What we want is open debate.

Another one of my very successful and also highly publicized meetings was the 'Image of Women in Literature.' It became the germ of my article being published in a collection at Stanford University. When everyone was denouncing Madame Mao, I suddenly wondered why a woman should be responsible for a whole system. I felt it was so typical from the time of the ancient empire, the Tang Empire, where the Fragrant Concubine, the royal concubine, was blamed for everything. It occurred to me that even reading the very liberated literature of the 1980s, when writers were ready to expose some of the abuses of communism, even some of the popular art form, they always started out very bravely and always ended very lamely, saying, 'It's pillow talk, it's the wife.' That's the safe characterization of the issue. I thought it was not only for reasons of political expedience. It runs very deep in the Chinese mentality, this fear of the woman and the tendency to always blame the woman. That's why I called this meeting the Image of Women and selected extensive literature. Dai Qing was also there. She had written a short story called 'No,' which reveals the practice of blaming the wife rather than the husband. The meeting was very lively, and there were many foreigners attending who were in Beijing. I also gave my talk and that was reported in the daily papers. At the time it was considered quite a novel idea to talk about the attitude which always makes the woman take the blame. It was dangerous because if you went one step further it would be like defending Madame Mao. I was not going in that direction. This mentality of making women bear the guilt is really a fear of women's power. There's a pattern: the powerful man repenting, and then it's the evil woman, the evil wife. Later, my idea was expanded into a paper called 'The Evil Wife,' published in a Chinese-language magazine in Canada, not in China. I presented it in Australia in 1988.

I have always been thinking of women's issues because of what I see around me and what I feel within myself. That conference was one of my earliest efforts. In addition, I always wanted to translate women telling their own stories because I wanted the West to know more about Chinese women and what they have to bear. A collection, *The Serenity of Whiteness*, was begun in China. Some stories were translated in Kent, England, some at the Bunting Institute [in Cambridge, Massachusetts], some in Bellagio [in Italy]. It's something I keep thinking about. I can't leave off even though I can't do it full time. Now, China has put out some anthologies of women writers, but most of the women in my collection were not well known. When people outside China talk about women writers, they always refer to one or two names. At the time, many women were coming out with their own stories in their own voice, and I just wanted the outside world to know. One of the criteria I adopted was that I really preferred women from the provinces, some of them from the outlying provinces, some of them quite obscure. There are so many tears in that collection.

Because of my background in Western literature I chose as the first story in the collection 'Gussie Grows Up,' by Chen Ruiqing. I selected that as the story of reverse initiation, opposed to the pattern of the female growing up, very often under the tutelage of the wiser male—either the father, the husband, or the older brother. You read it in all English literature. In Jane Austen, even earlier in Fanny Burney, there's always this young woman making mistakes and being guided. This pattern of young females groping in the revolution and being helped by the Party, sometimes by a man they worship and marry, was unconsciously adopted by Communists. I can tell you about ten well-known novels of that kind of genre. This is the reverse; Gussie's process of acquiring wisdom and being initiated into life is disengagement from the Party, the orthodoxy, the establishment. All her illusions are peeled off one by one. It also has a utopian element—every one of the women is equal because they each have that enemy label and can't report on each other. They have a spark of life which can't be stifled, so they go swimming naked in the pool and say, 'Oh, little fishes can't report us, isn't that lovely!' While the men in the story try to conform so that they will be let off earlier, the women are more natural in their behavior. I chose the stories for what they have to say about women's lives: childbirth, abortion, marriage, disillusionment with romantic love, mother-daughter relationships, women making decisions about their own lives. Every story has a theme.

For me, literature is a vehicle for values. I felt that I couldn't write fiction, so I wanted to bring out my message through other women writers. I couldn't do sociological studies because of lack of resources. I would have liked to do some research in China about those old wives who have been discarded. Immediately after liberation, all the Communist heroes got rid of their old wives and married young women from the city. We see them all alone in the countryside since nobody could marry them because their husbands were high cadres. This was the first betrayal of women by the Communists. Dai Qing's story 'No' touches on it. Sometimes we work alongside these pretty young city wives the cadres have married. It was like a movement because the Party made a law that if you have been apart from your wife for eight years, you could announce an automatic divorce. However, these poor women were country women and, of course, eight years covers the war with the Japanese. I wrote saying that this was the Communists' first liberation, to liberate themselves from their own wives. There is widespread rape in the countryside and also marital rape within the family. There are many things about women that are dark and very painful, hidden under Chinese society waiting to be unearthed.

Another thing I do through my work is to bring out the feminist message through my literary criticism. One of the things I am now writing about is the concept of shame. Because they are more associated with power, men have too little sense of shame and Chinese women have too much shame. An example is in the autobiography *Wild Swans*, where a woman felt so ashamed of becoming pregnant after she was raped that she hung herself.*

I [have drafted] a paper about one young woman who is the fallen woman of Chinese socialist society, Yu Luojin, now in political asylum in Germany. Her brother had been executed by a firing squad during the Cultural Revolution for writing against Mao's theories of class struggle, so the family members were social outcasts. Apart from that, she had to sell herself in marriage in order to survive and help her parents. Her father wrote out her description and posted it up for the first buyer who would marry her and support the family. She sold herself to a young man in northeast China, a rich and productive part of the country. When the Cultural Revolution was over, Mao had died, and her brother was reinstated as a martyr, she decided to tell the truth. The Communists under Deng Xiaoping took credit for reinstating her brother: 'Now we are so liberal minded, we reinstate this man.' Riding on the crest of that good fortune, she published her story and became the talk of the town. She wrote about her life and her first wedding night, how she was raped by her husband. She took up a pair of scissors and threat-

*Jung Chang, *Wild Swans: Three Daughters of China* (New York: Simon & Schuster, 1991).

ened to kill him if he approached her again after that devastating experience. She felt dirty and washed herself. All the prim and proper Chinese critical world rose up against her, not because she had been raped but because she wrote about it. They were outraged that she could write about such a shameful thing. Her book sold by the thousands, but she was never recognized by the official writers' union because she was so frank about herself and the fact that she felt she couldn't go on living with this man.

Afterward, Yu Luojin divorced the peasant and married a worker in the city. She became a writer and had a love affair with an older senior editor of a daily literary paper. She wanted to divorce her second husband and was writing a new story about her love affair. This was the first time she fell in love because marrying that worker was also expediency. The editor tried to block publication of her story, and it became very ugly. She admitted that she was in love with him, but he said that he had nothing to do with her and barely knew her. So she published all his love letters to her, Xeroxed them, and distributed them. In her writings she was very frank, not only about her first marital rape but about her own feelings. She was blamed for being so open about her feelings. Even though women do these things, they are not supposed to talk about it or should find another reason and say, 'He is not progressive enough, or doesn't work hard enough.'

There's a hypocritical and terrible streak of puritanism in the Party. Yu Luojin is considered the shameless woman of Chinese society. I want to use her as a wedge into the argument that Chinese women are really oppressed by a sense of shame. Another example occurred during 1986, when there were student movements and spontaneous demonstrations and marches. There was one young woman who was also involved. At first people defended her, saying, 'Why shouldn't she be the organizer of one of the marches?' Then she got into trouble for accusing her boss of raping her, and since then nobody wanted anything to do with a woman who could come up with all the dirty details of the rape. She was accused of libel when she described in graphic terms how her boss raped her. The more she went into detail to defend herself against libel, the more people were repelled by her. Women have been silenced by this sense of shame. Traditionally, women caught in adultery have to hang themselves.

There is so much to be done in other areas which are not even talked about, like child molestation. The reason that this abuse is hidden is because of shame. Dai Qing has written a piece about child molestation. A violated child is considered damaged goods, and even the parents reject her. Nobody comes forward on her behalf because the parents would not allow anyone to make the accusation of abuse.

I want to talk about this sense of shame that women should really liberate themselves from. I have been lecturing on it in the classroom. I have a paper on it as part of a collection I am gathering on this theme. The 'sick woman' is now an image that Chinese writers are using as a metaphor for political sickness. I picked it up through the fiction that I read.

Another thing I write about is gossip. I look upon female gossip not in the conventional view as backbiting. Rather, I see it as a kind of subversive language that women use. I have a title for my book, *A Room or a Broom of Her Own*, which uses examples from fiction. I also have ten to twelve titles for a work on relations between women and mother-daughter relations. Reading Western literature so extensively has made me realize that these are universal patterns.

Another one of my themes is called 'class struggle in the bedroom.' In Chinese society husbands use the weapon of class against their wives. It gives them an edge over their wives. There is a very moving story called 'The Well,' in which circumstances finally force a woman down the well. Suicide is the accepted way for women to get out of a difficult situation because there is no legal recourse against difficult marital relations. In this story, when the couple have an argument, the husband claims that his wife's views are an expression of her bourgeois outlook. Furthermore, the Party secretary and organization support the husband, so the woman is helpless. When you don't have the support of the all-powerful Party, you are like a fly caught in a web. The Party systematically oppresses women. First, Party officials divorce their old wives, and then they use the pretty young women they marry to serve them in bed and in the house. These women always have very lowly positions because their main responsibility is to the husband and the household. In most institutes there is always a personnel department which looks after files. They are wives of high cadres, but these jobs lead nowhere.

The reason I feel the women are doing badly in socialist society is that the law has not made many provisions for them. In the countryside there has been no legal provision for women who remarry to take away their children and the common property. The children stay with the in-laws. People feel that if these women are shameless enough to remarry, they are lucky just to go scot-free. In 1986 there was a much-publicized law allowing widows to take away their share of the property, but still it's very hard to be able to do that. The reason that women have such a raw deal under communism is that the Party wanted to maintain the status quo. So long as the Communists' own rule was ensured, the village system with its elders stayed in place. If a woman married out of the village, her private plot was lost. If you really want to change things for women, the whole structure has to be changed. The system of control is still through the village head, with the Party secretary sometimes doubling as the village head. There's still the problem of what a woman can do when she marries out of the family, of what belongs to her.

The problem is not only that the law is weak in China but also that the law doesn't get enforced. There are no lawyers, and it's only recently that you can find a few lawyers in the city. Women have a raw deal everywhere. Even in urban areas there is the problem of productivity and level of development. We are all so poor and there is so little mechanization, so all the housework falls on women. You see it everywhere. Men and women graduate together, marry, and then, ten years later, the man is a lecturer and the woman is still home expected to do all the housework and care for the children. It's a vicious circle. Then, of course, women don't get promotions because it's assumed they will devote their attention to the children and can't be trusted to pay attention to their work. Because of traditional attitudes, men have more promotions and more power. The law allots housing according to the place of work, but typically it is the man's workplace which provides the housing. Since the man's position is usually higher, it's to the advantage of the couple. Then the child must be registered with the mother, which means that if the mother still lives in the country and the child only visits his or her father periodically, he or she must be registered as rural. That is supposed to control the urban population, but many things are very arbitrary.

The first campaign ever launched by the Communists after liberation was the antiabortion campaign. There were strict laws passed against abortion. Women were just made to bear children one after another. Now, we are forced to have abortions, and nobody talks about our suffering. They talk about it in terms of economic and social effects. It varies from place to place. In principal, no matter how late, if it's a second child, you can have an abortion. Now, there are so many violations that the government thought it might as well make some concessions. If you have a girl, then after a number of years, in a rural area, you can try again. This is open discrimination. For the peasant it's not only to carry on the line, it's because even after fifty years of liberation the country is so poor, you just have to use your muscle to scrape a living out of the soil so, of course, you want sons.

There are other problems. Even if you have just one daughter and you want to take your son-in-law in, there are no provisions in the law so that the son-in-law can settle in a village and have his plot of land. Traditional attitudes and the absence of law reinforce each other. I think it's up to Chinese writers to focus on these problems. It's hard for a sociologist because it's so subversive a project, but writers can discuss them. That's why I feel that even by definition fiction is a deeper truth. As a critic I try to bring out the message in the fiction that women writers themselves are not aware of. I bring out how women suffer under communism.

Now women have become objects again and are experiencing the worst of both systems. With this new market economy, much of the old benefit network is being eroded as an outdated old system. The economic reforms have taken away some of the old provisions for women. I worked for a whole year as a cotton spinner as part of my thought reform, and I saw young mothers who had several months off for confinement and then one hour off for breastfeeding. There were always two surplus workers who walked around and replaced the young mothers who went off to feed their babies. Hiring two extra hands is now viewed as taking away from profits. Factories used to have a mother-child dorm, and there was a nursery for children while the mother was working. After work the mothers stayed in the dorm for the night. It was very drab, but it made working possible for these young women because they may have lived a two-hour bus ride away. These are extra expenses and cut into profits. All these practices are disappearing fast. It doesn't happen by changing laws because that means losing face. It occurs by changing practices.

What happens now is that women are not being hired and are being forced to retire who are not yet retiring age. That has created a practice of schools refusing to recruit women students. This was told to us in 1988 in Guansi province by the head of Normal College, the school of education, who said, 'We don't want any girls. We are raising the standards for girls to enter college. What are we to do when we can't assign them? When the girls get their jobs they want to marry, and then, of course, they want to have their one child. Then they will lavish so much care on their child and meanwhile we have to hire someone extra to take over their courses.'

To encourage people and reward them for having only one child, the government is prolonging the maternity leave to six months. But then the woman's career suffers because she can't find work, since an employer knows that in three years or so he would have to give her six months' leave. She can take six months' maternity leave with pay, and then take another six months without pay. Why shouldn't the husband be made to take the other six months? That practice is just not recognized, and it seems that nobody had thought of it in China. Women are underprivileged in many ways. It's the combination of imperfect laws and traditional attitudes.

Now, of course, a quick way for women to make money is prostitution. There are many forms of it and a lot of documentation about it. Concubinage is also one problem which is back in full force. Young women just consent to it because they can make a lot of money. Because of the breakdown of control, the police don't bother to track them down. Another form of prostitution is that of women being kept by businessmen who have an enterprise in China. They visit this enterprise every month or so and want a woman there waiting for them, and it's probably safer than a prostitute because now we have AIDS in China and venereal disease is back. Venereal disease is so serious that there are special hospitals to treat it. Young women can get paid several times what a full professor can make, 2,000 to 5,000 yuan a month. A full professor earns 1,000 yuan if he or she works night and day and weekends. For a young woman it's so easy. All she has to do is live in that hotel room or apartment, do her hair, play mah-jongg, and entertain the man when he's back. Some of these young women keep a young lover with all the money they make. Now, this is a problem posed for the law because this is voluntary, and these women are not forced into prostitution. What about the children that are born in this kind of relationship? The law has made no provisions because it just can't keep up with the new reality.

There may be successful women entrepreneurs making a lot of money, but for every successful businesswoman there must be at least ten thousand women who aren't doing well. However, they are not mentioned because the woman is still the exception; the other, the man, is the norm. Not every woman can make use of all these opportunities considering the traditional attitudes. Because females are burdened with so many limitations, an easy way to make money is selling sex.

In the countryside there's a new problem for women. Girls are taken out of school, even out of primary school, because now the family has the freedom to run their own little concern and make money, like making straw hats, for example. A girl of eleven or twelve can cook and look after her little brother and sister. Because she is going to marry out of the village anyway, there is less incentive to invest in her education. Now that women are less and less educated, they become less competitive when they grow up. It's a vicious circle.

The biggest problem, which is even against Chinese law, is the abduction and sale of women. There's a book called *The Sale and Abduction of Women.* I wrote a review about it, and that is my way of calling attention to the problem. It's happening on a very large scale. These country girls or small-town girls just go to a big city hoping to find jobs because now people are allowed to move about. In the old days a peasant couldn't buy a ticket and ride on a train. Now, girls go off having heard that there are employment agencies, but they are approached by men who tell them they will take them to an employment office or find them a cheap place to live. These men work in gangs, taking the young women hundreds of miles away to very poor areas where the men just can't afford wives because a wedding banquet and bridal presents are so expensive. It's cheaper to buy a woman. Once these woman are raped and pregnant, sometimes they accept it because their families don't want them back. Even though it's illegal, the local authorities register these women, which means that the Party is winking and accepting this situation. If they had gone after these gangs in the same way that they went after democracy activists, they would all have been rounded up and shot.

Sexual harassment is only now beginning to take on the idea of 'he pinched me, he said all these dirty words to me.' Of course, sexual favors have always been necessary for promotion. In my academy, during the Cultural Revolution, women were forced into sexual favors because they were accused of being in an enemy category or of doing something wrong. No one talks about these things. I think that Anita Hill is now bringing a revolution to China. Sexual harassment is widespread, and there is no legal recourse. Secretaries are expected to sleep with their bosses. I feel that if women would overcome their sense of shame and fear, there are dark corners that would be exposed. The oppression of women is most pervasive in China from discrimination in the workplace, in education, to the loss of a lot of benefits, down to marital rape.

There was a much-vaunted book, which was banned in China as subversive and which, of course, was hailed in the United States. It was called the *Hills of China* and mentions the ten crises which China is facing, including environmental issues and pollution. One of the crises is population. The problems are just seen in terms of economics and not in their human dimension. There is no mention of the suffering of women. In Tiananmen Square there were no slogans about women's problems. There was very little awareness of them.

For every thousand magazines with pinups of half-naked women, there will be about one or two serious articles and magazines on women's issues. There is the *World Women Review*, which carries articles translated from Western magazines dealing with women's rights and women's problems in the West. It's a way of introducing new concepts, for instance, that a woman can sue her husband for marital rape, something unheard of in China. There's not even a term for sexual harassment in China. It all began with Anita Hill.

I want to introduce American women's rights into China. I had collected and translated into Chinese the first volume of American women's fiction early in 1981, and it came out in 1983. Many women writers that I knew told me that they were influenced by some of those stories. When I go back to China, I'm hoping to be able to concentrate on women's writing so that I can do something significant and useful, like serving as a cultural bridge between women. Chinese women can bring much to American culture. I have made out a list of Chinese women's autobiographies that have been published in the last fifty years. I thought that American women could learn something from the way Chinese women look at their lives and the experiences they have endured, the mother-daughter relationships, handing down the strength and resourcefulness for survival. The bonds between women in China are quite strong. Conversely, bringing Western literature to China will introduce new concepts to Chinese women, so that they will look at their own reality through new eyes.”

Part V

Making the World Safe for Children

16 / Liv Ullmann

WHEN THINKING OF HUMAN RIGHTS, women immediately envision the rights of children. Many people, however, may think instead of the more traditional view of the right to freely participate in the political process and to express oneself without fear of reprisal, issues in the domain of adults. Most people rarely focus on the basic right of survival or are not even aware that 29 percent of the world's children are malnourished. Those of us who have children or nephews and nieces may regard them as our greatest treasure, our continuity, and our hope. But do we ever consider the world's children in this light? UNICEF believes that the human rights of children include access to adequate nutrition and basic health care, and that we should all be striving for this goal. In her work with UNICEF, Liv Ullmann reminds us that children should be our greatest concern.

Liv has devoted the past nineteen years of her life to the welfare of children in the developing world. As do many women activists, she stresses the importance of community and close relationships in the struggle for rights and helps us to see that responsibilities that we might consider burdensome are really a source of great joy. She also points out that just wanting to help is an important step. It opens us up to all of the opportunities to make a difference that we encounter in our daily lives.

Through her acting and her human rights work, Liv brings us a sense of our common humanity, that we are not only inextricably connected with events occurring around the world but also with the people we pass on the street. As such, she believes that our daily lives should include helping others in any way possible, thus expanding our humanity and the boundaries of our lives as privileged people. As she reveals in her many-faceted work, we each have a higher potential, which is expressed when we reach out to others.

Many people see Liv as the possessor of an enviable talent, success in her career, a glamorous life, and material ease. Yet, she demonstrates that all of this is nothing compared to the moments of quiet intimacy with a band of street children in Colombia, and she shows us that the way to overcome alienation in this world is by extending the commitment that we feel to our own families to those in need.

I first met Liv at an annual celebration of Amnesty International in Boston. She had been instrumental in helping to free a Cuban political prisoner, Armando Valladares, whose prison poetry I had translated. Her achievement was notable because many socialist parties in Europe at the time, with the exception of the French, were loath to criticize the Cuban regime and preferred not to address human rights issues in that country. Working on that case was just one of many projects that Liv was involved in at the time. Although she has demanding careers as a mother, writer, director, and actress, she views her many-sided life as seamless. She has one daughter, Linn, who graduated with honors in literature from New York University and has become a spokesperson for UNICEF and youth concerns.

Born of Norwegian parents in Japan, Liv spent her early childhood in Canada and New York, returning to the family home in Norway when World War II ended. In her late teens she began to study drama, devoting herself to developing a career in the theater. She left home and lived on her own during these formative years, setting a pattern of autonomy for her future life. Her first leading role, as the title character in a stage version of *The Diary of Anne Frank*, was a prophetic beginning for her life as an actress and an activist. Later in her career she would try to make not only Anne Frank but also all of the suffering children of the world live in our consciences.

Although Liv does not consider herself a feminist, she has accomplished what so many women have yearned for, following her own interests and passions in shaping her life. At times this has meant loneliness and confronting the conflicts between the demands of being a single parent and a career that brings her to so many parts of the world. She has not only taken these difficulties in stride but also has spoken of them with great honesty and has therefore encouraged many women to face their own problems with new insight.

Liv Ullmann became world famous for her roles in the films of Ingmar Bergman and has received many acting awards. In the past few years she has appeared in films in the United States, Canada, Australia, Italy, France, England, Germany, and Argentina as well as in theatrical productions in Europe and the United States. She frequently participates in artistic productions that have human rights and social justice as their central concern. For example, in conjunction with her long-standing support of the Mothers of the Plaza de Mayo in Argentina, she played the lead role in *La Amiga*,* a film about the *disappearances* under the military junta of 1976–1983.

While her acting career was flourishing, Liv turned her energies to another mode of expression and became a well-known writer. *Changing* was published in 1976 and has been translated into twenty-four languages. Her second book, *Choices*, was released in the United States and is available in Europe, Australia, the Far East, and Central America. She is currently working on a book about the relationship between mothers and daughters.

Since her appointment as a UNICEF goodwill ambassador in 1980, Liv has devoted much of her time to the work of the UN Children's Fund. She has visited UNICEF-assisted programs in Thailand, Bangladesh, India, and Sri Lanka and also has made field trips to drought-affected countries of eastern Africa, traveling to more than forty countries around the world.

In December 1986, Liv participated in UNICEF's fortieth anniversary celebrations. Addressing the UN General Assembly, she

**La Amiga* was written and directed by Jeanine Meerapfel and produced by Journal Film Klaus Volkenborn, in coproduction with Jorge Estrada Moral Producciones Buenos Aires and Alma Film GmbH in 1988.

said, "If the sad statistics are not enough to compel us to work for peace, let us think of the faces of the children. Think of the pleading face of a hungry boy in the Sudan, a frightened face of a little girl in Lebanon. Think, finally, of the face you love the most, the face of your own child."

Throughout her career, Liv also has traveled extensively in industrialized countries in order to increase public awareness of the critical problems that mothers and children face in developing regions, relating her experiences in the press and on radio and television as well as in lectures. She has appealed for government and private contributions to help UNICEF expand its work for child survival and development.

The king of Norway presented Liv with the Order of St. Olav, and she also holds several honorary degrees in the arts and the humanities in recognition of her humanitarian work. One of her greatest achievements, however, is to affirm our essential equality as human beings and to reveal that our smallest efforts can serve as the beginning of far-reaching improvements in this world, thereby reminding us of the spiritual dimension of human rights work.

LIV SPEAKS

Parenthood now, to me, involves all children.

"Before joining UNICEF, I had been on the periphery of human rights work. I gave money to Amnesty International, which is very helpful, but for me it was very easy because it somehow didn't involve me personally. I had never been face to face with individuals who might benefit from my contribution. Fund-raising is something I knew how to do, and which I had done a lot of. But in 1979, when I gave a check to Leo Cherne of the International Rescue Committee, he asked me if I would go down to Thailand and see what a refugee camp was and what the needs were. For me, the big difference was to make that journey and, in a sense, never return. It changed my life. It didn't change me, but it changed my priorities. Somehow I cannot picture the person I was before, whose life was so full of privileges and who only met privileged people.

When I came back from Thailand, Hong Kong, and Macao, I traveled in the United States for the International Rescue Committee but on a very limited basis. Because they didn't have the money to send me around, I was paying my own way as well as doing fund-raising. But it wasn't enough for me. I wanted to do more.

When I was wanting this the most, I got a call from the Office of Special Events at UNICEF. I had lunch with them, and they told me that they needed a spokesperson besides Danny Kaye and that they wanted a woman. They asked me if I would consider traveling as a volunteer for them, look at their projects, the needs in developing countries, and find ways to promote their aid. At the moment, I thought, 'Yes, that sounds good,' but I didn't really know what they were talking about. They were talking about water pumps and vaccinations, and it sounded a little boring; but I went to India and Bangladesh and Sri Lanka and then to Somalia and Ethiopia. It turned out that these things are so much more dramatic and so much more miraculous than anything I had experienced in my life until then. So that was my second journey.

The most profound experiences I have had in terms of giving and being given to have been from very unprivileged parts of the world. These were the touch, the smells, and the kindness that I seemed to remember from childhood and somehow didn't find in my adult life. During travels for UNICEF I always spend time with the children. When I am holding them, something opens up in me that has only been half-open in the life I have had as an adult, a place of reality, truth, and tenderness. A little child that is close to you and looks at you and talks to you shows an enormous trust. To me, that is among the most profound experiences one can have. It's to be in love, be in a moment of trust with someone you care deeply about. With children I can have this all the time. It's allowing Liv to really be Liv. I can be in Mexico with boys and girls who were strangers ten minutes before, and suddenly we are running after each other and laughing, and I'm tremendously happy. This is who I am. As a parent, if I sit with a mother and her child who is dying of measles because this child didn't have a vaccination or health care the way my child has, that little one is suddenly as precious to me as my own. Parenthood now, to me, involves all children.

There are two children whom I remember most. One was a little boy who just held my finger. His grasp around my finger was so similar to the grasps my own child gave, except this was a little boy in Africa who had no one and who was naked, carrying an empty plate. His little behind was wrinkled like an old man's, and he held onto my finger as if I could help him, lead him somewhere good. I couldn't help him because I couldn't lift him up and take him back with me. I knew he wouldn't survive that year because it was so devastated in that place, and there was no food. To know that somebody is grasping me and trusting that I can help because I am grown up and yet that I am not able to help is something that will always be with me. Although he probably didn't survive, he is a reminder of the children we can save.

That was in 1981, when there wasn't much on television about Ethiopia or Somalia or the Sudan. The drought and the famine were as bad then as they were later when it became "in" to talk about suffering, and as bad as it is now when it's half in and half out. There wasn't much about it on television, but we had a camera team and they took a lot of pictures, among them this little boy. The strange thing was that when Band Aid and Live Aid and all that happened, the television stations started to dig in their archives because they couldn't use the same thing as the BBC crew had taken in 1985. So, this same little boy from 1981, whom no one, almost, noticed, then was suddenly in all our homes. Although he had been dead for a long time, there he was, still alive to remind us, alive like Anne Frank and the children of the Holocaust.

Another time when I had this feeling of Liv, one of these strange times in life when suddenly your identity as a human being becomes very clear, happened when I was with some street children in Colombia. We spent an incredible evening. We shared a meal, and we shared stories. They were so little and had no parents and grownups around them. I remember all the little tricks they used to come close, like pretending to fall asleep and sitting so that their head would fall on my shoulder, and a little hand would rest on my lap. When they were going to bed, which was a street corner, they wanted me to tuck the dirty sack they brought along around them. They reached up their arms to be kissed, and I lay down just holding them. This enormous feeling of belonging, this is really who we are. Because Linn is my child and I am her parent, I am their parent. It's not possible that anyone can ever walk away from such a street corner.

It is not sentimental to care about others. It is not banal, although it somehow seems banal in these days to talk about compassion when it is really our opportunity as people to touch and be touched. We are so lonely and so desperate because we don't even touch in our own homes, let alone on our street corners. Maybe if we were allowed to develop, reaching out and being reached, maybe if television weren't always there instead, dehumanizing us at times, maybe then we would be able to hold each other in our own homes and in our own neighborhoods. We would reach out to people who have AIDS or are homeless, to those who are in great need. Then, we would find that we truly belong. We would be what human beings are supposed to be. Animals are like that with each other. At the moment, we are almost less than they. We don't have their pleasures. Look at our two cats, lying around and holding each other. We only do that when it's a sexual thing, and most people don't even do it when it's sexual anymore. What voids we allow in our lives that could so easily be filled!

In developing countries, perhaps because people have so little and it's either life or death, this sense of belonging by holding and touching and listening and by being together in a group is much more common. That's why certain community programs are easier to establish there. For example, just recently I have been talking to the Salvation Army [in the United States], and they explained some of their difficulties establishing community projects. It's difficult simply because people don't have feelings for their neighbors. They don't want a home for AIDS patients in their neighborhood, whereas that question wouldn't even arise in a poor Asian village because there the community feeling is strong. By tradition, culturally, we worry so much about our physical appearance. But beauty isn't external. We are losing our beauty because we don't care anymore. We use all our time to pursue the superficial, but *this* pursuit will either give us beauty back or happiness.

As women, we are allowed to shape our roles closer to who we are, whereas a man's model is more uniform and often far from his reality. I know that the capacity for compassion and caring is as great for a man as it is for a woman. I have seen men who have given up their careers and sold everything they have to enable them to work out there as doctors for no pay, and I've seen awful, uncaring mothers in my neighborhood. But it's easier for women to work for others. It's unquestioned by our society, and it conflicts less with who we are supposed to be. A woman does not have to prove herself by career-oriented actions.

It's a sad reflection on our ability for caring, and on our media, that our compassion somehow is awakened mostly by, for example, one little child who falls into a well when there are so many children that are falling into death every day. The bad thing about statistics and the one child falling into the well is that people seem to be only able to react to the one horror story. We follow more intently the paths of three whales than the fate of weeping mothers. On the other hand, statistics make us look away from the individual horror stories that are happening around us every day. It doesn't take much bravery or insight to see behind the statistics that there are children with names who are loved by their mothers and fathers, children who are not faceless. If you put the face of the one you love the most over a number in the statistic, you will forget the number. Statistics are really faces as loved and as hurting and as full of dreams as ours are.

It's not brave to do something good for the world. It's very brave not to do something, because if you do nothing, fifty years from now you will be defined by having done nothing. It's very brave to want to face up to that. If you happen to have a child or a grandchild who is very idealistic, and he or she asks you what you did during the time when forty thousand children died every day, could you answer, 'Well, I couldn't really do anything'?

The reason people get so wrapped up in themselves is that they don't know how wonderful it is to be wrapped up in someone else. I heard someone talking on television about his work for the homeless. He said, 'I am doing it for me.' That's a very good reason to do something. Nobody is asking anyone to be a saint.

I have been working for UNICEF since 1980. It has taken more and more of my time, but it's not taking more of my life because it is my life. I don't believe in compartmentalizing and saying, 'My life is really my career or my married life or whatever.' Everything you do is your life."

17 / *The International Gathering of Mothers and Women in Struggle*

In March 1994, Hebe de Bonafini, president of the Argentine Mothers of the Plaza de Mayo, sponsored an international conference of activist mothers' groups. The women gathered in Paris because of its central location and also because the coordinator of the Argentine Mothers' support groups is based there. The purpose of this extraordinary meeting was to forge an international movement of mothers and women on behalf of human rights that would both strengthen each organization within its respective country and create a new presence in international politics.

Hebe de Bonafini's travels around the world had brought her into contact with other Mothers' associations that were working on behalf of justice, while the Mothers' office in Argentina had hosted

Latin American Mothers who came to learn from their experiences. With her usual vision and courage, Hebe knew that assembling these different organizations would create a powerful alternative force in world politics. Once again, the Mothers forged an ambitious goal with few resources other than boundless hope.

The Mothers of the Plaza de Mayo, who were once referred to as *las locas* (crazy ones) for opposing a military dictatorship and speaking truth to power, have once again taken up what seems to be an unfulfillable goal—to achieve justice and peace and to help to establish political systems throughout the world that will assure the economic, social, and physical well-being of children. They have undertaken this task at a time when peoples of various nations are exhausted from war and revelations of corruption as well as from economic, social, and environmental injustices. However, they enter this struggle with the confidence gained through their long battle for human rights in dangerous circumstances.

Within Argentina the Mothers have continued to work toward a more humane society in the face of fluctuating public perceptions of their organization. Over the years they have gone from pariahs under the military junta, to heroines at the time of the junta's collapse, to stubbornly unrealistic idealists in the eye of the constitutional government for insisting that those guilty of the *disappearances* be brought to justice. In the spring of 1995, as military personnel came forward with confessions of brutal murders during the junta's rule, facts that the Mothers had been publicizing for many years, the Mothers were once again regarded as the bastions of credibility. Unfortunately, this new public discussion of what has been referred to as the Dirty War has not resulted in any follow-up action to the military's revelations, and it has not ended the security forces' intimidation of the Mothers. Like many of those who gathered with them in Paris, they brave death threats and assassination attempts, and they have continued their struggles after the murders of members of their association.

The Mothers of the Plaza de Mayo was founded in Argentina in response to the practices of the military junta that took power in 1976. The junta suspended political institutions and began antisubversive operations to capture and interrogate all members of suspect organizations, their sympathizers and associates, and anyone else who might oppose its rule. However, because it wished to avoid international censure, it resorted to the deadly practice of *disappearances*. During the Dirty War, the state-sponsored terror against innocent citizens of all ages, thousands of idealistic young adults vanished without a trace into the 340 clandestine concentration camps scattered throughout the country. In those dark days most people sought refuge from their fear in the belief that if one remained quiet and focused on personal matters, nothing would happen. The only ones who dared to protest publicly were the Mothers of the Plaza de Mayo, a group of housewives that began to demonstrate in the plaza outside the presidential palace in 1977. Their numbers soon swelled to the hundreds and included a network of mothers in the interior and support groups staffed by exiles and nationals throughout Western Europe. At a time when any opposition was banned, the Mothers openly constituted themselves in 1979 as an organization promoting democratic values.

In addition to threatening them physically and *disappearing* their president and two other members, the junta deliberately ridiculed them in order to isolate and weaken their organization and to set an example for groups contemplating opposing the regime. The Mothers soon realized that they needed to create an international presence, both to promote their goals and to protect their lives. They broadened their struggle during the late 1970s and early 1980s to include trips to the United Nations, the Vatican, and major points throughout Europe to denounce the *disappearances* and to seek the support of democratic political leaders. By the time the junta collapsed in 1983, the Mothers had gained international recognition for their bravery.

However, despite the establishment of a constitutional government in 1984, the Mothers remained part of the opposition and broadened their agenda to demand a complete transformation of the Argentine political system. They wanted to eliminate the scourge of the military presence in the country at a time when many human rights groups felt that too much pressure on the military might cause it to revolt and retake power. From the Mothers' perspective, insufficient pressure on the military would create the same result. They believed that the military had been the chief source of repression in the country and that no less than a complete dismantling of its power would ensure a true democracy. They also realized that the establishment of a political democracy did not ensure economic and social justice, and they began to campaign on behalf of these goals.

Their political effectiveness was a result of their ability to forge a new public language, proclaiming their own goals while revealing the hollowness of governmental policies. They also established their presence by creating their own newspaper and by their demonstrations in the streets and plazas throughout the country and at all important political events and military parades. In a system that wished to eliminate them, they remained an important political voice.

In April 1995 the Mothers of the Plaza de Mayo celebrated eighteen years of their struggle and their marches in the plaza. They have demonstrated that age can be a source of power and that a decentralized, quasi-anarchist organization can be an effective political force, not only within Argentina but also abroad. They were nominated for the Nobel Peace Prize in 1980 and shortly thereafter received the Norwegian Prize of the People for those who qualified for the Nobel prize but did not receive it. Among their many other awards is the Sakharov Prize for Freedom of Thought, which they received from the European Parliament in 1992.[1]

Expanding their movement to include grass-roots organizations of activist mothers from around the world seemed a logical follow-up to the Mothers' activities. Just as the Mothers had moved beyond their personal tragedies to discover patterns of oppression within their own country, they began to fathom the international forces helping to keep repressive regimes in power. Armed with their belief in the ability of committed women to effect changes in values and political practices, the Mothers set out to transform a troubled globe.

The difficulties of even contacting women's groups in war-torn countries such as Bosnia-Herzegovina, the Israeli Occupied Territories, the Western Sahara, and Sri Lanka, coupled with a lack of funds, meant that it took two years to arrange for the gathering. Ada Alessandro, who coordinates the Mothers' support groups in Europe, was given the responsibility of raising funds, finding housing, and corresponding with various Mothers' organizations around the world. She was helped financially by the Mothers' European support groups and by Mme. Danielle Mitterrand, the former French president's wife, who long has been active in human rights work and who heads the human rights organization France Libertés.

Between March 27 and 30, representatives of fourteen organizations met in Paris, including women who had flown from Sarajevo, Zagreb, Belgrade, Brazil, Kiev, Jerusalem, and other places around the world. There were women, such as the Sinhalese and Tamil members of the Mothers' Front in Sri Lanka, who could not leave their war-torn countries but who wanted to attend. Many of the participants had never left their countries before; a number of them risked their lives in leaving because their governments regarded their presence at the gathering as a traitorous act. Although they came from different cultural backgrounds, all shared the common bond of having suffered oppression and the loss of family, and were struggling against various forms of injustice. They were united by their activism, their ability to give each other affection and support, and their goal of ensuring human dignity.

Speaking to each other of the horrors they had endured and of their attempts to confront dangerous authoritarian governments, they broke the silence imposed by political persecution and social conventions. They also ended their national isolation, exchanging stories of *disappearances*, murder, and, in the case of the Mothers from Kiev, details on how only 30 percent of the children in the area near Chernobyl are actually healthy. Like the Mothers of the Plaza de Mayo, these women uphold a version of history that governments have kept secret. Disseminating these stories was both an act of courage and a form of power.

Although these women's political circumstances and cultures were highly diverse, their stories revealed a common path from personal tragedy to courageous activism. As they listened to each other over a three-day period, they recognized their own struggles and were able to form alliances transcending the barriers of language and geography. Israeli and Palestinian women overcame national hatred, and three women's organizations from the war-torn former Yugoslav republic found mutual support in their efforts to end armed conflicts and establish peace among Muslims, Croats, and Serbs.

Not all of the groups that participated in the conference were battling repressive governments or working in war-torn regions. Organizations from Italy, the Ukraine, and Spain were targeting specific problems endangering the youth of their countries. Rosetta Giaccone and Rita Borsellino of the Sicilian women's association against the Mafia confront an organization that successive Italian governments have been either unwilling or unable to stamp out. Like the other participants at the Paris meeting, their activism resulted from searing personal events. In 1982, Rosetta's husband, Paul Giaccone, a professor of forensic medicine and a doctor, refused to falsify a report that would have implicated the Mafia in an assassination. He believed that his profession as a doctor would shield him from the Mafia but one morning in August of that year, he left for work and later was found murdered. Rita Borsellino, a pharmacist and mother of three, lived peacefully in Palermo until 1992, when a bomb killed her brother, Judge Paolo Borsellino, and his five bodyguards, in addition to destroying the homes of 142 families. Her life shattered, Rita joined Rosetta in Women against the Mafia, which is dedicated to breaking the code of silence imposed by the Mafia, encouraging people to speak out, and, most of all, raising the consciousness of young people regarding the dangers of associating with the Mafia and the necessity of working toward justice and honesty. The members of Women against the Mafia believe that reaching out to young people is the way to eliminate the deep roots of the Mafia in Italian society. To this end, they lecture in the schools and attend important trials against the Mafia in support of public prosecutors, essentially devoting all of their time and funds to prevent the younger generation from falling prey to the Cosa Nostra.[2]

The mothers from the Ukraine who participated in the conference are also concerned about the very survival of young people in their region. Ann Synomina and Tamara Malkova live in Kiev, Ukraine, less than eighty-five miles from Chernobyl. When their children became ill and developed allergies, they began to investigate the food that they were eating and found that the milk, vegetables, and meat were contaminated. They also discovered a high level of pollution in that area, which was linked not only to Chernobyl but also to the use of pesticides that are produced but not used in Western countries because they are so dangerous. These women's homes soon became centers of information for thousands of concerned families, leading them to form Mama 86 in 1990 and to open the first free and independent laboratory in the country with the help of German and American foundations. The mortality rate in that region has grown by 15 percent in two years, the cases of pneumonia have increased sixfold, and instances of birth defects and brain cancer have tripled. Forty-four percent of the children in the Ukraine have been afflicted by thyroid cancer.[3] Mama 86 has helped four thousand children who suffer from the effects of radiation by providing summer camps for children and their mothers in "clean" areas of the Ukraine. It also maintains an information center, supplies children with vitamins and medication to counter radioactivity, and has created a program to monitor drinking water. To date, the Ukrainian parliament has failed to declare Kiev a disaster area or to shut down Chernobyl. The government regularly harasses the organization by cutting its electricity and destroying the test results from its laboratories but has failed to curtail its activities.

The creation of the Mothers in Green Scarves was prompted by the outrage of a small group of women against the effects of drug trafficking on Spanish children. Micaela Pérez Fernandez's daughter was only thirteen when she found her brother in a near coma with a syringe in his arm. Micaela launched an appeal on the radio and was soon joined by other women who wished to join the war against drugs. Their first public demonstration against drug dealers drew three thousand people and helped solidify a group of twenty activist mothers located in Concepción, near Gibraltar, the site of heavy drug trafficking. Group members target corrupt police officers who work with the dealers, demanding judicial inquiries. They demonstrate in public squares and in front of town halls and banks, which they believe are involved in laundering money. The group has affiliates all over Spain and is expanding. Like the Mothers of the Plaza de Mayo, they have been labeled as "crazy" and have received numerous death threats. As president of the organization, Micaela has been singled out, and her windows have been smashed. The police have told her that she is lucky that the local drug dealers are not powerful enough to kill her.[4]

Participating in the conference were mothers' groups that are working in war-torn countries to try to end hatred among battling ethnic groups. Although the former Yugoslav republic has been sundered by warring factions, mothers' groups in Croatia, Serbia, and Sarajevo are struggling to reunite their diverse populations and end the conflict. Palestinian and Israeli women are also seeking to bring peace between their peoples. Their stories reveal a rare courage in the face of tragedy.

Farida Musanovic, a piano teacher, and Beba Mahic, a former director of a bank, both members of the Women's Movement of Sarajevo, are trying to help women and children survive the horrors of war in that country. Although Farida and Beba, the presidents of the association, are Muslims, the vice presidents are Serbian and Croatian, in an effort to maintain the peaceful intermingling of different groups that existed before the war. Beba has said that, in Sarajevo, to cook bread one has to burn shoes. The laces serve as wicks for oil lamps.[5] When the offices of the Women's Movement were destroyed by shelling, Farida welcomed the members into her music school, where she continues to hold concerts as a response to the barbarity of the war. The association was created at the beginning of the war and, given the exigencies of wartime, has undertaken many different tasks, including finding shelter for refugees, the displaced, and children; helping women and girls who have been raped; equipping an ambulance that works around the clock; distributing food and clothing; visiting the wounded and sick in hospitals and homes and bringing them food and medicine; and finding stoves for refugees and the elderly. Also part of their program are the protection of public health for women, children, and the aged and the creation of organizations to help women and families. The members have been active in breaking Sarajevo's isolation, renewing relationships with Italians, Croatians, Slovenians, Macedonians, and Austrians. They also arrange for the return of the displaced and the expelled to their former homes.

Their activism is matched in Serbia, where every Wednesday since October 1991, Dubravka Velat, Neda Bozinovic, and fifty other women, dressed in black, demonstrate silently against the war and the Serbian government. Neda Bozinovic, a seventy-seven-year-old former supreme court judge and secretary of state, fought against fascism during World War II. She once told her daughters that if they did not fight for the smaller rights, they would lose the more important ones.[6] She has said that "it is madness to allow ethnic hatred, but the Women in Black will not tolerate this."[7] The Women in Black are supported by sister organizations throughout the world and attended a meeting of Women in Black in Venice in 1992, where they joined women from other republics of the former Yugoslavia and decided to hold an international meeting in Novi Sad, Vojvodina, the following July. They then launched a worldwide campaign against rape as a political policy and against militarism. The organization participates in antiwar actions in Belgrade and supports deserters and men opposed to the military. On March 8, 1993, International Women's Day, they organized a large antiwar demonstration in the heart of Belgrade and released their book, *Women for Peace*, which was written in Serbo-Croatian, Italian, and English. As do so many females who are working toward human rights, they point out that they are never included in decisions regarding war and peace, yet suffer disproportionately from the effects of war.

Dubravka Velat, mother of two, is the director of the Anti-War Center in Belgrade, Croatia. The Center represents the nucleus of a peace movement in the Balkans, and its activities are geared toward the creation of a civil society that respects human life, individual and minority rights, and democratic institutions. Its primary goal is to demilitarize the Balkan Peninsula and help establish peaceful coexistence among Balkan nations. Among its many activities are extending legal assistance to those who refuse conscription, defending conscientious objection, documenting human rights violations, and protecting the civilian population of Dubrovnik by providing humanitarian aid. Its members continually organize demonstrations, concerts, meetings, and public forums on behalf of peace. Despite the difficulties of communicating under wartime conditions, the mothers from Bosnia, Serbia, and Croatia have managed to work together.

Women's groups in the Middle East have also defied their governments by crossing cultural barriers. The Israeli Women in Black, whose members came to Paris, is an informal movement of women seeking to end the conflict between the Israelis and Palestinians. The members stand in vigils throughout Israel every Friday between one and two o'clock in the afternoon in the centers of towns and at the intersections of busy streets to protest Israeli policies that result in violence against the Palestinians. Before the peace talks between the two peoples, they carried signs demanding that the government end the occupation and begin talking to the PLO (Palestine Liberation Organization). The Women in Black was founded in 1988, and the organization has thirty affiliates throughout the country. Because there is no formal leadership or hierarchy, decisions are made by universal participation and discussion.[8] Like the Mothers of the Plaza de Mayo, members gravitate toward different responsibilities spontaneously, with some making banners and others negotiating with the police.

While these women had been protesting the occupation for many years and demanding a dialogue with the Palestinians, it was the Intifada that inspired them and helped them realize that they, too, could go out into the streets to empower themselves. They first attempted to visit refugee camps on the West Bank in order to see the situation for themselves and to express solidarity with Palestinian women but were stopped by the Israeli army. They then realized that censorship was being imposed on the public and that the media were not revealing the truth. To raise public consciousness, they collected slides of the horrors from journalists, installed a generator on a busy street in Tel Aviv, and began screening them. The Women in Black have criticized the Israeli government's policy of arrests, executions, and the establishment of detention camps to combat the Intifada and therefore characterize their own work as a positive reaction to that movement.[9] Their goal is for an independent Palestinian state in peaceful coexistence with Israel.

Ednna Yam, who traveled to Paris with the founder of the group, Hagar Roublev, lost her son during the war between Israel and

Lebanon. Both women came to Paris with stories of how the members of their group are routinely insulted, pelted with rocks and potatoes, and maltreated by the police. While passing soldiers regularly point their guns at them through car windows, in June 1993 a group of soldiers jumped out of a car and attacked the women, tearing their signs and hitting them while yelling and cursing.[10] Despite these threats the Women in Black continue to promote peace by sponsoring national peace conferences and regional conferences and discussions throughout their country.

During the Paris conference, these women were able to establish close contact with Palestinians such as the journalist Rouquia Alami, who lived in exile for sixteen years before returning to Jerusalem in 1992. She is an active member of the Palestinian Human Rights Center, established in Jerusalem in 1986. The Center is a nongovernmental organization (NGO) committed to the promotion and protection of human rights by monitoring and documenting violations based on field investigations and testimony that are then sent to UN agencies, NGOs, and the media. It also serves as an advocate for the victims of abuses and promotes human dignity through education, community-based projects, seminars, and publications.

Rouquia Alami was joined by Eman Khalil, one of the organizers of the Palestinian Federation of Women's Action Committee (PFWAC), which coordinates local initiatives within a socialist and feminist perspective. The Federation was formed in 1978 on International Women's Day and is active in the West Bank and the Gaza Strip and in Jerusalem. Composed of Palestinian females from all social classes, it works toward improving their economic, social, and political rights, thereby giving equal importance to uniting women in defense of the Palestinian people's right of self-determination.

Other participants at the Paris meeting were Embarka Hamoudi Hamdi, who fled the Western Sahara and sought refuge in Algeria when the Moroccans invaded her country, and Mama Sidi Addel Hadi, who was captured during the invasion. Mama spent two years in prison and suffered terrible tortures along with the eight hundred men, women, and children detained by the occupying forces. Six years later she and her older son were able to flee to the refugee camps of Tindouf, where she was reunited with her husband and the 160,000 Saharans who live there. She left her mother and her two-year-old daughter behind, knowing that she might never see them again. Mama and Embarka are activists with the Association of Families of Prisoners and the *Disappeared* of the Western Sahara, created in 1989.[11]

Their country was invaded by Moroccan forces eighteen years ago and is now divided into two parts, one of which is under Moroccan occupation. In the occupied sector hundreds of Saharans have been detained by Moroccan authorities, some for almost eighteen years and under the most terrible conditions. People are continually *disappeared* with no traces, including mothers who were separated from their children and even from newborns. Because there is no freedom of the press or of speech, it is very difficult to work against the regime. Moreover, the Moroccan occupiers have refused to allow Amnesty International or the Red Cross to enter the country.

The Association of Families of Prisoners and the *Disappeared* spent many months visiting people in refugee camps, gathering documentation and testimonies regarding the missing. It represents the families of the detained/*disappeared* before various NGOs, such as Amnesty International, and at the UN Human Rights Commission and the Organization of African Unity. Its goals include indemnity for families whose members died of torture at the hands of the authorities and the application of international conventions relating to torture, kidnappings, and arbitrary arrests in the occupied territories.

Mothers' groups at the conference also came from countries suffering violence and oppression at the hands of their own military forces, as is the case for the Honduran, Peruvian, and Guatemalan mothers. Also present were Brazilian mothers whose children were *disappeared* by security forces and Spanish women activists on behalf of conscientious objection.

Marilene Lima de Souza and Ver Lucia Flores Leite, both of whom live in the slums of Acari in Rio de Janeiro, had never left their country before coming to Paris. In 1991 their daughters were kidnapped, imprisoned, and executed by clandestine security police along with six other adolescents and three adults. The day after the *disappearances* of the two girls, eight women formed an organization, the Mothers of Acari, defying the climate of fear and oppression in a country where 656 children were assassinated in 1993. These Mothers also have taken up the cause of the many street children in Brazil who are either executed by the police in order to sell their organs or kidnapped and sold into prostitution.[12] One of the founding members of the Mothers of Acari, Edmeia da Silva, was shot down in broad daylight while leaving a prison in Rio where she sought information regarding the death of her son. Although brought to trial, her murderer was later acquitted, a not unusual circumstance in Brazil. The Mothers of Acari have moved beyond searching for the children to demanding justice and the end of impunity for the security police, whom they characterize as assassins, so that people will no longer have to live in fear.[13]

The Honduran Committee of Families of the *Disappeared* confronts a repressive military that routinely *disappears* young people. Members of that group had already visited the Mothers of the Plaza de Mayo in Argentina in the late 1980s to draw upon their experiences and skills. The Committee was created in 1982 in Tegucigalpa, the capital of Honduras. As in Argentina during the Dirty War, the Mothers first met each other while searching for a *disappeared* child in various governmental agencies. Fidelina Borjas de Pérez and Ludivina Hernandez, mothers of *disappeared* young adults, modeled themselves on the Mothers of the Plaza de Mayo. Like the Argentine Mothers, they have worked to raise public awareness of military behavior through press conferences, demonstrations, teach-ins, lectures, and conferences, and by gathering documentation on human rights violations in Honduras. They are also demanding that the guilty be tried and sentenced in court.

The Widows' National Committee of Guatemala [Coordinación Nacional de Viudas de Guatemala, or CONAVIGUA] faces issues similar to those tackled by the Honduran Mothers: oppression by the military and the assassination of innocent family members. Some forty-five thousand women have been widowed in Guatemala when the army kidnapped or assassinated their husbands. The majority of these women operate in villages controlled by civilian and army patrols and suffer dire economic circumstances. The organization was founded in 1988 and now includes 3,560 women, mostly Indians.

In 1992, Gisela Ortiz Perea's brother, who was studying at the University at La Cantuta in Lima, Peru, was captured with a group of students and one of their professors by an army-led death squad. From that moment, Gisela left the university and joined with the families of the *disappeared*, forming a group called Families of La Cantuta. The families searching for their children were continually rebuffed by the authorities until they contacted the Red Cross. Ultimately, they were able to establish both the army's involvement and the government's complicity and recovered nine brutally tortured bodies of students. Gisela also has joined the National Association of Families of Detained/*Disappeared* in Peru, founded in

1983 in Ayacucho, the home of the greatest number of *disappeared* in the country. As it has classified the president of that association, Angelica Mendoz de Ascarza, the Peruvian government has labeled Gisela as "an ambassador of terrorism in Europe" for attending the conference in Paris, and she now fears for her life. Angelica traveled to France in 1991 to give testimony on the *disappearances*, including that of her own son. Since then she has been continually threatened, and she decided not to come to the meeting for fear of not being able to reenter her country and continue her battle for human rights.

Eva Tejedor from Madrid and María Jesus Burban García from Saragossa, activists with the Associations of Mothers and Fathers on Behalf of Conscientious Objection, believe that even in democratic societies the military establishment is a source of injustice. Both their sons were imprisoned for refusing military service even though that prerogative is recognized by the United Nations as a fundamental human right. In Spain, after the war in Kuwait, 30 percent of conscripts declared themselves conscientious objectors; 5,000 of them refused alternative service, and 150 were imprisoned. The Mothers regard alternative service as a mere palliative that leaves the military structure untouched and have denounced the shocking inequalities between rich and poor nations, which they consider a result of governments' military policies.[14] They criticize the weapons trade and believe that the West's involvement in Third World military conflicts is a way of bolstering their economies. Their goal is to help create a society free of militarism and to ensure tolerance, peaceful coexistence, and compromise in dealing with social and political problems.

Although the women involved in the conference arrived from the four corners of the world, they claimed that they came from a single country—that of discrimination, persecution, torture, rape, and racism.[15] They experienced the same pain and were waging similar battles. They also share a vision of the world that is in direct contrast to prevailing views among governments; for them, peace is not just the absence of war but includes the sharing of power and resources. They have made connections between peace and their own lives and between their lives and those of other oppressed people. They gathered together in Paris to gain international visibility and to forge contacts with the United Nations, the European Community, and national officials, as well as with the media. The meeting helped them to marshal their political strength in order to become more effective in their own countries and also to enter the international arena as an alternative force. Given their limited resources and their poverty, these groups would have remained isolated voices in their own countries. Knowing that they were not alone in their struggles was a source of strength for each group.

The final communiqué of the International Gathering of Mothers and Women in Struggle was released to the press and then presented to governments around the world in October 1994, along with thousands of signatures from their supporters. They wanted no less than a new world order, free of oppressive governments and so-called democratic governments whose economies marginalized sectors of society and failed to provide adequate health care or to protect the environment. They insisted that hunger, pollution, and drug trafficking were as deadly as military repression. They demanded self-determination for all peoples but in a form that honored pluralism and peaceful coexistence. These mothers understand that "while there exists a single tortured or *disappeared* person, while there is a single child who dies of hunger or is assassinated on the streets, . . . and women are discriminated against and raped, there can be neither freedom nor democracy."[16] The goal that they have established for themselves is to work toward transforming human relations so that children will be properly nurtured and taught equality, freedom, and respect for the environment and human rights. What they propose is a revolution in the way those in power think and act. They encourage compromise as a means of settling disputes and as an end to militarism, racism, and exploitation. Their final statement is a cry that has come from women throughout history: "Given that there are those who wage death with such efficiency, let us, as women, make life."[17]

The various organizations that met in Paris will convene again in Italy in the spring of 1996, expanding to include African mothers' groups and intending eventually to achieve global representation. In the interim, they have undertaken a number of coordinated actions to promote their goals. The day after the meeting, a group of Mothers, including the Mothers of Sarajevo, went to the Presidential Palace in Paris to meet with President François Mitterrand. A delegation of Mothers later traveled to Brussels, Belgium, to meet with Mme. Catherine Lalumière, secretary-general of the European Commission and one of their staunch supporters, while another group met with the High Commission for Human Rights in Geneva. They presented petitions from each member organization and gained the support of the undersecretary-general for human rights of the High Commission.

When the group of seven industrial nations met in Naples in the fall of 1994, there was also an international gathering of Christian clergy, indigenous peoples, and Emmaus International, an organization founded by the French abbot Abbé Pierre that works on behalf of the homeless. Ada Alessandro and Women against the Mafia also were present and spoke on behalf of their movement. They then sent petitions to representatives of the seven nations.

After Naples, the Mothers' organizations began coordinating common actions. One of these was a petition by Mama 86 demanding that Chernobyl be shut down because the protective structure built around it after the disaster is already deteriorating. They also petitioned the government to sponsor more economically viable and ecologically safe energy policies. With Paris serving as the communications hub, signatures were gathered around the world and presented at the United Nations and to the Ukrainian government.

The Mothers of the Plaza de Mayo also circulated a petition against President Carlos Menem's proposed law to declare the *disappeared* dead and grant immunity to the military for crimes committed during the Dirty War. As Mama 86 had been, they were supported by the other organizations via Paris. The Mothers from Bosnia, Croatia, and Serbia, as well as the two organizations from Spain, have been able to stay in contact and work together because of their proximity.

Ada Alessandro is in constant touch with the Mothers of Sarajevo, endeavoring to send packages of food and medical supplies. Because of the war and the frequent closing of roads, Ada coordinates her efforts with UN officials, Mme. Lalumière, the Red Cross, and Médecins sans Frontières (Doctors without Borders) in order to ensure that the parcels arrive.

Through the extraordinary efforts of the participants, the International Gathering of Mothers and Women in Struggle has broadened the definition of justice and human rights, so that these remain all-inclusive, guaranteeing future generations social, economic, political, and environmental dignity. Given the fact that they operate without the conventional trappings of influence such as economic leverage or high-level contacts with political elites and organizations, their work does not fit into any schema of political action or contemporary definitions of power. Their power lies in the realm of the spirit: in their courage, the authenticity of their voices, and their truth telling. They gather strength from their ability to cross national and ethnic barriers to serve as role models and as a source of hope for the world. Because they believe deeply in the effectiveness of the ordinary person, their actions have been supported by signatures from concerned people around the world.

As a movement, the International Gathering of Mothers and Women in Struggle can be compared to peaceful democratic anarchism because it consists of federations of local, democratically based organizations that regulate their own affairs and adjust their diverse interests by free and spontaneous agreements. Historically, anarchism has embraced a variety of doctrines, practices, and attitudes toward social change. However, the unifying spirit in various strands of anarchism is that of rebellion against the established order. In the Mothers' case, their rebellion is a peaceful one and takes as its starting point the evaluation of contemporary society with respect to the fulfillment of human potential, freedom, and justice. Likewise, anarchism perceives repression not only in governments and the military establishments but also in multinational corporations and bureaucracies that create policies for an unwilling society. Above all, it opposes the imperviousness of existing institutions to the needs and desires of ordinary people.

The Mothers' movement has made a clear connection between the local and the global, while insisting upon continuity between the private and the public in assuring human rights. The members' lives are proof of how policies made by people in inaccessible political institutions have disrupted family life and violated human dignity. Like the founding Argentine Mothers, the International Gathering of Mothers and Women in Struggle has opened up a new space in the international political arena, circumventing national governments so that the voices on behalf of future generations can be proclaimed throughout the world.

HEBE SPEAKS

We are hoping to publicize a cry that comes from the core of our beings in order to change the terrible circumstances under which we all live. Murder is not always carried out with bullets but also with pollution and drugs. Unfortunately, it's always the young people who pay with their lives.

"Two years before the gathering in Paris we had been receiving letters from mothers' groups around the world wanting to know all about our organization and how we managed to survive under such great odds for so many years. We heard from mothers from Sri Lanka, from Honduras, throughout Latin America. Many of them wanted to meet us. Then we heard about a group of Ukrainian mothers who were marching with white scarves just like us. They were protesting the effects of the radiation from Chernobyl on their children but getting no response from their government.

That's when we decided to have a meeting with all these women in Paris. The director of our European support group, Ada Alessandro, lives there and, also, Paris is a central location. The French president's wife, Mme. Mitterrand, who has always championed our work, helped us in this project too. We decided that the participant groups had to be completely independent of any political party, revolutionary organization, or the church, just as we are. We asked for documentation to check that they were truly activist mothers and not connected to outside groups. We then selected sixteen groups who resembled us in organization and goals. They were all eager to come.

The most difficult logistical problem was with the mothers' groups from the former Yugoslav republics. The Mothers from Sarajevo couldn't come until the last day of the gathering because they had problems crossing the aerial bridge. We have a friend who talked to people at the United Nations, who lobbied various embassies and officials until we were able to assure them safe passage across that bridge. These women had had no communication with the outside world for six years. One of them had not talked to her daughters for four years because they were in the United States. As soon as she arrived in Paris, she called them. It was a very moving experience for us. When we served lunch, one of them began to cry because she had not seen a pear or a piece of fruit for so many years. During our gathering each mother explained the work of her organization and her country's situation. Our translators worked for free, telling us, 'How can we possibly charge the mothers of the world?'

We all stayed in the same place. We ate together and met for long hours, but we didn't always agree with each other. For instance, the women from Sarajevo were feminists and only wanted to speak about the rape women endured. We explained to them that in Argentina, during the time of the military junta, our young men were also raped. These women also told us that women were placed in camps where Serbian soldiers would rape them, and that those men who refused had their sexual organs cut off. Two of the younger women from the former Yugoslav republics invited us to visit them because they feel that nobody knows what is going on in their countries, that they have no water, gas, or electricity.

The most emotional moment occurred between the Palestinian and Israeli women. There were members of the Women in Black from Jerusalem with us as well as Palestinian activists. When an Israeli woman saw how upset one of the Palestinian mothers was, she said to her, 'Please tell me everything that you are feeling, because that is why we are all gathered here, to share our thoughts. Let's not hide anything. I understand your pain, and it hurts me, too. That is why we are gathering, to work against war.' The Palestinian woman didn't reply and then spoke about the suffering caused by the Israelis in the Occupied Territories. When she finished talking she saw the Israeli woman put on her black veil, and then she stood up. They hugged each other. You can't imagine how emotional that moment was for all of us.

The women from Sicily discussed their problems with the Mafia. It is so dangerous to oppose the Mafia that they cannot march. Instead, they place a white blanket on their balconies every Thursday.

At our meetings we discussed education toward peace. We have to revise our history books. We cannot talk about peace to people who are always at war. This was very clearly stated in our final communiqué, which we sent to the United Nations, the European Parliament, and the European Council. Mme. Lalumière received us at the European Commission. We gave her a list of our concerns: war, the arms race, nuclear contamination, and drugs. The Spanish Mothers were fighting drug dealers because they say that a child who uses drugs disappears from society.

We met with President Mitterrand and with Mme. Mitterrand, who spent the whole day with us. On October 6 [1995] we delivered this communiqué all over the world with the thousands of signatures we gathered in support of our work.”

Notes

1. Marguerite Guzmán Bouvard, *Revolutionizing Motherhood: The Mothers of the Plaza de Mayo* (Wilmington, DE: Scholarly Resources, 1994), 253.

2. Léa Rochford, "Des mères en lutte contre la violence du monde," *Marie Claire*, no. 52 (June 1994): 65.

3. Mariapia Bonanate, "Diritti umani, la battaglia delle madri," *Famiglia Christiana*, no. 19 (April 27, 1994).

4. Ibid., 68.

5. Ibid., 67.

6. Ibid.

7. "Mères de la Place de Mai," *Bulletin de Liaison de Solma*, no. 24–25 (April–May 1994): n.p.

8. Karen Kahn, "Israeli Feminists Look to the Future," *Sojourner: The Women's Forum* 20, no. 3 (November 1994).

9. Women in Black, *National Newsletter*, no. 6 (Fall 1993): 2–15.

10. Rochford, "Des mères," 65.

11. Yocheved Gonen, "A Good Day on the Haifa Vigil," Women in Black, *National Newsletter*, no. 6 (Fall 1993): 11.

12. Bonanate, "Diritti umani."

13. "Rencontre et témoignages des Mères de Mai," *Politis*, March 31, 1994.

14. Rochford, "Des mères," 68.

15. "Citoyennes de la planète," *Humanité Dimanche*, no. 22 (June 14–June 22, 1994): 35–41.

16. Final Declaration of the First International Meeting of Mothers and Women in Struggle, Paris, March 30, 1994.

17. Ibid.

Bibliography

Books and Articles

Anchee, Min. *Red Azalea*. New York: Pantheon Books, 1994.
Arrigo, Linda Gail. "Lu Hsiu-Lien: A Feminist in the Taiwan Democratic Movement." Unpublished paper, 1988.
Ascherson, Neal. *The Polish August: The Self-Limiting Revolution*. New York: Penguin Books, 1982.
Awiakta, Marilou. *Selu: Seeking the Corn Mother's Wisdom*. Golden, CO: Fulcrum Publishing, 1994.
Barmé, Geremie. "Using the Past to Save the Present: Dai Qing's Historiographical Dissent." *East Asian Studies* 1 (1991): 141–81.
Bates, Daisy L. *The Long Shadow of Little Rock*. Fayetteville: University of Arkansas Press, 1987.
Bertell, Rosalie. "Charting a New Environmental Course." *Women and Environments: Charting a New Environmental Course* (Winter/Spring 1991): 6–9.
Bouvard, Marguerite Guzmán. *Revolutionizing Motherhood: The Mothers of the Plaza de Mayo*. Wilmington, DE: Scholarly Resources, 1994.
Brown, Rosemary. "Matching Women, Environment, and Development around the World." *Women and Environments: Charting a New Environmental Course* (Winter/Spring 1991): 37–41.
Bullard, Robert D., ed. *Unequal Protection: Environmental Justice and Communities of Color*. San Francisco: Sierra Club, 1993.
Byrnes, Andrew. "Women, Feminism, and International Human Rights Law—Methodological Myopia, Fundamental Flaws, or Meaningful Marginalisation? Some Current Issues." *The Australian Year Book of International Law* 12 (1992): 205–42.
Chang, Jung. *Wild Swans: Three Daughters of China*. New York: Simon & Schuster, 1991.
Charlesworth, Hilary. "The Public/Private Distinction and the Rights to Development in International Law." *The Australian Year Book of International Law* 12 (1992): 190–205.
Charlesworth, Hilary, Christine Chinkin, and Shelley Wright. "Feminist Approaches to International Law." *American Journal of International Law* 85 (1991): 613–46.

Dai Qing. *Yangtze! Yangtze! Controversy over the Three Gorges Dam Project*, ed. Patricia Adams and John Thibodeau. Toronto: Earthscan Publications, 1994.

———. *Wang Shiwei and "Wild Lilies": Rectification and Purges in the Chinese Communist Party, 1942–1944*, ed. David E. Apter and Timothy Cheek, 1–93. Amonk, NY: M. E. Sharp, 1993.

———. "The Three Gorges Dam Project and Free Speech in China." *Chicago Review*, no. 39 (December 1993): 275–78.

Gardam, Judith. "A Feminist Analysis of Certain Aspects of International Humanitarian Law." *The Australian Year Book of International Law* 12 (1992): 265–79.

Gonen, Yocheved. "A Good Day on the Haifa Vigil." Women in Black, *National Newsletter*, no. 6 (Fall 1993): 11.

Gutiérrez, Gabriel. "The Mothers of East Los Angeles Strike Back." In *Unequal Protection: Environmental Justice and Communities of Color*, ed. Robert D. Bullard. San Francisco: Sierra Club, 1993.

Held, Virginia. *Feminist Morality: Transforming Culture, Society, and Politics*. Chicago: University of Chicago Press, 1993.

Hosek, Caviva. "Coming Together." *Women and Environments: Charting a New Environmental Course* (Winter/Spring 1991): 14–17.

Labalme, Jenny. *A Road to Walk: A Struggle for Environmental Justice*. Durham, NC: Regulator Press, 1987.

LaDuke, Winona, and Churchill Ward. "Native America: The Political Economy of Radioactive Colonialism." *The Insurgent Sociologist* 13, no. 3 (Spring 1986): 51–79.

———. "Native Environmentalism." *Cultural Survival Quarterly* (Winter 1994): 46–48.

Laska, Vera, ed. *Women in the Resistance and in the Holocaust: The Voices of Eyewitnesses*. Westport, CT: Greenwood Press, 1983.

LeBourdais, Linda. "Women and Environmental Activity." *Women and Environments: Charting a New Environmental Course* (Winter/Spring 1991): 4–5.

Lelyveld, Joseph. *Move Your Shadow: South Africa, Black and White*. New York: Random House, 1985.

Meisner, Maurice J. *Mao's China and After: A History of the People's Republic*. New York: Free Press, 1986.

"Mères de la Place de Mai." *Bulletin de Liaison de Solma*, no. 24–25 (April–May 1994).

Okin, Susan Moller. *Women in Western Political Thought*. Princeton, NJ: Princeton University Press, 1979.

———. *Justice, Gender, and the Family*. New York: Basic Books, 1989.

Pardo, Mary. "Creating Community: Mexican American Women in Eastside Los Angeles." *Aztlan: A Journal of Chicano Studies* 20, nos. 1 and 2: 39–67.

———. "Mexican-American Women Grass-Roots Community Activists: Mothers of East Los Angeles." *Frontiers: A Journal of Women's Studies* 11, no. 1 (1990): 1–8.

Pillay, Navanethem. "Equal Rights for Women." *African Law Review* 3 (April 1992): 14–25.
———. "The Role of a Conscientious Lawyer in the South African Legal System." *African Law Review* (October 1990): 24–27. (See Chapter 8.)
Ratushinskaya, Irina. *Grey Is the Color of Hope*. New York: Knopf, 1988.
Rochford, Léa. "Des mères en lutte contre la violence du monde." *Marie Claire*, no. 52 (June 1994): 65–72.
Ruddick, Sara. *Maternal Thinking: Toward a Politics of Peace*. Boston: Beacon, 1989.
Salisbury, Harrison E. *The New Emperors: China in the Era of Mao and Deng*. Boston: Little, Brown, 1992.
Schneider, Mary Jane. *Persistent Poisons: Chemical Pollutants in the Environment*. New York: New York Academy of Sciences, 1979.
Seager, Joni. *Earth Follies: Coming to Terms with the Global Environmental Crisis*. New York: Routledge, 1993.
Shorris, Earl. *Latinos: A Biography of the People*. New York: W. W. Norton & Company, 1992.
Wallace, Aubrey. *Eco-Heroes: Twelve Tales of Environmental Victory*. San Francisco: Mercury House, 1993.
Wallach, John and Janet. *The New Palestinians: The Emerging Generation of Leaders*. Rocklin, CA: Prima Publishing, 1992.
Waring, Marilyn. "Gender and International Law: Women and the Right to Development." *The Australian Year Book of International Law* 12 (1992): 177–90.
"Why Talk about Women and the Environment? A Panel Discussion." Kate Davies, Joy Fedorick, Elizabeth May, Fiona Nelson, and Liz Amer. *Women and Environments: Charting a New Environmental Course* (Winter/Spring 1991): 10–20.
Williams, Juan. *Eyes on the Prize: America's Civil Rights Years, 1954–1965*. New York: Viking, 1987.
Women in Black (Israel). *National Newsletter* 5 (Spring 1993).
———. *National Newsletter* 6 (Fall 1993).
Wright, Shelly. "Economic Rights and Social Justice: A Feminist Analysis of Some International Rights Conventions." *The Australian Year Book of International Law* 12 (1992): 242–65.
Zhu Hong, trans. *The Serenity of Whiteness: Stories by and about Women in Contemporary China*. New York: Ballantine, 1991.

Newspapers

Acuna, Rodolfo. "The Armageddon in Our Backyard." *Los Angeles Herald Examiner*, July 7, 1989.
Barmé, Geremie. "The Trouble with Dai Qing." *Index on Censorship* 8 (August 1992).

Bonanate, Mariapia. "Diritti umani, la battaglia delle madri." *Famiglia Christiana*, no. 19, April 27, 1994.
"Citoyennes de la planète." *Humanité Dimanche*, no. 22 (June 16–June 22, 1994).
Dai Qing. "My Imprisonment." *Index on Censorship* 8 (August 1992).
"Deadly Nuclear Waste Piles Up with No Clear Solution at Hand." *New York Times*, March 14, 1995.
Kahn, Karen. "Israeli Feminists Look to the Future." *Sojourner: The Women's Forum* 20, no. 3 (November 1994).
"La sorella di Borsellino accade qualcosa di grave." *Il Nostro Tempo*, April 4, 1994.
Lathan, Adaora. "Dollie Burwell: Standing Up for What's Right." *Audubon Activist* 7, no. 8 (May 1993).
Lek Hor Tan. "Caught in the Memory Hole." *Weekend Guardian* (November 11–12, 1989).
Liu Jernow, Allison. "China's Dai Qing: Nothing But a Pawn." *Communist Party Journal Update*, December 1989.
"Mères de tous pays, unissez-vouz!" *Non-Violence Actualité*, May 1994.
Moore, Jeanne. "Chinese Writer Makes Journey from Prison to Harvard." *Boston Globe*, January 18, 1992.
Palmer, Barbara. "Treading on Sacred Ground." *Oklahoma Today* (May–June 1993).
Regan, Tom. "Chinese Nieman Fellow Wins Golden Pen Award." *Nieman Reports*, Spring 1992.
"Rencontre et témoignages des Mères de Mai." *Politis*, March 31, 1994.
"70 Nuclear Plants on Route to Being Radioactive Dumps." *New York Times*, February 15, 1995.
Stewart, Jill. "Society Matrons and South-Central Moms Take on the Gun Lobby." *Los Angeles Weekly* 18, no. 24 (May 12–18, 1994).
"U.N. Said to Deny Equal Employment to Women." *New York Times*, April 10, 1995.
"Free the Press!" Interview with Sophia Woodman, *Human Rights Tribune*, Spring 1992.
Wudunn, Cheryl. "Trading Cloak and Dagger for Pen and New Ideals." *New York Times*, December 27, 1991.

Documents

Amnesty International USA. Prepared statement. Hearings on Human Rights Abuses against Women before Subcommittee on Human Rights and International Organizations, Committee on Foreign Affairs, U.S. House of Representatives, 101st Cong., March 21, 1990.
California Environmental Protection Agency, Los Angeles County. List of solid waste disposal facilities from which there is known migration of hazardous waste. Section 18051 of Title 14, California Administrative Code, pp. 97–98.

Commission for Racial Justice, United Church of Christ. *Toxic Wastes and Race in the United States: A National Report on the Racial and Socio-Economic Characteristics of Communities with Hazardous Waste Sites*. New York: Commission for Racial Justice, 1987.

First International Meeting of Mothers and Women in Struggle. Final Declaration. Paris, March 30, 1994.

Flathead Nation Confederated Salish and Kootenai Tribes. Tribal Council meeting, excerpted minutes, pp. 3–6. Pablo, Montana, July 12, 1984.

Gouna, Kalaat-M. *El Tazmamart de los Saharauis*. Asociación de Familiares de Prisioneros y Desaparecidos Saharauis (A. FA. PRIE. DE. SA.). January 1993.

Mole Lake Sokaogan Chippewa Community. "Resolution in Support of Nuclear Free Zones on Tribal Lands." Fifth Annual Indigenous Environmental Network "Protecting Mother Earth Conference" and Ninth Annual Midwest Treaty Organization "Protect the Earth Gathering." June 15–19, 1994.

Probe International. Press release regarding the construction of the Three Gorges Dam, Toronto, Canada, April 19, 1993.

Thorpe, Grace. "Statement to National Congress of American Indians." Sparks, Nevada, December 1, 1993.

United Nations, Commission on the Status of Women. *The Nairobi Forward-Looking Strategies for the Advancement of Women. Adopted by the World Conference to Review and Appraise the Achievements of the United Nations Decade for Women: Equality, Development, and Peace, Nairobi, Kenya, July 15–26, 1985* (DPI/926-4176-September 1993-10M).

———. *Preparations for the Fourth World Conference on Women: Action for Equality, Development, and Peace* (38e°CN.6/1994/10).

———. *Report of the Commission on the Status of Women* (E/1994/27).

White Mountain Apache Tribe of the Fort Apache Indian Reservation. Tribal Council Resolution No. 09-93-246.

Women's National Coalition. *Women's National Coalition Research Issues* (Johannesburg, South Africa), n.d., n.p.

Interviews

Hebe de Bonafini, telephone interview, Argentina, May 10, 1994.

Ada Alessandro, telephone interview, Paris, February 9, 1995.

About the Author

Marguerite Guzmán Bouvard was born in Trieste, Italy. She has been a professor of political science and of poetry for many years and is currently a resident scholar with the Women's Studies Program at Brandeis University. She is the author of books in the fields of political science, psychology, women's studies, and poetry. Her first volume of poems, *Journeys over Water*, was a winner in the *Quarterly Review of Literature* contest (1982); and her chapbook, *The Body's Burning Fields*, recently received an honorable mention in the Wind Publications contest. Professor Bouvard's book *Revolutionizing Motherhood: The Mothers of the Plaza de Mayo* appeared in 1994.